In Justice, *inAccord*

Shauna Ries & Susan Harter

Published by BookLocker.com, Inc., Bradenton, FL.

Printed in the United States of America on acid-free paper.

BookLocker.com, Inc.
2012

First Edition

In Justice, *inAccord*

Shauna Ries & Susan Harter

We dedicate this book to all of those in search of justice

Acknowledgements

On the Shoulders of Those Who Came Before

No work is an island in and of itself. This book is informed by the centuries of creative scholarship, theory, and practice of those who came before. We acknowledge that our book, *In Justice, inAccord,* stands on the shoulders of many of these seminal thinkers. And so, we would like to acknowledge the creativity and scholarly work by many of the great contributors in the fields of psychology and sociology in the last century that helped inform our book. First and foremost, our book was influenced Morton Deutsch, it is his concern for social justice and commitment to sound research that made him one of the leading social theorists of the twentieth century. We would also like to extend our thanks to other leaders in their presentation of justice and conflict resolution through scholarly efforts: Alison Taylor, Jay Rothman, Evelin Lindner, Ken Cloke, Lawrence Kriesberg, Jay Folger, Robert Bush, Bill Ury, O.J.Coogler, John Haynes, Jeffrey Z. Rubin, Mel Cohn, Bernie Mayer, Christopher Moore, Paul Lederach and many other essential contributors to the field of justice and conflict resolution, who are too numerous to list here.

Acknowledgements of Those Who Supported Mediators without Borders

First and foremost, we would like to thank the co-founder of Mediators Without Borders, Genna Murphy. Genna's artistry and competence are at the core of our Mediators Without Borders leadership team. We thank her for the many hours she dedicated to reviewing and editing this book. And, from Shauna, I send Genna my gratitude for helping me find the words to tell the stories.

A special heartfelt "thank you" goes to the esteemed teacher and early pioneer in the field of mediation, Alison Taylor, for her thoughtful review of this work and her special insights which helped inform the final product. Alison is both a valued member of Mediators Without Borders faculty and serves on our advisory team. Our documentary team, headed by Susie Arnett, is striving provide an international audience. Thank you Susie you are awesome. With gratitude to David O'Donnell, our captain for our Mediators Without Borders University Initiative. Your capable hands have expanded our capacity for planful growth and opened pathways for additional capital.

We would like to thank the loving support of and confidence in this mission; the first author's (Ries) Father, Edward Ries and his partner Grace Baron. Brother, Thomas Ries and his wife Velda, his sons Edward and Patrick, sister Kathy Friebis and her husband Dave, and children Christie, Amy, Thomas, Jeffery and all of their children's children.

We would also like to thank our team member and statistician, Shauna Rienks who trained with Susan Harter and has brought a new dimension to the research component of our work and mission. A special thanks to our current consultants Travis Chillemi, Jennifer Rogers, Chris Cosgrove and Kat Downend for their creativity and collaboration with our team.

We are pleased to thank our entire faculty who dedicated their time to bring our materials to over 2000 student alumni and the hundreds of clients they are now serving. We want to begin by acknowledging our current faculty. Brian Luther whose excellence in training and online teaching inspires each of his students, along with his wife, Danielle, a Certified Mediator who supports the dream of Mediators Without Borders. Thanks also to our San Francisco ADR Center Director, Mark Gum and his partner, Mary Simpson; Rachel Felbeck our ADR Center Director in Washington, Susan Duba Hayes, Kara Breese, Jackie Wood and Eric Baribeau each of whom will be carrying the torch for Center openings in our future.

We thank Instructor Rebecca Daniels, whose depth of teaching experience and years as a military spouse has provided Mediators Without Borders with flexibility, cultural sensitivity and great care, especially with our students who serve in the military abroad. Rebecca also reviewed this book to help us bring forth a cohesive vision. We thank colleague and friend, Jim Siefkin, who has been like a brother to the first author and steadfast in his work with our team. Kindred soul, Christie Carroll brings a contagious enthusiasm and heartfelt genuineness to every class she teaches. Lynn Lee and her teaching assistant Robin Spaulding created a wonderful Restorative Justice course which they impart to their students with great care. We thank Jennifer Barber for her spark, tenacity, and belief in Mediators without Borders. We thank Kamani Desai, for our future Train the Trainer program.

Each of our advisors has served as friends and mentors for Mediators Without Borders: Ambassador Joseph Ayalogu, Alison Taylor, Michael Carper Ann Jenkins, Durham McCauley, Michael Herrick, Barbara McCombs, Jonathon Ormes, Mark Carson, Deb Zeigler, Robin Finch, Roger Soweid and Will Hunzinker. We thank those as well who came before to teach our early courses both online and in live classroom settings, and so we thank Robin Amadei, Christie Coates, Carrie Heltzel, Claire Riley, Michael Caplan, Gary Crist, Annie Cohen, Dirk Biermann, and Kathryn Swearingen. We appreciate the time they dedicated to our students and to our vision along the way.

We would like to thank many others who helped build the dream, including Sat Tara Kaur Khalsa, Marianna Ali, Tamar Benavraham, Vincent Harding, Former Prime Minister of Ethiopia Tamarat Layne, Wallace Pond, Mathew King, Ruth Parsons, Anita Khaldy and her son Alex, Amy Kelsall, Jill Cantor Lee, Sean Rutledge, Bill Eager, Amrit Desai, Starshine Nolan, Henry Guy, Judy Knight, Frankie Benning, Josh Marks, Andrew Roppel, Dana Sednek, Jennifer Grassini, Cheryl Bass, David Leisure, Mark Pfeiffer, Josh Marks, Josh Vowell, Jim Olmstead, Benjamin Denee, Tamara Banks, Reverend Heidi McGinness, Ian McNeel, Jake Demarco, Carey Hartman, Betsy Thomas, Michael Suit, Brian Scott Henry, Ambassador OzichiAlimole. A special thanks to Ashlin Malouf-Spinden, who started as an intern with Mediators Without Borders and then served as administrator to help forge our first university partnership with Arcadia University.

We thank our growing group of new friends in Romania who are bringing the ADR Center initiative to their country. This outreach would not have been possible without leadership of Mediators Without Borders International Liaison Michelle Moran, Brian Luther and his wife Danielle, Suzie Arnett working with co-founder Genna Murphy to produce and direct our *In Justice, inAccord* documentary , along with our Romanian Collogues; Elena, Alexandru, and Andrei Handolescu,

RaduFurnica, of Leadership Development Solutions; Ionelia, Edward and Delia-Maria Vison, Ionel Olteanu, Oana Sorescu- specializing in Human rights law, Codruta for assisting as our legal liaison, Liana Elefterie, Dragos and Florina Baraisaru, Richard and Mirela Rudas, serving our team for our Mediators Without Borders in Romania in our goal of a network of ADR Centers throughout Romania as sister centers to other International Centers. We thank our first group of graduates in Constanta with the assistance of Alex Catlin Grigoras and Corina Andrei – our Botosani ADR Center Directors, along with David, Verginica and Alexandru Burnei- our Constanta Center Directors. We are delighted to introduce our newest Center in Santu Mare, with Costel Dohasuc, Stela Marian and Codruta Forea. It is this team who provided tireless efforts in bringing the first *inAccord* training to Romania. Finally, we thank Sorin Angheluta, the Head of the Ministry of Education and Cornel Pavel the Executive Director and his collogue Gabriela Gyongy Mihut for the Consilul De Mediere.

We thank our friends in Africa who continue their struggles for peace and economic equality, including Ambassador Joseph Ayalogu, Uche Igwe, Obiora Obeagu, Uche Anichkwe, Dorcas Akawakusi, Oyoyo Ogbor-Omorie, Ibru Nejuvie, Sam Dimka, Tobias Agbaegbu, Dickson Orji, Dominic Adabuiro, Lekan Da-Cocodia and Robert Idahosa.

We would like to thank Arcadia University for believing in our first of its kind online graduate certificate program in mediation and conflict resolution and offering it through their International Peace and Conflict resolution Graduate program. A special thanks to their director Warren Haffar for shepherding this former partnership.

We would like to thank Omega Institute for offering our conflict resolution courses in Rhinebeck, New York, where they inspire and promote a better world, including graduates Tae Takahashi, Benedetta Barabino, Elise Freed-Fagan, Linda Gutterman, Jenny Silver, Willa Breese, Mary Mathai, Mary Ann Stearns, Kate Abbott, Robin Hills, Lee Schwebel and others who are changing the world with their life work. We would also like to thank the over three thousand graduates of our program who are now serving hundreds requiring conflict resolution.

We thank our investors, without whom Mediators Without Borders would not have come to be: Shawn Hanson, Genna Murphy, Linnea Carlson, Durham McCauley, Peter and Barbara Dyson, Felicia Malsby, Louise Wildee, Keith Swan, Sharon Stanley, Michael Stewart, Wendy Pardo, Tammy and George Ackerman, and those who will become involved in our future.

We would like to thank those who have left us but whose memories continue to lift us up and inspire us, Alma Harter, Professor Lincoln Harter, Var Harter, Betty Ries, Edward L. Ries, Dorothy Rudolph Ries, Thomas Brady, and Irma Brady-Scheel.

Finally and with deep gratitude, we would like to thank the first author's son, Michael Herrick and the second author's daughter, Karen Callahan, for providing each of us with the hope for a happy ending in this lifelong pursuit of justice. We wanted to provide you with your best chance to become stewards of a better future for all.

Table of Contents

Foreword by Alison Taylor

The struggle to create a just solution to problems in which they are involved is the task of every person. Mediators sit with others who are attempting to come to a just and workable solution to issues and concerns that affect them. Mediators become the midwife to peace and justices, helping the disputants give birth to understanding and behavior that takes on a life of its own, formed, like a child, from the contributions of both. Agreements made in mediation, like a child, continue to exist over time, and reflect the personalities and abilities of those who created and now nurture them.

In this volume, Shauna Ries and Susan Harter have articulated a method of providing mediation in a way that honors the full capacities of each individual disputant, including their emotions as well as their thoughts, their feelings and their bottom-lines. The *inAccord* model, as explained here, can serve to remind mediators of important values and beliefs – empowerment, transparency, a set of *Touchstone Skills*, and the role of balancing head with heart, for outcomes that can last.

Based on the experience of undertaking mediation and teaching this method of mediation, the authors describe the fundamentals. The *inAccord* model has as its core the concept that individuals can find the shared means to create the interpersonal justice that they desire. The authors believe this model works in interpersonal disputes, as well as disputes between organizations, and large-scale disputes involving entities such as nations, even when the disputants are representatives negotiating for a constituency. Like a midwife, a mediator can help or hinder the process. The method outlined in this book is meant to help mediators understand their roles, to do enough but not too much, and focus on the most important things for skillful intervention at the right time.

While many of the mediation concepts and techniques embedded in this *inAccord* model are based on previous research, the way in which they are used becomes a unique style. The model is unique in that it directly assesses disputants' self-reports of emotional states in the beginning stages of mediation process and links these reports of emotional states to predictive outcomes in the mediation process. This may prove an important contribution for disputant outcomes and contribute significantly to the fields of justice and mediation.

The *inAccord* model requires mediators to collect data during the process as an intrinsic part of the method, which could lead to better outcomes and more hard data that can form the basis of further research and development. It is good to see empirical methods brought to bear in a field that has often been lacking in research. Just as medical science, with its empirical imperative, has used research for better results, there is every reason to believe that mediators who are monitoring and quantifying what they and the clients do using the self- reports built into this model will be able to improve their results over time. Just like the trend in medicine to use holistic approaches, mediators also must go back to the essentials of the relationship and feelings during the process as essential components and this is a strong emphasis of the *inAccord* model as it emphasizes both the use of data-gathering and the focus on feelings.

The authors explain how groups, organizations, and societies can build resolution centers using the *inAccord* model, where conflicts and disputes can be honorably and effectively handled using their mediation methodology, without the cost and infrastructure required by our traditional procedural justice systems. Most disputes can be handled using the less cumbersome apparatus of the mediation process rather than resort to court. This move back to the idea that smaller systems can empower individuals to resolve disputes using the least restrictive (and least expensive) means to create more individual response to conflict, is a philosophical move that fits with these economic and social times.

Mediation can work in many diverse cultures; perhaps some adaptations will be found using the built-in research capacity to make it even more culturally consistent. Instructing and empowering local people in mediation centers is like bringing justice back to the village elders – letting the people who have learned this method provide the help and support to others. Learners become teachers as well as doers. The centers are set up, the first learners become the mediators, the mediators teach others, and so the center becomes self-sustaining, without intervention or support from outside sources.

The actions, of the disputants as well as mediators, *do* matter, and we can perfect our methods of mediation, just as we can work together as societies to promote the use of appropriate conflict resolution methods for greater access to justice for all. All justice starts with us, where we are. This book is an important contribution for promoting the use of mediation with a feedback loop for increased effectiveness, which may well lead not only to better outcomes for disputants, but to a more vital development in the field of conflict resolution.

Foreword by Kenneth Cloke

"So long as society is founded on injustice, the function of the laws will be to defend injustice. And the more unjust they are the more respectable they will seem."
Anatole France

"Each time someone stands up for an ideal, or acts to improve the lot of others, or strikes out against injustice he sends forth a tiny ripple of hope."
Robert F. Kennedy

"Justice" is the great catchword, the past's promise to posterity, humanity's hope. It is the indignant cry, the lost illusion, the selfless dedication, the bitter and the sweet. It is the last word of millions who suffer, and the first demand of those who seek change. It has stood for revenge and forgiveness, punishment and rehabilitation, compensation and closure, mercy and terror.

These are the themes that Shauna Ries and Susan Harter highlight in their thoughtfully crafted book. Yet justice has been cited in support of integration and segregation, gay marriage and criminalizing homosexuality, pro-choice and pro-life. It graces the facades of law schools and decorates courthouses, but is rarely predominant inside. It is a fixture in the rhetoric of politicians the world over, including the most right-wing supporters of dictatorship and the most left-wing proponents of democracy. How then can we know what it means?

Shakespeare, for example, wrote that "mercy seasons justice," while Robespierre declared that "Terror is nothing else than justice, prompt, secure and inflexible." Plato described Thrasymachus debating Socrates over whether justice was "the interest of the stronger," while Aristotle argued that justice was "the highest virtue of the state," and a kind of "due proportion" in the assignment of rewards and punishments. Aristotle also wrote that justice was "someone else's self-interest," while Franz Kafka felt it was "a fugitive from the winning camp," and comedian Lenny Bruce quipped that "the only justice in the halls of justice is in the halls."

Yet, as Ries and Harter show, calls for justice are not without content or meaning. By no means can it be claimed equally by those who demand equality and those who insist on discrimination and privilege; those who support liberty and those who oppress others; those who favor the rich and those who advocate for the poor. Instead, ruling parties speak of "law and order," "obedience," and "rights and responsibilities," without inquiring "whose laws?", "what kind of order?" "obedience to whom?", and "responsibility for what?"

Applying these ideas to the modern world, the Occupy movement has dramatically cited the injustice and inequality of wealth between the top 1% and the remaining 99%, politicians are battling over gay marriage, and religious and political divisions are becoming increasingly violent. Even widespread acceptance of unjust laws implies acquiescence to inequality and injustice, and an ongoing need to mediate the chronic, recurring conflicts that arise over them.

It is precisely here that mediation parts company with the law in its approach to justice. Rather than declare abstract universal principles or impose these ideas on both parties unequally as the law does, it seeks to resolve the practical issues that make each side believe what is happening is unjust, and asks the parties to decide for themselves what is fair and just using procedures that invite everyone impacted by the problem to the table to negotiate how it should be solved. Ries and Harter offer a viable alternative in their approach to mediation.

Mediation represents a significant, transformational departure from law in its approach to justice, not only by equalizing the roles of the parties and offering them a veto power over whatever is proposed, but more subtly by inviting conversations based on interests rather than rights or power; acknowledging emotions, listening and encouraging respectful communications, and building more collaborative relationships. In these ways, mediation allows parties to write their *own* laws based on what they believe to be just, rather than allowing legal principles to determine in advance and for everyone what is just. This is what Ries and Harter seek to reveal.

It is a truism, yet no less true as a result, that we cannot create lasting peace in the absence of justice. Merely attempting to do so validates anthropologist Laura Nader's critique of mediation for "trading justice for harmony," and turning peace into something fleeting, fragile, and phony. Novelist Toni Morrison offers a more useful definition of peace:

There is a certain kind of peace that is not merely the absence of war. It is larger than that. The peace I am thinking of is not at the mercy of history's rule, nor is it a passive surrender to the status quo. The peace I am thinking of is the dance of an open mind when it engages another equally open one ...

We cannot achieve *either* a sustainable peace or an integrated, equitable and just social order that makes such peace possible unless opposing sides are encouraged to listen, learn and genuinely seek to understand each other. There can be no lasting justice without harmony, or harmony without justice. Without it, we become unable to solve our common problems, collaboratively negotiate our differences, seek genuine truth and reconciliation, or dismantle our prejudices. More importantly, we become unable to prevent, resolve, transform, or transcend chronic conflicts by unlocking them at their systemic source. This applies not only to large-scale global conflicts, but to the small-scale interpersonal conflicts experienced by all of us, as revealed herein, as Ries and Harter also argue.

Real, lasting peace is impossible in the absence of justice. Indeed, the deepest form of evil *is* injustice, and as long as it continues, peace will always be fleeting, fragile, and a disappointing reminder of everything people have suffered and lost. Where injustice prevails, peace merely becomes a way of masking and compounding prior injustices, impeding necessary changes, and rationalizing the continuation of domination, aggression, and war. As the Trappist monk Thomas Merton presciently observed:

To some men peace merely means the liberty to exploit other people without fear of retaliation or interference. To others peace means the freedom to rob others without interruption. To still others it means the leisure to devour the goods of the earth without being compelled to interrupt their pleasures to feed those whom their greed is starving.

And to practically everybody peace simply means the absence of any physical violence that might cast a shadow over lives devoted to the satisfaction of their animal appetites for comfort and leisure ... [T]heir idea of peace was only another form of war.

Where millions lack the essentials of life, peace gives legitimacy to continued suffering, and compromise offers a rationale for capitulation, passivity, and tolerance of injustice. True peace requires a search for justice and a dedication to harmoniously satisfying fundamental human needs; otherwise, it becomes the self-interest of the satisfied, the ruling clique, the oppressors, the victors in search of additional spoils.

For peace to be achieved, it is essential that we neither trivialize the sources of conflict nor become stuck in the language of good and evil, but work collaboratively and compassionately to redress the underlying injustices and pain *each* side has caused the other. Ultimately, this means sharing power and resources, advantages and disadvantages, successes and failures, and satisfying every group's legitimate interests. It means collaborating and making decisions together. It means giving up the assumption that what is legal is therefore just. It means taking time to work through differences, and making our opponent's *human* interests our own. It means standing up for the rights of others as though it were *our* lives that were affected.

While shantytowns coexist with country clubs, peace cannot be lasting or secure. Where some go hungry while others are well fed, terror and violence will be nourished. In the end, it comes down to a question of sharing status, wealth, and power, realizing that we are all part of a single human family, and understanding that an injury to one is truly an injury to all.

Making the search for justice an integral part of conflict resolution therefore means not merely *settling* conflicts, but turning them into levers of dialogue and learning, catalysts of community and collaboration, and commitments to social, economic, and political change. By failing to take these steps, we make justice secondary to peace, undermine both, guarantee the continuation of conflict, and lay the groundwork for more to come. By taking these steps, as the authors of this book do, we help to create a better world.

Finally, why, as a founder and first president of Mediators Beyond Borders, an organization often confused with Mediators Without Borders, am I writing a foreword to a book promoting a different organization? The answers are quite simple but need to be stated: First, the world is highly conflicted and we need all the help we can get in resolving global differences. Second, this book raises important issues that we all need to grapple with and suggests approaches that have validity beyond narrow, self-serving organizational goals. Third, justice and conflict resolution techniques belong to no one, and we do both a disservice when we are unable to stand for the principles we advocate in the world.

Introduction

It is by understanding the differing perspectives and the emotions that each person brings to a conflict situation that we are able to empower all parties and, as a result, attain a lasting resolution, and with it true justice.

- Shauna Ries, President, Mediators without Borders®

The global community today is more united in the desire to expand peaceful resolution of conflict than at any other time in history. The instantaneous transmission of events through the media, among once-isolated societies, has exposed a growing sense of commonality and a deep desire for shared peace, yet we struggle to understand, to connect, and to bring our common desire for justice into more sustainable economic, political, and social models.

The cost of violent solutions to conflict has reached the point where they are irretrievably weakening the economies of the most powerful nations. There are not enough sanctions, guns, bombs, or prisons to control such a diverse and culturally rich worldwide community. Nations and societies who seek to control and force others to view the world from their perspective are doomed to collapse under the economic weight of the destructive devices designed to maintain such control. There are countless examples of this folly: a series of costly wars that contributed to a global recession; the leveling of Beirut that all but destroyed a thriving economic tourist destination and weakened both sides involved in the conflict; the genocide in Darfur and the inability of the global community to effectively respond; and, the totalitarian rule in North Korea that created a country of nuclear might while its citizens starve and languish in labor camps.

In this book, we present the *inAccord Conflict Analysis™ model*, hereafter referred to as the *inAccord* model, operated within the Mediators without Borders International Alternative Dispute Resolution (IADR®) Centers as one answer that can help us connect and share ideas that will help build a more peaceable world, one society at a time. Briefly, these International ADR Centers are established globally, linked by a virtual campus, and directed by local citizens.

Each Center provides facilitation, mediation, and arbitration services to a regional population while promoting the *inAccord* educational model. At the heart of the our model and International ADR Center project of connection and sharing, is an ever increasing understanding of the important role of emotions in shaping perceptions, reactions, and solutions to conflict. By understanding the important role of emotions in both escalating and resolving disputes, we may be able to systematically tackle even the most intractable conflicts. This is a foundational concept of this book and the *inAccord* model.

Overview of In Justice, inAccord

Many leaders in the field of conflict resolution and peace programs accept that conflict is not only an *inevitable* condition of human interaction, it is a *good* condition. In this book, the authors will extend the conviction that conflict can be a powerful force of systemic change for the betterment of a society by exploring the value of honoring not only divergent perspectives of conflict but the potential contrast of emotional reactions to the conflict by each of the disputants. Conflict can help open minds to divergent thinking and help disputants understand how differences in their cognitions and emotions offer exposure to unique options that might otherwise not be imagined.

This book explores critical questions linked to the exploration of solutions to conflict such as, (1) How might justice be served, given the differing perspectives and emotions inextricably tied to each version of a conflict? (2) Are we able to enhance the current justice systems with alternatives such as International ADR Centers designed to ameliorate conflict between disputing parties, once their individual negotiation attempts failed them? (3) How do we evaluate the efficacy of these new International ADR Centers and other interventions? and, (4) What mechanisms must be instituted to guarantee the ongoing sustainability of intervention models?

By answering these questions and others, the authors make a case that the Mediators Without Borders International ADR Centers and their forms of direct alternative dispute resolution processes may offer an invaluable vehicle to deliver justice to the underserved in society, whether that underserved be a disempowered individual or a company unable to find the funds to battle a larger or more economically resourced institution. On a broader level, this book considers how to help resolve conflicts to disputes as seemingly intractable and complex as those between and within countries.

The guiding premises and assumptions of the *inAccord* model include: (a) conflict is inevitable, normal, and workable; (b) disputants can be empowered to work successfully with conflict; (c) empowerment derives from transparency in the mediation process and from teaching the *disputants* the *Touchstone Skills* of reflecting, re-framing, and questioning; and (e) mediators must help disputants explore the role of emotions, which then enables parties to create enduring agreements.

In Justice, inAccord is written as a text for the foundational mediation course at Mediators Without Borders, as a resource book for any practitioner in the field, and as a book for anyone desiring to learn about the fields of justice and conflict resolution. The book is organized into three parts beginning with Part One where the reader is taken through an overview of the field of justice and alternative dispute resolution, how the *inAccord* model complements and fits into these fields, and the three central functions of the model. In Part Two, the book focuses on placing the foundations and processes of our model into practice during mediation sessions. Part Three concludes the book by presenting the *inAccord* research component and its application through the networked Mediators Without Borders International ADR Centers.

Part One: Foundations of the inAccord Model

It is the authors' contention that justice delayed is justice denied and so Part One begins with a focus on the overarching concepts of justice and why new and complimentary systems to existing conflict resolution approaches are imperative to create a more peaceable world. This includes a discussion of the difficulties inherent in the criminal justice system, focusing on the United States crisis of funding which is seriously debilitating local, state, and federal courts. The discussion then moves to the remedies and complimentary systems of alternative dispute resolution that can certainly help with this ongoing crisis in the courts.

Chapter Two of Part One presents both the field of ADR and an introduction to the *inAccord* model, emphasizing the fact that it departs from traditional ADR methods through a concerted focus on how the disputant understands and is satisfied with the procedure. *inAccord* is a disputant- centered facilitation model, meaning that it examines the needs of the disputants, what they require emotionally (this informs the facilitative technique chosen), and what is required economically to reach settlement. Ultimately, the settlement of the conflict is a goal in the *inAccord* model.

The *inAccord* model is referred to throughout this book as a facilitation model because it best designates the process as a form of alternative dispute resolution with a third party neutral "facilitating" mediation between disputants. Although we refer to this facilitator as a "mediator" in this particular text, we will apply the *inAccord* facilitation model to arbitration, negotiation, and conciliation methods of dispute resolution in our other Mediators Without Borders courses and textbooks. Throughout the book, we use the words "party" and "disputant" interchangeably as terms for the participants involved in conflict. Part One concludes with two chapters that cover the foundational concepts of transparency, empowerment, and the role of emotions which form the central foundational functions of our model. We will discuss these functions briefly in the following pages.

Central Function One: Transparency. Transparency, one of three central functions that support the *inAccord* model, is presented in detail in Chapter Three, including discussions of neutrality and impartiality in theory and in practice, differentiation and self-regulation, transference and counter-transference, and the links of transparency to authenticity. *Transparency* applies to each of three phases of our model, to each party engaged in the conflict, and to the mediator. Transparency means making the covert overt. It includes shedding the mediator's role as the expert in the parties' dispute because it is the disputants who ultimately understand their perception of the injustice and what they are wanting in the form of an apology and/or remuneration to reach a solution.

Mediators are not the primary problem solvers to a disputant's problem; this role falls to the disputants themselves. Transparency is facilitated in the *inAccord* model through a sequence of surveys at each of the 4 stages, including surveys the mediator fills out. The model further promotes transparency by teaching the disputants the same *Touchstone Skills* the mediator uses to clarify and frame the underlying interests, understanding, and satisfaction of each party.

All parties are encouraged to communicate from an authentic stance based on increased self-awareness and increased awareness of the perspective of the "other" party. The goal is to reach a negotiated agreement to the conflict and to use an informational, more transparent process. Examining the approach to the mediation itself at certain points in the process and making necessary adjustments to the choice of intervention strategy, helps facilitate movement to a negotiated agreement. It is our hypothesis that transparency is critical for examining the role of emotions, because it exposes power imbalances that are critical to address when empowering the disputants. This power balancing process thus becomes a vehicle that helps disputants achieve equal footing in the negotiations. Once this is achieved, it is possible to come to a Memorandum of Agreement, with which the parties will realistically comply over time after the process concludes.

Central Function Two: Empowerment and Systemic Change. Chapter Three also covers the second of the central functions, empowerment, in terms of how to use the *directive* and *relational* techniques (described in subsequent chapters), along with sharing the *Touchstone Skills*, to maintain a balance of power between the disputants. The chapter concludes with a discussion of how facilitators can influence positive disputant power and the links between empowerment and the concept of "self-efficacy". Empowerment applies to each phase of the model. Empowering the parties and facilitator to find their own personal voice in the dispute is also a central component to the *inAccord* model, as the process encourages parties to take an active role in the resolution of *their* dispute.

Although many alternative dispute resolution models seek empowerment, what is central to our model is teaching the *Touchstone Skills* of *reflecting, reframe, and questioning* directly to the parties at the end of Stage 1 in Phase Two. This prepares the disputants for negotiation with each other. The *Touchstone Skills* are designed to increase self-empowering emotions and self-awareness, along with understanding the other party's perspective. This may have the added benefit of creating greater compassion and open-mindedness among the disputants. These *Touchstone Skills* are not unique to the *inAccord* model and were written about extensively in books such as *The Making of a Mediator* (Lang & Taylor, 2002). What distinguishes our model is that we not only encourage the facilitator to "model" these skills but direct them to take time to *teach* these skills to each disputant to use throughout the 4 stage process.

Why is empowerment such a critical concept of our model? Because, the feeling of disempowerment is so universally negative and debilitating that many people, groups and nations who feel disempowered will do anything to feel even a little more empowered. Anything may include taking away someone else's property or rights, taking their life, or waging a war. Often, these styles of conflict resolution to address an injustice create a cyclical system of violence where one party is constantly trying to regain power over the other. This type of power over another is not empowerment. It is a hollow victory built on violence toward the other. What is needed is a systemic change, including an empowerment process which encourages people to constructively release their own overt or dormant personal power and gain the skills and knowledge to overcome obstacles in their lives. Ultimately, this should help them develop and create this change within themselves and their societies.

Central Function Three: The Critical Role of Emotions to Inform Facilitator Technique. The central function of the role of emotions in the *inAccord* model is the focus of Chapter Four which presents the emotional scale used in the model and the *My Feelings* pre- and post-survey instruments. This scale is based on the first-hand practice experience of first author Ries as well as the scales presented in *Ask and it is Given* (Hicks & Hicks, 2004) and *Power vs. Force* (Hawkins, 2002). This presentation is followed by discussions of self-conscious emotions, emotional competence, hope theory as applied to facilitation, and the function of positive emotions. Emotions are powerful forces that disputants bring to the table. Others such as Bolton (1970), Deutsch (2006), Furlong (2005), and Taylor (2002) have also highlighted the importance of addressing strong disputant emotions at the outset of conflict. One novel contribution of the *inAccord* model is the identification of emotions that are empowering (e.g. optimistic, happy) as well as emotions conceptualized as disempowering (e.g. depression, humiliation), namely, negative effects that can disrupt the success of the process. Our expectations, if the model is effective, is that empowering emotions would increase in strength and disempowering emotions would decrease in strength as a result of the *inAccord* model for facilitation.

An important feature of the model includes the implications of the emotions that disputants report at the outset of the facilitation. We shall see how the particular emotions of each party dictate the intervention strategy employed by the facilitators. In addition, we will explore recent theorizing about the role of positive emotions, including cognitive-emotion hybrids such as hope and optimism. In our sessions, we find most disputants are seeking a feeling of emotional relief, which may be important to consider as we examine the role of emotions in Chapter Four.

Part Two: The Practice of inAccord Facilitation

Part Two of this book will present a more comprehensive discussion of how mediation practitioners can practice the *inAccord* model. Chapter Five, in this section, will focus on the mediation skills necessary to successfully guide disputants to a resolution of their conflict and begins with a discussion of the competency cycle and how it relates to the need for ongoing self-reflection in the maturity and development of any practicing professional. This is followed by an examination of three essential skills sets that are used throughout the model including building rapport with each disputant, employing the *Touchstone Skills* of reflecting, reframing, and questioning, and conducting fair and impartial caucuses when needed. The chapter concludes by introducing pre-mediation protocols that offer a solid structure to help contain the inevitable intensity of any dispute.

Chapter Six of Part Two takes the reader through the three phases and four stages of the *inAccord* model, highlighting specific techniques and interventions to use at each stage. These two main components include: (1) the Three Phases including Phase One, the pre-facilitative assessment, Phase Two, the 4 disputant-focused stages, and Phase Three the post-facilitation; and (2) a deeper clarification of the 4 stages of facilitation in Phase Two. These 4 stages include: *Stage 1*: Sharing of Perspectives: Issues, Positions, and Interest Identification- teaching the *Touchstone Skills*, *Stage 2*: Developing the Agenda and Option Generation, *Stage 3*: Joint Solution Statements, Testing the Agreements in Principle, and *Stage 4*: Crafting the Memorandum of Agreement (MOA). See Table One below for a summary of these phases.

Table 1: Overview of Phases and Associated Surveys to Assess the inAccord Model

PHASE ONE Pre-Facilitation Assessment	PHASE TWO 4 Stage Intervention Scores	PHASE THREE Post-Facilitation Outcomes
Conflict Styles Survey* -Avoidance - Competition -Compromise -Accommodation -Collaboration	**Stage 1**: Sharing of Perspectives: Issues, Positions, and Interest Identification**(caucus; review touchstone skill sets) - Understanding - Satisfaction	**Signed versus did not sign** **Exit Survey**** - inAccord Model successful, party satisfied -Can understand, implement inAccord Model -Mediator fair/impartial -Process transparent -Process empowering
My Feelings Pre Survey* -Empowering Feelings -Disempowering Feelings	**Stage 2**: Developing the Agenda and Option Generation** -Understanding -Satisfaction	
My Expectations Scale* -Saving money -Saving time -Saving the relationship	**Stage 3**: Joint Solution Statements: Testing the Agreements in Principle** -Understanding -Satisfaction	**My Feelings** Post Survey* -Empowering Feelings -Disempowering Feelings
	Stage 4: Crafting the MOA* -Understanding -Satisfaction	**My Expectations** Scale* -Saved money -Saved time -Saved the relationship

*Mediator evaluates disputant responses to survey
**Mediator completes a parallel version of this survey

Part Three: *inAccord Research and International Applications through ADR Centers*

Another unique contribution of this book is the inclusion of a research evaluation component in Part Three. As with any intervention, we believe it is critical to evaluate, through appropriate research designs and statistical techniques, whether the components of the *inAccord model* are effective in producing the desired outcomes. We will share our specific research endeavors to the *inAccord* model in Chapter Seven. Conclusions from our initial research are presented here as well as plans for future research in this ongoing effort.

Our book often references Morton Deutsch (Bunker & Rubin, 1995), a social psychologist, considered to be a leading contributor to the field of conflict, cooperation, and justice. He pointed out that there is "an appalling lack of research on various aspects of training in the field of conflict resolution" (p. 128). He laments that this lack of research has left us with many unanswered questions about who benefits, what is effective, when and where, in what circumstances, and through what mediation processes. We agree that these questions along with many other practice-related issues and issues of efficacy need well-designed research and data to back up any potential answers. In this spirit, we introduce not only the *inAccord* model of facilitation but its research component that will help us determine the effectiveness of this model in the United States and abroad.

Mediators Without Borders is in the early stages of creating a foundation of study for empirically-demonstrated findings. We are in the beginning phase of testing our International ADR Center research component and our second edition will produce data sets with more active international cases. Our initial research results were based on a study using the results of mock disputant trainees from *inAccord* onsite trainings and from role play practice through our weekly teleconferenced practice sessions. We chose this venue as a practice area to refine the survey instruments created by the authors and to see if these had initial validity. We have noted similar results with disputants from actual facilitation sessions and we felt it was imperative to publish a first edition while we await the results with a larger sample from the

International ADR Centers. Although, we do not yet have the requisite number of these actual surveys to report statistically significant findings, the live surveys we have administered mirror the results from the mock disputant findings. A more comprehensive study will be included in our second edition.

Chapter Eight of Part Three focuses on the business model of globally networked ADR Centers and the proposed International University for Professional Studies as vehicles for disseminating the *inAccord* model and research study. In this chapter, we present an overview of the ADR Center Project and the University of Professional Studies founded by Mediators Without Borders including the importance of bridging the divide between corporate and non-profit organizations, the emphasis on local direction of ADR Centers, and the underlying business model of fair profit and sustainability for thriving centers. In addition, we apply the central functions of transparency and empowerment from *inAccord* to the International ADR Center project and outline some of the challenges ahead as we launch this model on the world stage. Our ADR Centers are the current delivery systems for our model, and they will work collaboratively with one another to expand the research study and University goals on an international level.

We believe our business model of partnering with local citizens and institutions to co-create a fair-profit model of conflict resolution, education, and service will help create a more peaceable and just world. We also recognize that a broader application of the model will bring greater challenges as we deliver the courses and services in other nations and cultures. From the psychological literature, we present some of these specific challenges to the ADR Center project such as the intractability of certain conflicts, identity-based conflict, issues of self-verification and how they impact conflict resolution interventions, the implications of false self-behavior, and folk theories about whether people can change. We conclude this chapter and *In Justice, inAccord* with a look at the path forward, one that we see as immensely hopeful.

Mediators without Borders: The Mission

The highest possible stage in moral culture is when we recognize that we ought to control our thoughts. - Charles Darwin

Just trust yourself, then you will know how to live. -Goethe

Mediators Without Borders is a part of a growing movement, nationally and internationally, toward increasing our awareness of the unique interests that accompany diverse perspectives and positions in a conflict. The world is increasingly interconnected, socially, politically, and economically, yet there remain serious limitations in the distribution of fairness and justice. This is an important time in the evolution of professionals who deal with those in conflict. It is necessary for each of us to continue efforts to work collaboratively and creatively, building trusted, impartial frameworks for the global and national delivery of dispute resolution services to families, organizations, or nations. This mission underscores the authors' creation of the *inAccord* research survey instruments to gather early data to support the hypothesis that a disputant-focused facilitation model could embed fundamental and trusted concepts such as transparency and empowerment in the quest for justice and procedural fairness in resolving disputes. With our professional roots in psychology, we seek to measure the role of emotions and how these emotions might inform a facilitator and the disputants of reliable techniques to move them to agreement, how to move through four measureable disputant-focused stages of facilitation, and how these two efforts might combine to create research-based methods in the quest for justice. This initiated the creation of our three phases and 4 stages of the *inAccord* research methodology.

The *inAccord* model is part of a natural progression of creating more effective and comprehensive training for students, by providing a measured, procedurally-fair, disputant-centered model for those in conflict. The model is built to address the need to measure our efficacy as facilitators, mediators, and arbitrators and as a call to action to create a research-based process that is straightforward in its approach, rigorous in its measurement, and always centered on the empowerment of all parties. Our approach includes the identification of theories and skills from psychology and sociology which might support interventions for disputants, and to build on the groundbreaking, classic work of leaders in the field of mediation such as Morton Deutsch, Alison Taylor, Jay Rothman, Evelin Lindner, Ken Cloke, Lawrence Kriesberg, Jay Folger, Robert Bush, Bernie Mayer, Bill Ury, O.J.Coogler, John Haynes, Jeffrey Z. Rubin, John Paul Lederach and many others. These pioneers have been an inspiration to our work and set the early call for a serious consideration of alternatives to litigation and war in the quest for justice.

Mediators Without Borders is continually seeking answers to the question of what can be done to promote justice. Old ways of handling conflict, with what many consider to be the alpha male, winner-takes-all mentality, are no longer an option. Social media is opening our minds and hearts to the plight of those in conflict internationally. As we witness vast societal and regional problems, the inordinate need for effective methods for conflict resolution to bring about justice becomes apparent. The *inAccord* model, and the Mediators Without Borders International ADR Center project introduced in Chapter Eight, may be one alternative to intervene early and provide a viable alternative to lengthy litigation or continuing hostilities that can at worst, lead to war.

It is the continuing mission of Mediators Without Borders to identify new and innovative approaches for positive, sustainable change in the field of conflict resolution grounded in research-based techniques. If both seasoned and young democracies in the West and abroad are to thrive, we must be able to connect and share new paradigms to deal with conflicts and continue to pursue effective and stable mechanisms to deliver justice for our citizenry, even for disputes that are by nature interpersonal rather than political or social. To this end, Mediators Without Borders continues to add increasing specializations and credentialing as the field of conflict resolution continues its rapid expansion around the world. With new models and delivery platforms for our courses, our courses are able to be efficiently and effectively transmitted to this growing global audience.

Conclusion

It is important to reiterate that this new, more just world does not translate to an absence of conflict. Conflict is a necessary process in human interaction. It is an essential component of social evolution as challenges and disputes across the globe compel us to find more creative and affirming ways to expand our humanity. The processes created for justice must embrace conflict in this manner. We must understand that war is almost always waged as an answer to a conflict that has no other defined resolution. In this sense, models of justice must begin to build alternatives to violence that become embedded in the institutions of each nation and people. If you take away guns, people will fight with sticks and stones. If you offer more constructive alternatives to the gun, people will have more options when they inevitably react to conflict. Moreover, if we define peace as a direction rather than an end to conflict, any diversion from that direction can be resolved through a simple course correction.

There were many times during the birth and growth of *inAccord* and Mediators Without Borders where forces acting against it threatened the leadership team with paralysis, with despair, and sometimes with a strong urge to abandon the dream. But we, along with our team, were fortunate to be what Rand and Cheavens (2009) refer to as "high hope" individuals, who worked diligently to transform stressors into challenges, even opportunities to soldier on. Hope, for most of us, is a sense where even the possibility of a happy ending is desirable goal.

In *The Better Angels of our* Nature, Pinker (2011) states that outside forces which transform individuals and the world include technology, demographics, commerce and growth. However, he also observes that ". . . they also originate in the intellectual realm, as new ideas are conceived and take on a life of their own" (p. xxiii). *In Justice, inAccord* and the new ideas embodied within will help with what we see as the continuing positive transformation of our world.

It is certain that no single world leader, regardless of his or her passion or charisma, can affect the broad change that is needed for justice. We must all find ways to act by crafting thoughtful

14

interventions, delivering these through creative private and public models, and carefully studying the results of each unique attempt to create a peaceful global community. With the folly of our antiquated solutions more clearly defined, how do we best respond? We do this by acts of construction rather than destruction, by finding ways to link us to one another so we can continue to share our common desire for peace. We do this by honoring our differences and celebrating the unique perspectives and solutions that each nation and people have to offer. We do this, most importantly, in ways that ensure that our solutions will survive the forces that seek to continually disrupt their positive effects. We believe that Mediators Without Borders®, its project of networked International ADR Centers, its future University of Professional Studies, and its evaluative research on the *inAccord* model will create a continuous source of constructive solutions to help this shared vision become a celebrated reality.

PART ONE:
Foundations of the *inAccord* Model

Chapter One: Justice and Alternative Dispute Resolution

Justice and Injustice

Presentations of facilitation, mediation, and other similar interventions into conflict have their roots in the broader discussion of justice and injustice. And so we ask, "Is justice alive and well?" For many people around the world, the answer is a resounding "no." In some instances, citizens find themselves in a nation that has no justice system, save for the rich and powerful. In others, the legal system focuses too narrowly on the law and not on justice. This stems, in part, from the confusion between what is *just* and what is *law*, two words that may or may not be compatible. Peter Wall (2009), a thoughtful attorney, remarks, "The law matters, but justice matters more. That may not be fair or even right, but it highlights the tension between law and justice. Most people want justice for themselves, but they want the law applied to others. Law simplifies reality. Law dictates that some things are admissible in court, whereas others are not; you can consider these things, but not those things. But justice requires you to think about all those other things. We're all intimately familiar with the mitigating factors that should result in justice for ourselves, but for others, we want everything simplified. You stole a loaf of bread? Criminal conviction for you" (2009, Law versus Justice, para.1).

In this sense, the legal system of courts and judges, battling attorneys, and winners and losers may actually work against the promotion of justice. Even in the United States' legal system, one founded on equal access to a fair trial for every citizen, the principle of equitable justice is often thwarted. This happens through no malice of forethought, but because the sheer number of disputes cannot possibly be served through a cumbersome and antiquated "justice" system. It is often said that justice delayed is justice denied. Justice is often denied through overcrowded courts that cannot possibly serve all its citizens, by court schedules that serve employees of the court and not disputants, and by the simple fact that the best representation often goes to those with the most money. As Folberg and Taylor (1984) observe, litigation procedures are ". . . too often used coercively to supplant self-determination, with no evidence that the disputants have been encouraged and helped to resolve their differences" (p. 35). They go on to point out that once lawyers and judges intrude upon the decision-making role between those in conflict, the disputants are less likely to function independently in the future.

The Injustice in our Courts

America's prisons and jails hold more people, in sheer numbers and on a per-capita basis, than any country on earth, including China, Cuba and Iran. Those prisons and jails are kept full through the ceaseless work of a massive criminal justice apparatus that processes the 14 million people arrested every year, on an average of about 26 every minute, according to the Justice Department. The vast majority of those arrested are poor, often desperately so; many are mentally ill, homeless or addicted to drugs and alcohol. Only a small percentage can afford a private attorney. (Rudolph, 2012, Pennsylvania Public Defenders Rebel against Crushing Caseloads, par. 1)

In 1962, the United States Supreme Court heard the case of an indigent man who was forced to represent himself in a felony robbery case. The court ruled, in a landmark decision, that should he be forced to defend himself, it would be in direct violation of his right to a fair trial under the Bill of Rights. This decision led to the creation of a nationwide public defense system that would guarantee every person a right to a fair trial, regardless of their station in life. Today, this system is failing, and failing rapidly, forcing public defenders to take on far too many cases, working long hours and watching funding for staff and salaries decrease with each passing budget. According to John Rudolph, writing for the Huffington Post in the summer of 2012, the already stressed public defense systems throughout the United States are being pushed to the brink of collapse.

One example of this collapse can be found in Los Angeles, the United States' largest superior court system, where state budget cuts forced the launching of massive job layoffs, pay cuts and transfers in June of 2012. John Clarke, the executive officer and clerk of the court in Los Angeles lamented that these changes would affect the ability of officers and staff of the court system to preserve access to justice. In an ironic development, this nationwide collapse of funding for the courts has forced a small but growing number of public defender offices to bring suit against the states and counties over the excessive caseloads that are working to deny clients the right to effective representation.

The American Bar Association (ABA) in 2011 addressed the growing crisis in the courts in a report to the US House of Delegates. The report summarized some chilling events taking place in courts across the US which includes (1) Twenty six states have delayed filling judicial vacancies; thirty one, judicial support positions, and thirty-four, vacancies in clerks' offices; (2) Thirty-one states have frozen or reduced judicial and staff salaries; (3) Fourteen states have laid off staff entirely; (4) Twenty-two states have tried to offset budget cuts by increasing fines and filing fees, and (5) Fourteen state court systems have had to curtail hours of operation, in some instances, closing for an entire day each week.

The ABA Task Force highlighted the damaging effects of these trends using Georgia as a lamentable example. Since watching their court budget shrink 25% over a two year period, criminal cases in Georgia now take more than a year to resolve, crowding the local jails with innocent and guilty alike. These delays cause an even greater reduction in court time for civil cases with one Georgia judicial circuit closing its doors entirely to all civil cases, with the result that any divorce, child custody, business and personal injury cases are simply not heard. Until something can be done to repair this broken system of justice, there is a desperate need for other complimentary systems to fill the void.

The Interdisciplinary Nature of ADR

We acknowledge litigation and traditional court systems as valuable services that can contribute positively to the highly interdisciplinary nature of the field of conflict resolution. Moreover, we are hopeful about the growth of alternative dispute resolution options within the ever growing ranks of North American attorneys. Julie MacFarlane (2008), in her book *The New Lawyer,* notes, "A growing reluctance to spend very large amounts of time and money on litigation has provided an impetus for another highly significant change: justice reform. The most important of these reforms have introduced mandatory settlement processes into the civil courts in the form of mediation and judicial settlement conferences" (p.xi) The author argues that lawyers need to begin to adjust their image from "warrior" to "conflict resolver." To this end, MacFarlane envisions herself as a role model and coach, moving away from providing only narrow legal, technical advice toward providing a more holistic, practical, and efficient approach to conflict resolution for her clients.

We concur with MacFarlane (2008) and with other recent thinking that has focused on the merits of what Rees (2010) refers to as the newer field of mediation and the continued importance of civil litigation. Rees observes, "I do not in any way seek to suggest that mediation is a better option than litigation nor to downplay the significance of litigation. Rather, I argue that mediation can be a viable and legitimate alternative in a broad range of situations…the emphasis is on its legitimacy as an *alternative* and understanding the strengths it may offer. It is therefore important to consider where the real challenges for mediation may lie, if they are not, as argued here, in the very nature of human rights. Three issues in particular require consideration: power balances; systemic change; and transparency" (pp. 3-4). Other authors such as Day (as cited in Rees, 2010), have taken an even stronger stand in favor of mediation and against litigation, claiming that, "As a process that empowers claimants, and ensures they are fully involved, mediation beats a court trial hands down" (p. 12).

Although we agree with Day (2008) as well as Folberg and Taylor (1984) on their points about the negative effects of litigation, our intention is to find a balanced approach to this topic. That is, although litigation is necessary at times, it is important that parties in conflict do not *begin* to solve their dispute in this manner. Rather, the starting point to resolving a conflict should begin with a more negotiative venue.

However, we agree with Rees (2010) that although there are situations and a legitimate time and place in which involving the court may be appropriate, it should not be considered the best process.

Just as mediation can be distinguished from litigation, it can also be contrasted to traditional therapies employed in clinical practice. As in therapy and counseling, mediation focuses on the incorporation of critical communication skill sets, such as the *inAccord Touchstone Skills*, designed to move disputants to a Memorandum of Agreement. However, mediation does not delve extensively into an analysis of potentially deep-seated "issues" that have been suppressed or repressed. Folberg and Taylor (1984) suggest that mediation involves creating a plan to resolve the conflict between disputants rather than delving into their personal history. Toward this goal, it is not intended to produce "therapeutic insights" into one's past nor alter the disputants' personalities. We concur with these authors that mediation is not designed to foster a therapeutic relationship between the mediator and the disputing parties. It is task-directed and goal-oriented, and as in the *inAccord* model, it attempts to produce results, namely, a solution to the conflict, through the active participation of the disputants rather than by forcing a decision upon them.

The *inAccord* model for mediation and arbitration cases often use processes that focus on issue-specific, short-term aspects and can, therefore, have the positive benefit of addressing issues that arise, *as* they arise. This is in contrast to long-term therapy, which delves into historical grief, loss, and more general personality traits of the disputants. The *inAccord* model shares therapeutic emphasis on emotions, transparency and empowerment. This importance is highlighted throughout this book as we examine empowering emotions such as serenity, understanding, forgiveness, optimism, hopefulness, contentment, trust, and happiness and disempowering emotions such as discouragement, jealousy, anger, depression, insecurity, despair, blame, and humiliation. In addition, we explore theories that influence these emotions centered on a disputant's self-concept such as identify- based conflicts and self-verification theory, noting how these theories support the research of the *inAccord* disputant-focused model.

There are some cases where mediation may be a preferable intervention to therapy because it does not necessarily stigmatize the disputant. Mediation, in general, does not view the disputant as pathological, as someone whose personality or behavior patterns need to be seriously altered or "fixed." This approach may be particularly welcome if adolescents are involved in a conflict that brings them into the mediation picture. Although many adolescents are in an age-appropriate period of self-reflection, their concerns are immediate, in the here-and-now crisis of the day or moment. They do not view their adolescent problems as deep-seated or requiring a personality adjustment because their personalities have yet to be fully developed. They are prime candidates for solutions that address current conflicts and thus mediation may offer some relief from their distress.

Although mediation derives much of its foundational knowledge from therapeutic, sociological and legal sources, it can offer an alternative path to changing habitual ways of reacting to people's natural disputes. The assumption underlying our model is that everyone and anyone can take ownership of the dilemma and its resolution using the *inAccord* process. People can effectively respond to the conflict they are experiencing, because, in many cases, they are the ones who participated in creating the situation of conflict. In Chapter Eight, we will expand this conversation as we discuss concepts such as self-identity and self-verification that may help practicing mediators understand how to assist disputants in reaching lasting agreements.

Alternative Remedies

What then is justice? The term justice is often broadly defined by individuals, organizations, and politicians, yet few of us understand the underlying complexities of this powerful word. Justice is typically defined as a principle of moral rightness, an upholding of what is fair treatment and due reward in accordance with honor, standards, or law, including a stance of equitableness and fairness. There are three common terms used in justice literature that all speak to the issue of fairness but in distinctly different ways: distributive justice, procedural justice, and retributive justice.

Distributive justice emerged from social exchange theory (Emerson, 1976) and refers to an individual's perception of the reward structure and his or her rightful portion of it. Procedural justice is concerned with the fairness and the transparency of the processes by which decisions are made. The *inAccord* model's three phases and 4 stages are designed to address the fairness and transparency of procedural justice. Justice theorist Morton Deutsch (2006) has written extensively on this subject and notes that when justice is implemented in accordance with fair processes, treating those concerned with respect and dignity, those affected will more easily accept the processes, even when the outcomes are not in their favor. This is in contrast to distributive justice which is more concerned with fairness in the distribution of rights and resources or retributive justice which is concerned with fairness in the punishment of wrongs.

Bunker and Rubin (1995) present procedural justice in terms of group value theory which links self-identity as it relates to groups in conflict, namely, that people are interested in crafting a favorable self-identity and use interactions to shape their sense of identity. This theory suggests that in addition to the goal of resource acquisition, people have the goal of identity affirmation. Bunker and Rubin refer to Tyler and Lind (1992) who suggest that concerns about identity affirmation lead people to focus on relational issues when dealing with others. The authors' research suggests three relational issues are important in this context: the belief that procedures are neutral, the belief that others are trustworthy, and the recognition of personal standing by others through respectful, dignified, treatment, that is, status recognition (Tyler, 1989; Tyler and Lind, 1992). These relational issues have been linked directly to evaluations of procedural fairness (Tyler, 1989). Tyler and Belliveau (1995) demonstrate that the relational concerns outlined are, in fact, a distinct second justice motive, which differs from the resource-based concerns that develop from social exchange models. They demonstrate that there are two distinct justice motives: one resource-based, the other relational in character. Resource concerns influence assessments of distributive justice; relational concerns influence assessments of both distributive and procedural justice. In other words, procedural justice judgments are purely relational in character.

It is not enough to simply question whether justice is alive and well for most people and point to the many ways it is subverted. More importantly, we must turn our efforts to questions of remedy such as: How do we create thriving systems of justice within our communities and, more importantly, how do we maintain them? Our social media is replete with stories of civil rights violations and injustices, to which many of the masses numb themselves. It is the norm in many societies for conflict to be avoided or denied. There is often an attitude that "this is not my problem" and a hope someone else will address these disputes. Yet, for those brave enough to meet conflict head on, there can be an opportunity to face not only the conflict but the person or persons with whom they are in opposition. More importantly, conflict offers individuals the opportunity to face themselves and their ability, or lack thereof, to change and flourish.

Mediation, although not a panacea, can function as one powerful remedy to injustice. However, mediation, as a procedural process of justice, must be, according to Deutsch (2006) and other theorists, perceived as fair by those it serves. It must also address relational issues and ensure that procedures are perceived as neutral, that disputants perceive others are trustworthy, and that they believe they are treated with respect and dignity. The *inAccord* model must meet these interpersonal criteria in order to create enduring settlements to conflict based on fairness, respect, and dignity. The model accomplishes this, in part, through the use of survey instruments that allow disputants to report back to the mediator on whether the interpersonal issues highlighted above were realized and that the procedure is being perceived as fair.

Never before has there been such an urgent need to find effective methods to handle our injustices and disagreements. On the larger societal level, countries and entire regions with internal conflicts, boundary disputes with other nations, nationality and religious disputes, shared natural resource disputes, and other growing pressures certainly need alternatives to repression and violence, or inadequate legal and social mechanisms for dispute resolution. They also require less time-consuming and less-costly complimentary systems to the burdensome pursuit of justice through overwhelmed traditional criminal justice venues.

On the organizational level of conflict that involves companies and employees embattled in conflict with each other where rights have clearly been violated on either side, one or both sides are sometimes forced to pay exorbitant retainers for legal representation, and are often spending up to five years of litigation before the rights violated can be corrected and compensated for. Even though a company or an employee demonstrates a strong case, they may be forced to either ignore the violation by another, or proceed with litigation while risking the economic and psychological health of their livelihood.

On the interpersonal level, couples divorcing, eldercare issues, neighborhood disputes and other small claims issues are taxing the underfunded and backlogged court system. Families and community members are finding themselves on court dockets spanning many months, with overwhelming legal fees. And, as the case study will illustrate, this process often leaves scars that can last decades.

Couples and Families

There is no other place more in need of an alternative to litigation than that of couples and families in conflict, whether that is in divorce, child custody disputes, eldercare and probate conflicts, or other deeply emotional disagreements between people who have, at one time, loved one another. In Chapter Four, we will discuss the role of emotions in disputes and how these can impact the ability of disputants to come to an equitable agreement. Certainly, our case for including the role of emotions in the mediation process is even more critical when it comes to those disputes that are with our closest loved ones, our friends, and our community members. These are conflicts that, left untended or amplified by litigation, can result in lasting and devastating wounds to all involved.

Foreclosure: Joshua and Soriah's Story

Joshua and Soriah have been happily married for twenty years and are no longer able to make their house payment. As the economic

27

pressure builds, tempers flare. The bank is preparing to foreclose on their family home, resulting in a dispute between the couple and the bank. The emotional conflict begins to spill over between the couple, and many unquestioned behaviors that were not problematic during periods of low stress, suddenly become unbearable. In this case, the financial pressures forced the emotional foundations of their relationship to crumble at the same time the economic cement in their comfortable home began to dissolve.

Joshua and Soriah, along with the banker, are now at a crossroad. They can choose to work together for a solution, or to work in opposition to each other. Across the country, situations like these are playing out against the backdrop of unprecedented foreclosures and family economic distress. One of our Mediators Without Borders graduates embraced this tragic type of situation and devoted his conflict resolution training to serving as a mediator within banks, to help people in similar circumstances to Joshua and Soriah. Mediation efforts can certainly help couples themselves, and families faced with difficult economic circumstances that must interact with outside organizations such as a bank, school, or governmental body.

The dynamics of the story above, based on a true story, is all too common in many family disputes whether they focus on divorce, eldercare, or finance. Although there is a strong push from judges to mandate those involved in non-criminal disputes to first choose mediation, this change is hampered by a lack of public awareness of mediation and a woeful lack of comprehensive training of family and divorce mediators. The *inAccord* model offers a more comprehensive education for family mediators, one that helps them assess their effectiveness in what are often highly emotional disputes. The procedural consistency of the 4 stages of the *inAccord* model can provide a reliable structure for disputants that can hold the intensity and variability of their emotions in check. In addition, the disputants can be systematically taken into caucus where they can report, on our surveys, the levels of their understanding and satisfaction at each stage. These breaks may also provide a time-out from the intensity of joint sessions where they can reflect on their previous progress.

Companies

Kals and Jiranek (2012) speak directly to the issue of "organizational justice" (see Greenberg, 1987) with regard to companies and corporations. Organizational justice describes the perception and understanding of fairness with an organization. They underscore the three types of justice, within the workplace, *distributive*, *procedural*, and *interactional* justice. They reiterate that distributive justice refers to the fairness judgments as they relate to distributions or allocations (e.g., of wages, responsibilities, privileges, rights, etc.) and that procedural justice addresses issues about the fairness of the *decision-making process* that leads to how distributions are determined. They add the term interactional justice which speaks to the regard for people's interpersonal concerns about the fairness of such decisions, and often involves the employee's *trust* of the employer. Kals and Jiranek tout the role of mediation as an alternative to litigation, in helping to resolve perceived injustices that involve these three forms of fairness, arguing that effective interventions can result in a win-win situation. They observe that the thoughtful mediator can be viewed as ". . . an escort in the thicket of conflict" (p. 229).

In 2011, first author Ries conducted a workplace training in mediation and conflict resolution skills in the workplace for a regional office of a governmental organization. Although mediation is a cornerstone of this organization's intervention within the workplace on the national level, many of the regional personnel did not have the advanced skills possessed by those in the organization who actually mediate cases that are referred to them. Recent budget cuts and the uncertainty of government shut downs placed this regional staff under much more stress than usual. Their hours were longer and their caseloads were becoming unmanageable. The staff participated in a two-day workshop that focused largely on the *Touchstone Skills* of reflecting, reframing and open-ended questioning, as well as the best practices to use in specific conflict situations with those involved in investigating both disputants in a case.

The training was effective for this organization because the participants in the program not only employed these skills in their cases, but they made a commitment to use them in the office for disputes and misunderstandings. In follow-up conversations with several other organizations, Ries learned that the use of reflecting, reframing and questioning had greatly reduced workplace tension and improved the communication of the entire staff. These examples demonstrate that the *inAccord* model and other forms of conflict resolution do not have to be instituted in system- wide interventions in order to positively affect a company's morale and productivity. Just a drop in the pond can create rippling effects.

Countries

The *Arab Spring* is a marvelous example of how citizens within a country can use the anger at injustice and inequality to completely transform a nation and a region. Many nations, historically as well as recently, have witnessed relentless opposition and conflict, challenging the status quo in a manner that has forever changed the face of the Middle East and Northern Africa. Amazingly, despite the differences in national structures and historical issues, these conflicts occur over very similar goals, such as ousting the current leaders and promoting freedom, yet transforming each country in a markedly different way. In 2011, Tunisia celebrated its first free elections in over 40 years; Egypt awaited the final verdict of whether one authoritarian rule would be supplanted by another or, alternatively, if a democratic system would emerge; Libya won its freedom through long months of bloodshed and violence although the new government was fragile and tentative; Syria grew more explosive teetering on civil war; and other Arab nations faced a slow simmer of opposition.

Often, there is little recourse for the disempowered whose rights have been violated except to rise up and defy the oppressors. But at what cost? One must acknowledge the tremendous toll that such uprisings take on the people who rebel against their current political, economic or social circumstances. Lives are lost, families are splintered, home and work life may be totally disrupted, homes and property are destroyed, adequate food and healthcare may no longer be available, all of which make the people more vulnerable.

Kriesberg (2007) addresses the need for more constructive conflict resolution efforts to deal with large scale violent conflicts within such countries, conflicts that have been highly destructive. He urges that leaders and opposing factions in such uprisings attempt to better understand each other's concerns. This involves the *avoidance* of violence, of the dehumanizing members of the opposing side, and of coercive tactics that rely on power. With some optimism, he provides examples within the last two decades where many large scale conflicts were prevented from escalating destructively, citing the illustration of how Lithuania, Estonia, and Latvia became non-violently independent of the former Soviet Union. Moreover, he sees a vital role for mediators who can explore the possibilities of avoiding destructive escalation, by constructing, as an alternative, a mutually acceptable agreement to help transform the conflict.

These are examples of situations where the power of facilitation and mediation may potentially ameliorate or address injustices leading to conflict. Any person, organization, or nation can embrace the options of going to court or going to war; alternatively, they may turn to more peaceable options to potentially make systemic, lasting change. The quest for answers to perceived or real injustices becomes not an "if" we can resolve the conflict, but rather "how" do we resolve the conflict in question. *In Justice, InAccord* will address the "how" question in resolving conflicts when the parties holding two opposing positions are each assumed to be right by the respective parties. Often times, the quest for a higher ground and common cause for those in conflict, opens a world of possibilities never before imagined.

Chapter Two:
The *inAccord* Model in Context of the Broader Field of ADR

Chapter Overview

In this chapter, we will discuss the broader processes of alternative dispute resolution and where the *inAccord* model fits into these expanding, and sometimes ambiguous fields of practice and study. Before we define the four major ADR processes of negotiation, mediation, arbitration, and litigation, we will present an overview of negotiation and bargaining including the definitions of issues, positions and interests, which many beginning mediators struggle to differentiate. The discussion then moves to a presentation of the spectrum of ADR from simple negotiation between two or more parties to the entry of a third party facilitator for the process of mediation to the more complex processes of arbitration and litigation where the entry of outside experts take the decision making process away from the disputants.

With the ADR spectrum and related terms defined, we move to a discussion of the field of mediation, offering a brief overview of major models (also called styles, approaches and theories depending on which mediation academic or practitioner is describing the process). This is followed by a description of how the *inAccord* model draws from three of the major models (facilitative, transformative, and evaluative) and where and why it deviates from them, making it a unique model in and of its own.

Overview of Bargaining and Negotiation

Negotiation is defined as a process in which the parties involved in a dispute or transaction, communicate with one another directly or indirectly to resolve the dispute or consummate the transaction. It is important for mediators, as facilitators of parties engaged in negotiation, to be knowledgeable about major negotiation principles.

There are two major styles of negotiation that can be placed on a spectrum, interest-based negotiation and positional bargaining.

Negotiation Spectrum

Positional Bargaining vs. Interest-Based Negotiation
(positional can be referred to as distributive, versus interest-based which can be referred to as integrative, negotiations)

Although most negotiations contain elements of both positional bargaining and interest-based negotiation, for our purposes we will distinguish these as two ends of a spectrum. Fisher and Ury's (1991) book, *Getting to Yes,* has been used for almost three decades to explain interest-based bargaining and argue for its effectiveness over positional negotiations. It is important to make a distinction between what the author's refer to as principled or interest-based negotiation and its opposite, positional negotiation.

Positional Bargaining. To illustrate positional bargaining, consider the proverbial purchase of a used car. Typically, this type of purchase is distributive in nature, in that the main issue involved is the resource of money. The seller wants to sell the car for as much as he or she can, while the buyer wants to pay the least amount possible for the car. There is usually no relationship between the parties, they often do not trust one another, and there are few incentives to be open and honest.

In this type of negotiation, parties will often examine their strengths and weaknesses to establish maximum and minimum figures before going into the negotiation. In our car purchase example, the seller might be relatively strong and the buyer relatively weak if the car is a collector's edition, which will influence each party's price range. During the course of the negotiation, parties will strategically reveal information and go back and forth on price. If the deal is to be successful, the parties will incrementally move towards each other's negotiation figure to arrive at a mutually acceptable compromise.

Positional bargaining may be appropriate when:
a. There is a definite fixed sum in a dispute
b. No continuing relationship is anticipated
c. There are no related issues
d. There are no underlying interests and needs other than money
e. There are no overlapping interests
f. Emotions are not important
g. A climate of trust is not possible

Interest-Based Negotiation. The defining difference between interest-based and positional bargaining terms is that interest-based focuses on negotiating the parties' interests. One of the most difficult distinctions for new mediators to make is the difference between issues, positions and interests, so we will spend a little time clarifying this. An *issue* is what brings the disputants to mediation, namely, the conflict to be resolved. For example, in divorce mediation a common issue is what to do with the shared house. Typically this is one of many issues to be resolved in a full mediation. A *position* is a stand one takes on a certain issue. It is often one-dimensional, defined in black and white terms, and can be emotionally charged. In the house example, a position might be the husband's insistence that the house be sold in contrast to the wife's position that she be able to keep it. In positional bargaining, it is very difficult to engage in a more collaborative process to resolve each party's positions.

Interests are the needs beneath positions that can often be used to forge compromises and build bridges between persons in disagreement. People are committed to positions in varying degrees, which means there may be a deeper concern underlying hardened positions that might open a dialogue, facilitated by the use of the *Touchstone Skills* of communication. In the issue of the house, the position of the wife is her demand that she keep the house. In contrast, the husband is demanding that they sell the house. To understand the underlying interests of each party, a mediator would employ the *Touchstone Skill* of questioning to ask the wife, "Help me understand your reason for *keeping* the house?" The wife may answer something such as, "The children have had enough change in their lives, if we sell the house they must change school districts." The mediator asks the husband the same question regarding his position on selling the home, "Help me understand the reason for selling the house. The husband may answer, "The house is our largest asset, if we do not sell the house, I will not be able to buy my own home for the children to come to."

What begins to happen in this interest-based process is a broadening of options and building of agreements in principle which we will talk more about in Chapter Six. One option may be that the couple sells the house and the wife purchases a home in the same neighborhood at a lesser price. This, indeed, opens options and meets the interest of keeping the children in the same school district. It also meets the interest of liquidity for the husband to buy his own home for the children to come to stay with him.

The following workplace case offers another illustration of the differences between issues, positions, and interests and how they emerge in mediation.

Company Case Study

Sam is middle manager at a software firm who has had a difficult few months with a new hire, Brian. The two men cannot seem to agree on anything and spend countless hours arguing over schedules, protocol, and delegation of duties while projects continue to stack up. Sam and Brian have filed separate grievances with Human Resources, both insisting they will not remain at the company unless the other is fired. The Human Resources mediator has decided to conduct an interview in hopes of finding a compromise. Both men initially held to their intractable positions. The mediator carefully pressed for more and more information until a few underlying interests began to emerge. It seems that Sam believed that Brian was a plant or a spy sent from management who was only there to gather all of Sam's knowledge and expertise, at which point Sam would be fired. Brian, on the other hand, could not understand why Sam was so hostile towards him. He believed Sam was trying to sabotage his efforts and get him fired. The mediator was further able to ascertain that both men valued collaborative, supportive work relationships.

Issues: *Schedules, Protocol, and Delegation of Duties*
Sam's Position:*Fire Brian or I quit!*
Brian's Position:*Fire Sam or I quit!*
Sam's interests: Keeping his job
Working collaboratively
Getting the projects completed
Being supported
Brian's interests:Working collaboratively
Having excellent and timely results at work
Having fun at work

Notice how the positions do not allow for much negotiation or compromise. However, upon further examination, it is revealed that the men have certain interests in common. This movement from positions to interests leads to the creation of an agenda, which captures joint solutions and builds agreements in principle, leading to the crafting of a Memorandum of Agreement. In this case, Sam and Brian were able to agree that they wanted to work collaboratively and with timely completion of projects. After some time, Sam was able to voice his fears about losing his job to Brian. Brian was surprised and confessed that he never wants a management position no matter where he works. With the interests clearly identified, the men were able to relax and work out a more cooperative relationship leading to the formalization of the *agenda items* to be resolved: (1) Schedules, (2) Protocol, and (3) Delegation of Duties. These are then addressed in the Memorandum of Agreement.

The Spectrum of ADR

Alternative Dispute Resolution (ADR) consists of a variety of approaches and processes including, but not limited to, negotiation, facilitation, mediation, and arbitration. In order to understand how the *inAccord* model fits into the broader spectrum of ADR, it is important to understand the range of dispute resolution processes and where mediation rests along the continuum. The chart below shows a progression from negotiation to litigation that is marked by ever decreasing power of the disputants to be in charge of the decision making and resolution processes.

| Negotiation | Mediation | Arbitration | Litigation |

ADR processes differ in their formality and placement of decision-making power. In litigation and arbitration, the decision-making power lies with a neutral third party who will weigh the presented evidence and make a decision based on who has presented the stronger case. This approach applies identified laws and historic judgments to the resolution of the conflict. This may or may not align with the disputants' unique situations, positions, or what they each would prefer to see happen. In the mediation and negotiation process, the decision-making power resides at all times with the parties. Let's begin by reviewing negotiation.

Negotiation. As we stated earlier, negotiation is defined as a process in which the parties involved in a dispute or transaction communicate with one another directly or indirectly in order to resolve a dispute or consummate a transaction. Although negotiation is a process used in mediation, pure negotiation occurs without the use of a third party neutral such as a mediator. In this process, the party with the best negotiation skills will often emerge as the winner, especially if they can keep a calm emotional stance. In negotiation, there is a saying, "Don't get angry, get your way." Parties tend to be more successful if they learn not to become overly emotional and not to disclose too much, too fast. This can be akin to what poker players refer to as a "poker face," which refers to keeping a countenance that does not reveal what may be occurring internally.

Mediation. Mediation is most often defined as "the intervention in a negotiation or a conflict of an acceptable third party who has limited or no authoritative decision-making power but who assists the involved parties in voluntarily reaching a mutually acceptable settlement of issues in dispute." (Moore,1985). Negotiation is always a component of mediation; however, mediation extends the bargaining process into a new format by introducing a third party who can contribute different negotiation strategies and ways of looking at the conflict.

Arbitration. Arbitration is based on the competitive presentation of evidence to a decision-maker who is often selected voluntarily by the parties for an award (decision). The arbitration is held according to procedural and evidentiary rules that the parties agree upon. Arbitration decisions may be either advisory or legally binding. This process may be conducted by one person or a panel with the distinction that the third party exists outside of the conflict relationship. (In a forth coming book about *inAccord* Arbitration, we will explore these issues in greater depth, applying the *inAccord model* directly to this ADR process.)

Litigation. Litigation, also referred to as an adjudication process, is the presentation of evidence to a judge through a competitive process. This presentation, usually by opposing lawyers results in a court order, judgment, or decree (win/lose decision). The decision-maker is often elected by the local community and decides cases according to community legal standards. The judge must follow formal rules of procedure and evidence and his or her decision is appealable.

The following graphic illustrates the often convoluted communication process inherent in an adversarial litigation process. As an example, Party A and Party B are at an impasse and each had decided to hire their own lawyers. A complex, and expensive, communication pattern begins wherein Lawyer A and Lawyer B counsel their respective parties not to communicate with one another, thus the diagonal across the arrow between Party A and Party B. Instead, Party A communicates with his attorney, Party A's attorney with Party B's lawyer, Party B's lawyer communicates with Party B, Party B responses to Party B's lawyer, Party B's lawyer responds back to Party A's lawyer, Party A's lawyer responds to Party A, Party A replies to Party A's lawyers, Party A's lawyer replies to Party B's lawyer, Party B's lawyer replies to Party B, Party B responds to Party B's lawyer, and the circle of communication continues in this fashion. If this seems unwieldy and confusing, it is. More importantly, it is a very costly process that involves expensive billable hours by each lawyer.

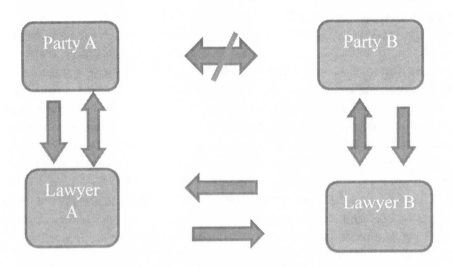

Litigation is often not the most desirable option in cases of conflict. Besides the expense, this type of communication can widen the gap between disputants, lead to a hardening of positions, and provoke more disempowering emotions. It also fosters a reliance on a system that is often antiquated, taking months and years of the disputants' time, not to mention a great deal of their money. However, litigation is often more appropriate than arbitration, especially when the arbitration is binding for two reasons. Unlike litigation, in binding arbitration there is no ability to appeal a decision that may be perceived as partial and unfair. Second, unlike mediation where the power stays with the disputants giving them the choice to sign or not sign the Memorandum of Agreement, in binding arbitration, an award is submitted that binds both parties.

Models, Theories, and Approaches

The *inAccord* model directs mediators to choose one of two approaches, directive or relational, based on the results of the *My Feelings* survey given prior to the mediation. In order to understand these approaches, we will begin with a broader discussion of what mediators mean by models, theories, and approaches. One of the most common questions that presents, as mediators deepen their knowledge base, is whether certain mediation practices derive from theories, approaches, models, or applications. This lack of clarity comes from the many different ways certain practice nomenclature is used for transformative, narrative, evaluative, or facilitative mediation.

Leonard Riskin (1996) attempted to bring clarity to the debate to this nomenclature problem by postulating that approaches exist along a continuum that encompass both the role of the mediator moving between evaluative (a more directive approach) and facilitative (a more relational approach), and the definition of the problem moving from narrow to broad. Critics of Riskin's approach argue that any evaluative (directive) activity on the part of a mediator denigrates and undermines mediation concepts such as empowerment, participation, and the freedom of disputants to craft their own solutions (Kovach and Love, 1996).

We agree with Stuhlberg (1997), in his critique of Riskin's presentation of mediation approaches on a continuum (1996), notes that there is a much more important issue at stake than which orientation or approach to use. As he states, the "missing piece is the inability of his (Riskin's) analysis to assist the practitioner in knowing why she should move or is justified in moving from one orientation to another" (p. 989). The *inAccord* model provides the mediator with this missing link through the use of survey instruments that measure empowering and disempowering emotions. Instead of adopting either a directive or relational approach, based only on evidence derived from listening to the disputants and their stories, the *inAccord* survey instruments provide measurement tools to support or challenge the mediator's intuitive assumptions.

Facilitative Mediation. The formal practice of mediation in the United States began in the 1960s and 1970s. What is now referred to as "facilitative" mediation was the only form or approach of mediation practiced at that time. In this type of approach to mediation, the mediator structures a process that helps disputants reach a mutually agreeable resolution to their conflict. This approach is based on the belief that, with neutral assistance, people can work through and resolve their own conflicts. In a facilitative mediation, the mediator will take an active role in controlling the "process", which in the case of the *inAccord* model includes setting a formal four stage structure with the systematic use of surveys to measure satisfaction and understanding. The mediator also directs the process by asking questions to identify the interests of the parties and the real issues in the disagreement. The mediator helps the parties explore solutions that benefit both parties (sometimes called "win/win" solutions).

It must be noted that the facilitative mediator does not have complete neutrality nor complete impartiality. By merely being present at a conflict, any mediator, regardless of orientation or style, influences the process and the outcome. The facilitative mediator can do this in a number of ways: by controlling the subjects that are addressed in negotiation, by ordering the topics on an agenda, by creating rules for communication, by helping parties generate options, and by establishing ground rules of behavior and fairness. We will discuss the issues of impartiality and neutrality in Chapter Three.

Transformative, Evaluative, and Narrative Mediation. The majority of the criticism leveled at facilitative mediation comes from the transformative mediation field. Many criticize facilitative mediation as primarily a problem solving approach which leaves the mediator with too much power to direct the process. They also argue that although all decisions are, in theory, left in the hands of the disputants, problem solving mediators often play a large role in crafting settlement terms and obtaining the parties' agreement. However, facilitative mediation is taught in most mediation programs and seems moderately acceptable to the vast majority of practitioners, although some, particularly those using the evaluative approach, find it less useful or more time consuming.

The debate among different practitioners of mediation about the best model or style is ultimately good for the field when it brings in new perspectives, challenges assumptions, and deepens the overall understanding of conflict. However, most practitioners do not practice a pure model or approach but choose an eclectic style where the type of case, complexity of the issues, and emotional state of the disputants dictate the approach or direction they use. Recognizing this reality, the *inAccord* model adopts an overarching approach of facilitation while providing the mediator with options to be more directive or more relational based on the pre-mediation assessment.

The inAccord Model and its use of Approaches and Techniques

The use of the relational and directive approaches in the *inAccord* model has implications for the choice of techniques employed by the mediator. The mediator decides which approach to use based on the results of the Phase One pre-mediation *My Feelings* survey which identifies two blocks of emotions, those viewed as empowering (happiness, serenity, optimism) as well as those viewed as disempowering (guilt, shame, anger). A match of emotions is indicated when both disputants report empowering emotions or both report disempowering emotions. Alternatively, there may be a *mismatch* of emotions when one disputant reports empowering emotions and the other disputant reports disempowering emotions.

Use of the directive approach results from a mismatch of emotions reported by each disputant on the *My Feelings* survey, and settlements are more heavily emphasized, caucuses are more frequent, and attempts to narrow issues, promote compromise, and synthesize arguments are more common (Folger, Poole, & Stutman, 2001). In contrast, the relational approach is employed when there is a match of emotions reported by each disputant on the *My Feelings* survey.. There is a strong emphasis on face-to-face contact to promote understanding rather than bargain or negotiate for one's needs. The goal is not simply to reach agreements but to use the intervention as an opportunity to improve communication and to develop a foundation for addressing problems in general (Folger, Poole, & Stutman, 2001).

Overarching Facilitative Approach. The *inAccord* model is a facilitative approach in as far as it follows three phases and 4 specific stages that are facilitated by the mediator. This facilitative approach is based on the belief that people can work through and resolve their own disputes with the help of a neutral third party. The *inAccord* mediator will actively control the Three Phases and 4 Stages (see Table 1) but not control the disputants or their settlements. The process refers to the mediator's control of the movement through the survey instruments and includes an emphasis on helping parties to gain perspective on the conflict. The *inAccord* mediator will use and teach the *Touchstone Skills* of reflecting, reframing, and questioning to set up a safe and secure environment for the sessions, clarify the issues, positions and underlying interests, help set up a formal agenda and generate options, move the clients to settle on agreements in principle and further assist them in creating a resolution formalized in a contract called the Memorandum of Agreement.

How inAccord deviates from the Facilitative Approach. The *inAccord* mediator hopes to direct the process to settlement while recognizing that the parties are always in charge of the outcome. Most of the time spent in this mediation is guided by the Three Phases and 4 stage intervention process. However, the *inAccord* model separates itself from a purely facilitative approach because it employs a "hybrid" of what we refer to as directive and relational approaches to facilitate the dialogue between the disputants. The use of these approaches is based on the disputant emotions as reported in the *My Feelings Pre Survey*.

The inAccord Relational Approach. A central function of the *inAccord* model is the empowerment of the disputants and the mediator. Because of this emphasis, there is a bias toward using a relational approach if at all possible. The relational approach to the *inAccord* model seeks the empowerment and mutual recognition of the parties involved. In the context of mediation, the word empowerment means enabling the parties to define their own issues and to seek their own solutions (Bush & Folger, 1994). The *inAccord* relational approach concurs with transformative mediations emphasis on recognition and perspective-taking, which refers to enabling the disputants to see and understand the other person's point of view, as well as their personal beliefs and emotions associated with the conflict. This entails helping disputants understand how they "frame" the problem and assist them in identifying underlying interests that may lead to options for resolution.

44

The relational approach is used in the *inAccord* model with disputants who would like to pursue a continued future relationship because it involves a more collaborative, face-to-face process. However, there must be a match in the *My Feelings* survey in order for the mediator to agree to a relational approach. The *inAccord* mediator using this technique may be guided by the acronym **WAIT**: WHY AM **I** TALKING. The mediator is only actively participating in the dialogue with the disputants about fifteen percent of the time; it is conversation between the disputants, which should occupy about eighty five percent of the dialogue, especially when preserving the relationship is the primary focus.

The *inAccord* model relies on a relational approach if the *My Feelings* pre surveys show that the disputants' emotions match, meaning they either both feel empowered or both feel disempowered. However, the *inAccord* model moves from a purely relational approach by requiring the disputants to follow a structured process. Although, it seeks empowerment and measures this through the use of surveys, it does not focus, as purely transformative mediation does, on preserving the relationship, unless this is a stated goal of the disputants. A final deviation from a purely transformative approach is that the *inAccord* model is focused on settlement more centrally than transformation of the individuals.

The inAccord Directive Approach. A directive mediator is focused on identifying the weaknesses and strengths of each party's position in order to help them reach resolution. This process is an option for a mismatch of emotions reported in the Phase One *My Feelings* pre-survey or in high conflict cases in which joint sessions might lead to an escalation of the conflict or to disempowerment of one or all parties. For instance, in situations of domestic violence, a divorce mediator might use this option as the only form of mediation that would be viable in order to create safety for the victim party. The directive technique is often used in construction disputes and commercial disputes, especially when the parties do not foresee an ongoing relationship. In contrast to the relational approach where the mediator tends to only be actively participating in discussions fifteen percent of the time, the mediator using this directive technique is usually actively engaged in the process approximately eighty-five percent of the time.

The *inAccord* mediator uses a directive approach after Phase One and directly following Stage 1 of Phase Two, when the sharing of perspectives, held in a joint session, has concluded and when there is a mismatch of emotions as a result of the *My Feelings pre-survey* results. The *inAccord* model moves away from a purely directive approach by having the sharing of perspectives occur in joint session where the disputants share their issues, positions, and interests in the presence of one another. Sometimes, this is the first time the disputants have had a chance to actually hear the other person's perspective and it can be a very powerful moment in the mediation session.

Discerning Rights-based versus Interest-based Approaches

Another way of framing ADR processes is to identify those that focus on interest-based approaches to conflict resolution and those that focus on more rights-based approaches. Traditionally, in a rights-based process, the opposite sides of a conflict are competing to convince a decision-maker such as a judge or arbitrator to decide on the outcome of the conflict in a way that favors one party over the other. The judge or arbitrator focuses on the disputants' claims and the facts that either support or contradict these claims. These approaches may be appropriate when the right in violation is one upheld by federal law such as the Americans with Disability Act. When there is a clear violation of such an act, it is neither ethical nor, in some cases legal, to take the offended party into a process to negotiate their rights away.

Rights-based conflicts are often considered taboo for mediation, yet some author's such as Rees (2010) argue that although rights cannot be bargained away, there still may be times when, even in these cases, mediation is a more viable alternative than litigation. Rees argues that, "Where disputes that arise between companies and communities or individuals represent a tension between different rights, it is not for the company to decree how different rights should be treated--it has no legitimacy to do so. Yet it would be hasty to conclude that a judicial process is therefore the only appropriate avenue, or necessarily the best one in terms of remedy" (p. 8). We agree with Rees and argue that, although rights-based cases may proceed more readily to litigation, this is not a guarantee that the rights of anyone person or entity will actually be upheld in a court of law. Given the uncertainly of outcome, mediation, using a directive approach might offer a better solution for some rights-based conflicts.

In summary, the *inAccord* model's use of survey instruments moves the choice of approach out of the realm of intuition into a decision making process based on a measure of the disputant's emotional states. Although some critics such as Kovach and Love (1996) argue that directive techniques are incompatible with mediation, we counter this argument and state that the use of directive techniques in the *inAccord* model actually reinforces the mediation process when used in response to a mismatch of emotions by the parties indicated in the *My Feelings* pre-survey instrument. We chose the words relational and directive to describe the direction of negotiations in the *inAccord* model because we want mediator to be unchained from any one theoretical orientation or proscribed style. This allows the mediator greater freedom to respond creatively to each unique mediation case and disputant.

Chapter Three:
Transparency, Empowerment, and Systemic Change

Chapter Overview

This chapter begins with a discussion of transparency, why it is so critical to the success of mediation, and how it can co-exist with the seeming contradictory notion of confidentiality. The term transparency inevitably evokes a conversation over neutrality and impartiality in mediation and we present differing opinions in this ongoing debate including whether neutrality is even possible. Because the choice of directive and relational approaches in the *inAccord* model influences transparency as it relates to the issue of neutrality and impartiality, we will discuss this influence in terms of expanded and limited uses of neutrality and impartiality and how power balancing plays into this mix. The discussion of these two terms as they relate to transparency are deepened through an examination of systems theory, concepts of differentiation and self-regulation, transference and counter-transference, and their links to authenticity.

Transparency

Transparency means making the covert overt, shedding the roles of expert, and being open to mistakes and new awareness at every level of the process. Transparency is a universal concept in our model, because it applies to each stage of the mediation, to each disputant in the conflict, to the mediator, and to the model itself. The concept of transparency is foundational to most mediation models, yet is applied in different manners and degrees. Moffitt (1998) points out that, in most cases, a mediator's internal questioning throughout mediation (the result of years of training and experience) is usually not presented to the clients, which he believes is not in keeping with a transparent process. The *inAccord* model offers greater opportunity for a mediator to bring this internal wisdom to the surface by promoting transparency throughout the entire mediation process through carefully tracking the disputants understanding and satisfaction each step of the way. This begins with the mediator examining the results of the *My Feelings* survey, determining whether to begin with a relational or directive approach based on the survey results, and sharing this decision-making with the disputants. From the very beginning of a mediation case, *inAccord* takes much of the mystery out of the mediator's interventions by bringing the disputants' feedback into the entire four-stage process. This makes for a more transparent and empowering course for the disputants by granting them a window into process decisions that remain private in most mediation models.

Transparency in the *inAccord* model is accomplished through a sequential series of stages in which the mediator remains focused on the interests, understanding, and satisfaction of each party. Further, all parties are encouraged to communicate from an authentic stance based on increased self-awareness and increased awareness of the perspective of the other person. The goal is to reach a negotiated settlement to the conflict. Finally, clarifying the process at certain points in the mediation in order to make necessary adjustments to the approach, helps facilitate movement to an agreement. It is our hypothesis that transparency is critical for the empowerment of those involved in any dispute.

Transparency is accomplished through a continual cycle of: (a) remaining focused on the interests, understanding, and satisfaction of each party; (b) encouraging all parties to communicate from an authentic stance based on developing increased self-awareness, increased awareness of the other party's perspective, and achieving a mutual goal of a negotiated settlement in the form of a memorandum of agreement or MOA; (c) empowering the parties and mediator to find their *unique voice* in the dispute, to brainstorm options without judgment, to learn skills that will increase self-confidence, and to develop the ability to accept and understand varying points of view; and (d) reflecting on the process at certain points in order to make necessary adjustments to the progression, content, and interventions used in moving to a negotiated settlement.

According to Rees (2010), identifying the transparency is a significant challenge that mediation its credibility as a pathway for addressing a variety acknowledges that the question of transparency regard   ⌐ines of mediated disputes remains one of the trickiest areas to navigate. As she notes, "Just as confidentiality is a means to a particular and important end enabling parties to reach agreement, so transparency must be a means and not an end in itself. The ends that transparency can most clearly serve in the context of dispute resolution is two-fold: (a) enabling public confidence that the outcomes of such processes respect a minimum human rights standards and that complainants are not being pressured to concede these rights; (b) enabling others in society to benefit from a growing body of knowledge of how disputes are being resolved, with the objective of disseminating the learning and supporting future dispute prevention" (p.19).

We concur with Rees that confidentiality is an essential hallmark of mediation. It is also clear that there is a tension between transparency and confidentiality that arises because there are competing needs. On the one hand, mediators require complete transparency in the negotiation process from each of the disputants. On the other hand, this is at odds with the needs of confidentiality. There may be situations when you want to bring public awareness to a particular dispute, such as a civil rights issue regarding sexual harassment within a given company. Mediation efforts are usually private to the people who are experiencing the dispute, and often the outcome of mediation is also confidential. Therefore, mediation does not share the degree of lawful value of setting precedence in court cases or other public venues that employ conflict resolution.

Because of mediation confidentiality, it could be more challenging to use mediation as a teaching example to others. However, the cumulative effect of mediation can be discussed, and the observable changes and behaviors after mediation efforts can serve as the guideposts to onlookers and others in the organization. This is one impetus behind the creation of the measurement tools of the *inAccord* model. Conducting a study that aggregates the survey data across disputants can demonstrate the efficacy of the model and create guideposts for the effectiveness of the model without violating the confidentiality of individual disputants.

Another example of public awareness might involve publicly disclosing a water rights dispute in the Western United States, which may help someone in the Niger Delta, where water is a critical resource and its use a potentially contentious issue. However, when we bring in the transparency component, we must ask if it violates someone's rights to share the outcome of mediation. According to Braithwaite and Parker (1999), ". . .research suggests that where individual mediations can also be projected into some form of public narrative, this can both enhance law-making processes and help change attitudes across groups, communities or societies in support of human rights and other social norms" (p.86). What must be considered for issues of confidentiality with individual case studies is how to present these types of cases as an aggregate, putting forward the lessons learned or the accumulative effect of these mediations in a group presentation of the case and findings, to assure mediation confidentiality.

The issue of transparency versus confidentiality looms large in our work with the *inAccord* research surveys and study. A researcher wishes to publicize important results from a given study, through professional publications and the dissemination of findings to the public through various media outlets such as newspaper or magazine articles, the Internet, and other public media interviews. However, one also needs to uphold or ensure the confidentiality of the research participants who are also disputants. Sturm and Gadlin (2007) suggest that there are strategies for balancing the competing needs of transparency and confidentiality in such a situation. They observe that ". . . there are ways of aggregating data without revealing the identity of individuals. There are general points that can be drawn from the particulars . . . without breaching confidentiality" (Sturm and Gadlin, p. 38). The particulars in this case, refer to the specific findings from individual study participants. This has been our approach, in presenting the results of our own research, as noted in Chapter Seven.

Transference and Counter-transference

Immersion in the crisis and conflict of a dispute can expose a mediator to unexpected emotional ebbs and flow on the part of both disputants as well as on the part of the mediator. This immersion into the conflict requires a great amount of skill and seasoned experience. The mediator should be prepared for the emergence from disputants of powerful emotions that can also involve unwarranted idealization and affection projected onto the mediator. Disputants may have positive expectations that the mediator will be their hero or savior. Such exuberant positive reactions toward the mediator are what Freud (1952) called *transference* (based on the original concept of the interactions between therapist and patient.)

In classic transference theory, the client in therapy projects feelings onto the therapist that are, in fact, based on the past interpersonal relationships in the disputant's own life or where there were idealizations of real family members including affections in loving relationships. This concept can be viewed in the mediation context as well, with the disputants projecting their current or past struggles onto the mediator, in an unrealistic fashion. One of the tenants of mediation is that disputants and mediators do not develop natural emotional bonds, or long-term relationships like those between a therapist and patient, because they are task-oriented in a short-term process. Sometimes such feelings and unconscious processes can unfortunately arise in the mediation context, and must be dealt with by the mediator in a transparent way. Since the concerns are not about the actual relationship with the mediator, they are most likely "transferred" from past familial or love relationships.

It is important for the mediator to be vigilant about undue idealization by disputants throughout the process. The mediator should use the practical aspects of transparency to make it very clear to the disputants what is real and what is a projection upon the mediator by the disputant(s). For example, first author Ries noted in a particularly high conflict divorce that the wife was deferring to her constantly in the negotiations through either a direct plea for help or through imploring looks. Ries broke into caucus with the woman and asked her how she was feeling, noting that she seemed to be looking to the mediator for answers to her dilemma. The woman confided that she thought Ries was there to give her the answers since she was "the expert." Ries let her know that the goal of mediation was to help create an atmosphere wherein the woman could speak her mind, noting that only she had the true wisdom about her particular case. This seemed to ease the disputant's anxiety and the transference of her own authority onto the mediator, and she gradually began to take more control of her part of the negotiations.

Freud also pointed out that sometimes there can be negative transference, a less happy experience for the therapist, which can also be translated into the mediation process. Negative transference applied to mediation refers to unwarranted negative reactions by disputants toward the mediator and can be based on unfortunate experiences in the disputant's life; for example, there may be distrust toward a parent or a loved one that was distressing and unresolved, and now plays out with a new authority figure, the mediator. Thus, the mediator has to learn skills to defuse these inappropriate projections. The mediator can become caught in an inappropriate accusation about being distrustful. Here, mediation skills come to the foreground, namely clarity and transparency. The disputant and the mediator must come to an agreement that the process of mediation is not intended to delve into the disputant's past, that the mediation process is immediate and present-focused around the current conflict that has brought both disputants to mediation.

In another divorce case that first author Ries mediated, the husband began transferring his negative feelings about his soon to be ex-wife onto her by sneering and rolling his eyes whenever she tried to paraphrase what the wife was trying to say. In order to ensure this did not derail the process, Ries called for a caucus and related exactly what she noticed and asked what was going on for him. In this case, the husband was furious about his wife's affair that had led to the divorce and did not feel Ries was giving this "crime" the attention it mandated. "You women all band together", he complained. Ries was able to remind him that he and his wife were not in couples counseling but in divorce mediation. His reasons for wanting a divorce were reasonable but this process was not about airing grievances, it was about finding a way to parent their two young children without emotionally injuring them. In that quest, she was not siding with anyone but helping them find a way to set aside their anger and disappointment in the best interests of the children.

Freud and his followers have also pointed to the flip-side of transference, namely what he labeled "counter-transference." Counter-transference in mediation refers to the fact that the mediator may have feelings or reactions toward the disputants, based on his or her own past experiences. They could be positive, for example, unwarranted idealization or affection that are projected onto a disputant, based upon the mediator's former relationships with family members, a spouse, and other important significant others (e.g.," He reminds me of the strength that I admired in my father, so surely his position is more tenable."). Negative mediator experiences in their own life could be projected inappropriately onto the disputant, (e.g., "She is exactly like my nagging mother, so I will ignore her"). This could be particularly problematic, if there is one mediator and two disputants, as the mediator could develop some temporary counter-transference reactions toward one disputant, but not the other, making the mediator potentially biased in terms of the guidance he or she is offering.

Although much of Freudian thinking has come under considerable scrutiny in recent years by the clinical community, certain tenets have withstood criticism. These include Freud's views on defense mechanisms as well as his identification of the processes of transference and countertransference in the therapist - patient relationship (see Fonagy, Target, Steele, & Gerber, 1995). Those neo-Freudians who followed in the tradition of Klein (1976) continue to stress the relevance of the transference and counter-transference processes we have described. They acknowledge that while these mechanisms involve considerable projection from the client's or therapist's own life into the therapeutic relationship, they are powerful forces that need to be acknowledged, understood, interpreted, and managed. The same applies to the mediator - disputant relationship, where the mediator must take the lead in clarifying, interpreting, and communicating any such occurrences, if the mediator feels that they are interfering with the mediation process. This could be most usefully accomplished in the stages during which the *Touchstone Skills* of reflecting, reframing, and questioning are emphasized. As such, this clarification would contribute to the important role of transparency.

Mediator training must emphasize being particularly sensitive to unwarranted attractions or idealizations that disputants may develop during the process, and, alternatively, inappropriate idealizations and attractions that mediators may develop toward disputants. The short-term model of mediation should work, if carefully presented, to obviate these reactions. The *inAccord* internship course, which is required in order to be certified through our organization, encourages trainees to bring these types of issues to their instructor for consultation. In this way, we hope to model the importance of having an objective third party help with powerful issues such as transference and countertransference.

Links to Authenticity

There are two core aspects of transparency embedded in our model. The first is that the stages of the *inAccord* mediation process itself are clear to participants, that they are accessible and understandable. The second core aspect is that both mediators and disputants present themselves as the persons who they profess to be, as honestly as they can, and that they try to disclose certain relevant aspects of their true selves.

This second objective takes us into the realm of personal authenticity. Toward this goal, disputants are encouraged to identify and communicate their true interests, their underlying thoughts and emotions. Such authentic trade of information using the transparency of the mediation process can better move toward a sustainable, negotiated, settlement. However, authenticity is a psychological commodity that would appear to be in short supply in contemporary society (Harter, 2012; Leary, 2004). In its place we find that many of today's mediators and disputants engage in self-distorting behavior, in the form of self-enhancing strategies and self-serving biases that they bring to the conflict. In the extreme, self-aggrandizement shades into narcissism. These self-inflation tactics interfere with true self-awareness of the disputants' contribution to the conflict and what the mediator may contribute.

Why else might the lack of authenticity be a liability during the *inAccord* mediation process? Distorted perceptions of a person's thoughts and feelings may cause the disputant (or the mediator) to draw faulty conclusions that prompt bad decision making. As a social psychologist, Leary (2004) also observes that an egocentric approach to processing information can blind us to our shortcomings and undermine relationships with others. Self-distortion can also contribute to the misunderstanding and mismanagement of the struggles and conflicts that confront us in our daily lives (Harter, 2012). Clearly, this will be an impediment for the mediator in identifying authentic thoughts and feelings as well as promoting an awareness of the issues and interests of the self and that of each disputant, so critical to the *inAccord* mediation process.

A related concern in contemporary culture is our constant unproductive preoccupation with the self (Harter, 2012; Leary, 2004). Inner monologues and excessive rumination can be detrimental for those in conflict. The disputant fails to check out assumptions, not only about what they imagine is happening in the conflict, but what they imagine the other person is thinking. Without checking out this inner monologue through dialogue with another, it is hard to know what is possible for resolution versus what is imagined. Leary concludes that the distortion of the self, in the form of an overestimation of one's positive qualities, coupled with a preoccupation with such attributes, absorbs people in a ". . . cacophony of irrelevant self-generated thoughts" (p. 32). Such a process leaves little cognitive room for other mental processes, including attention to, and a realistic awareness, of others. This, in turn, will obviously interfere with those skills critical to the *inAccord* mediation process (for example, accurately identifying the underlying causes of a conflict, reframing the issues and clarifying interests, and taking responsibility for one's role in the dispute).

The *inAccord* survey instruments themselves can serve as a welcome interruption in both the disputants' preoccupation with the self and the presumed superiority of his/her position, as well as each disputant's self-distortion. At the close of Stage 1 during the first caucus, the mediator implements the *inAccord Touchstone Skills* of reflection, reframing and questioning, whereby the mediator promotes authenticity from the disputants. The mediator encourages disputants to get in touch with their true feelings and cognitions, through using these skills.

A common language is created wherein disputants may begin to listen to each other, as the use of these skills prepares a climate for authentic communication. The *inAccord* model takes authenticity a step further by providing constant interaction through the surveys, which measure understanding and satisfaction at each stage of the mediation process. The survey tools also create a self-checkpoint for the mediator, thereby preventing him/her from also falling into the trap of inner monologues and excessive rumination.

Leary (2004) also observes that self-biases often go undetected by an individual, as he or she overestimates the value of his or her self-worth, and that certain people are much more likely to acknowledge biases in others. That is, they feel that they have greater insights into other people's psyches and shortcomings than these people do. This aspect of self-deception carries with it the perception that one has a greater ability to respond rationally compared to others. This can lead to the interpretation that others' behavior may be irrational, while they deny their own irrationality. This psychological stance can obviously interfere with the goals of the mediation, and the mediator should recognize if a given disputant erroneously feels that he or she is more perceptive than the opposing party.

However, a sensitive mediator may be able to impact such normative biases. The very process of the *inAccord* model, with an emphasis on self-awareness and an appreciation for the perspectives of others, can help to temper these biases. Furthermore, our procedure of embedding our *inAccord* surveys into the mediation process itself serves to heighten the awareness of disputants' satisfaction and understanding, clarifying their perceptions, and making them more amenable to realistic solutions. When the mediator demonstrates his or her authenticity, each of the parties involved are able to witness the empowering force created by bringing one's authentic self to the room in the spirit of finding common ground and higher purpose.

Empowerment

Empowerment is another central function of the *inAccord* model. It is a common term used in disciplines that work with clients or communities and refers to the process by which people, organizations, and communities gain mastery over issues of concern to them. According to Rappaport (1987), "Empowering processes are those where people create or are given opportunities to control their own destiny and influence the decisions that affect their lives. They are a series of experiences in which individuals learn to see a closer correspondence between their goals and a sense of how to achieve them, gain greater access to and control over resources, and where people, organizations, and communities gain mastery over their lives" (p.119).

In time, empowerment develops into a broader understanding as a process of change (Cornell Empowerment Group, 1989). The empowerment process is defined as one that compels individuals and groups to think in terms of wellness rather than illness, strengths rather than weaknesses, and competencies rather than deficiencies. Empowerment is all about helping people and communities to gain the skills and resources they need to take control of their own lives or reach their full potential. The role of an outside expert is not one who intervenes with their own ideas of progress or change but rather a facilitator who guides people or the community to their own generated ideas and solutions. *Empowerment theory* is a common term used in disciplines that work with clients or communities and refers to the process by which people, organizations, and communities gain mastery over issues of concern to them. The *empowerment process* is defined as one that compels individuals and groups to take control of their own lives.

Empowerment and Mediation

According to Spreitzer and Doneson (2005), the modern concept of empowerment is derived from the civil and women's rights movements of the 1960s in the United States. However, the authors regard the concept of empowerment as stemming from a long progression within political philosophy beginning with the democratic ideas of Sir Francis Bacon in the sixteenth century. As they noted, empowerment theory is ". . . concerned with elucidating and applying the answers to the timeless questions of political philosophy itself – namely, the nature of power, the role of the citizen in the polis, and the achievement of justice in civic life. From this vantage point, empowerment is a continuation of this theoretical search for elusive, but critical, answers to timeless human questions" (p. 3).

The concept of empowerment was first brought into the field of mediation in 1994 by Bush and Folger (1994, 2005 in their groundbreaking book, *The Promise of Mediation: Responding to Conflict through Empowerment and Recognition.* The *inAccord* model expands on this theory by applying empowerment, in the form of disputants' emotions, to the entry and exit survey instruments completed by the disputants prior to and after the mediation process. These tools measure empowerment based upon a survey of empowering versus disempowering emotions. The surveys offer the mediator a gauge of empowerment prior to the mediation session allowing them to more thoughtfully choose the approach (more relational or more directive) that they will apply to specific cases.

Empowering the parties and mediator to find their own personal voice also applies to each of the Three Phases of the *inAccord* Model. Empowerment occurs when the mediator encourages parties to take a more active role in the mediation. Many mediation trainings teach variations of the *Touchstone Skills* of reflecting, reframing, and questioning. What is unique to the *inAccord* model is having the mediator, not simply modeling these skills, but *teaching* the disputants to use them in the first phase of the case. These three skills prepare the disputants to effectively negotiate with one another as the *inAccord* mediator encourages them to use them throughout the entire mediation process. These skills also increase self-confidence and self-awareness, and may engender compassion and an expanded perspective for the participants. Directly teaching these skills not only empowers the process and the disputants, but provides them with important *Touchstone Skills* they can apply to other conflict situations in their lives.

A discussion of empowerment in the field of mediation must invariably center on the debate between proponents of various mediation styles or methods. Although empowerment is most often associated with the model of transformative mediation which is more relational in direction, it is only in the most extreme cases of the model of evaluative mediation, which is directive in nature, that empowerment is entirely avoided. We would argue that most mediation models seek, in some measure, the empowerment of the disputants because it is commonly accepted that empowerment is necessary for effective mediation.

Mediator Neutrality and Impartiality

Much of the debate about the use of mediation models invariably centers on mediator neutrality and impartiality, which are issues that are under greater professional scrutiny than perhaps any other single issue in the field of mediation. It is reminiscent of challenges to the scientific field of objective experimentation that held sway during the period of Modernism which, in the twentieth century, ushered in numerous scientific and technological advances. With regard to human nature, rationality and reason became the essence of defining humanity, as the laws of science and reason prevailed (Harter, 2012; Hoffman, Steward, Warren, Meek, 2009). Modernism has, in recent years, given way to our current period of Postmodernism, during which objective reality and scientific reasoning have lost some of their luster, particularly as applied to human behavior and to psychological constructs such as the self (Harter, 2012).

As applied to mediation, ascribing terms like objective, neutral, and impartial to human behavior can be misleading. Nowhere is this more evident than in considering the issue of the neutrality and impartiality of the mediator in a dispute between two parties. Although the concept of a conflict of interest means that the mediator should not have another relationship with one of the parties, the concept of neutrality generally means that the mediator has no personal stake in the outcome. It is often used to describe a mediator's sense of disinterest in taking sides in a dispute, or in having a pre-existing bias toward the ultimate outcome, as well as lack of prior knowledge about the parties.

Impartiality generally means that the mediator exhibits no bias toward one of the parties or the concerns that they bring to the dispute. It often is used to refer to being even-handed, objective, and fair. Impartiality also requires the mediator's lack of prior knowledge of the dispute or the parties and the absence of judgment by the mediator about the parties and their conflict.

Neutrality and Impartiality in Theory and in Practice

In theory, these terms have several different elements of meaning. Most books on mediation practice and theory acknowledge that a broad notion of neutrality may be ideal in the abstract but may not be possible. These texts seem to assume that some mediator interventions and actions in the mediation process may violate the notion of neutrality. In contrast, with the *inAccord* model, we believe the mediation process and survey instruments are part of the process to encourage and evaluate mediator fairness, neutrality and impartiality. The mediator assesses these themes in each of the overarching phases and throughout the individual four stages of mediation. It is also included in the disputant's surveys at the conclusion of the mediation case.

From Strict Neutrality to Expanded Neutrality

In her 2002 book, *The Handbook of Family Dispute Resolution: Mediation Theory and Practice*, Taylor encourages mediators to think of neutrality along a continuum, or scale, from one extreme of strict neutrality to the other extreme of expanded neutrality. Strict neutrality is necessary in some contexts of mediation, where there are sophisticated negotiators who know their constituency's positions. It is less applicable in family and interpersonal disputes involving unsophisticated disputants who may or may not understand their own interests. In these instances, a mediator may need to control the process in order to give the disputant time to think.

We agree with Taylor, and have modified this concept of neutrality as it applies to our *inAccord* model. For example, when first author Ries knows that saving the relationship is a more critical goal than signing a Memorandum of Agreement, she will convene the mediation in joint session. Using this relational approach, she estimates she contributes about fifteen percent of actual direct communication whereas the disputants are actively engaged in the conversations approximately eighty-five percent of the time. The definition of expanded neutrality allows the mediator to play a much more active role in the case of a more directive approach, by more directly intervening and refocusing the mediation on personal and social change. When using this approach, Ries finds the reverse calculation is true and she contributes about eighty-five percent of actual direct communication whereas the disputants are actively engaged in the conversations approximately fifteen percent of the time.

The approach, implemented by the mediator, is either relational or directive as guided by the *Pre-Feelings Survey*, indicating where disputants fall regarding the strength of empowered or disempowered emotions. If there is a match of empowerment levels, meaning both parties are feeling empowered or both parties are feeling disempowered, the mediator selects a more relational approach and keeps all parties in the same room. For example, in the case of an eldercare dispute where two siblings are in conflict over how to care for their aging parents, surveys showed that both disputants were largely feeling disempowered by the ongoing animosity. In this case, the mediator started in joint session as she deduced that neither sibling had the upper hand in terms of feeling more empowered and could therefore dominate the other.

In contrast, if one party is empowered and the other party is disempowered, meaning that there is a mismatch of emotions, the mediator selects a more directive approach to address this perceived imbalance of power. Mediators in our model use a more controlling process, and therefore a more expanded level of neutrality that allows greater intervention by the mediator. For instance, a mediator will be more directive if he or she believes it will serve the emotional needs of the participants. This assessment is based on the self-reports filled out at the beginning of the session. If the disputants are at different emotional levels the person who is disempowered may be less rational whereas the person who is feeling empowered becomes *more* rational. In this case, the mediator will intervene by using a directive approach to begin the mediation. For example, a mediator in a divorce dispute found that one spouse reported anger about the divorce while the other, who initiated the divorce, is feeling hopeful. In this case, the mediator decided to begin the process with shuttle mediation.

Mediators employing a relational approach, based on the similar levels of empowering or disempowering feelings, will be closer to the expanded concept of neutrality because they tend to actively intervene and use their considerable influence to affect the process and the people directly. In relational mediation approaches, mediators tend to treat each person as an individual who may need a particular intervention, which makes it very difficult for them to maintain strict neutrality or impartiality. When the *My Feelings Pre-Survey* reveals a mismatch of empowerment levels, mediators use a directive approach employing greater direct problem solving skills and tending to stay much closer to strict concepts of neutrality.

It is important to reiterate that although the *inAccord My Feelings Pre-Survey* guides the initial choice of an approach, be it either relational or directive, this can change throughout the process. For example, a mediator might decide to begin with a directive approach but then notes that the more disempowered party is beginning to move to a more empowered stance. At this point, the mediator might ask this person if they would be agreeable to moving into a joint session for the remainder of the process. In this sense, the choice of approach should be considered fluid rather than set in stone as it focuses on continuing attempts to maintain the balance of empowerment among the disputants.

Empowerment and Power Balancing

The *inAccord* model, in its use of both relational and directive approaches to make up for power differences, is a form of power balancing. Power balancing refers to the mediator's attempts to rectify imbalances in power that will render an unfair settlement. However, the only strategy through which a mediator can address an imbalance of power is if he or she openly foregoes the neutrality/impartiality requirement. There are mediators who feel that any attempts at power balancing are a violation of the true intent of the mediation process, which is to keep the ultimate authority for the resolution in the hands of the clients. In contrast, others argue that the mediator must focus on leveling the power because negotiations may result in uneven and grossly unfair resolutions.

Deutsch (2006) concurs, pointing out that *asymmetries* in the interdependence in a relationship ultimately play out in a power differential, where one party has greater power than the other, and, as a result, tends to dominate in the negotiations. Moreover, he observes that if the disputing parties have adopted a competitive stance, the conflicting parties will seek to enhance their own power and to reduce the power of the other. This, in turn, provokes a power struggle which can lead to unconstructive coercive tactics, physical threats, and violence on the part of the dominant party. He notes that attempts to balance the power by the mediator will prove more constructive.

Our position is that balancing power is a better alternative than strict neutrality for most disputes utilizing the *inAccord* model. However, it is important to distinguish between a rights-based issue and an interest-based issue in terms of power balancing. Rights-based issues are not conducive to a pure relational approach, which uses the more strict neutrality concept. It is critical that the mediator using the *inAccord* model employ the directive approach when mediating rights as opposed to interests. As Rees (2010) notes, ". . . the theory and practice of mediation have sought to evolve to allow for the inevitable co-existence of rights and interests in practice. It has done so by defining different modes or styles of mediation to address each, according to the parties' preferences or the exigencies of the situation.

Evaluative mediation leans the process towards so-called 'rights-based approaches', and is indeed referred to by some as 'rights-based mediation' "(p.4).

In the ongoing conflict between citizens of the Niger Delta and the Shell Oil Company, millions of dollars and years of time have been spent pursuing the case through legal channels. To some, this case may seem too complex and "rights-based" to be well served through mediation. However, we would argue that a directive mediation approach might have been, and indeed still could be, a better option for resolution. As it is, the case has become a battle that will inevitably be won by those with the deepest pockets and the most time to spend in appeal after appeal.

Empowerment and its Link to the Concept of "Self-Efficacy"

A basic assumption in the *inAccord* model of mediation is that conflict is inevitable, regardless of whether it occurs with couples, within companies, or within and across countries (see also Lang and Taylor, 2000.) It is a normal human process, given the construction of social networks that define cultures. That said, it is also assumed that conflict is a workable phenomenon that can be impacted positively through mediation, by *empowering* disputants to play a major role in the process. Toward this goal, disputants play an active role in identifying the issues underlying the conflict that they bring to the table. Moreover, they are encouraged to engage in a number of skills to facilitate the process, including transparency, self-awareness, reflection, honest communication with the other party, and the understanding of the others' perspective, all of which can lead to a more realistic negotiation. The mastery of these skills is guided by a skilled mediator, trained in the *inAccord* model which fosters the empowerment process, placing these abilities within the grasp of the disputants, paving the way toward a resolution of the conflict.

However, the acquisition of these skills is not totally in the hands of the mediator, for the disputant cannot simply be a passive learner. The disputant must bring particular personal qualities to the process. One such characteristic is *self-efficacy*, a belief in one's own capabilities and skills, so essential to the concept of empowerment. *Self-efficacy* is a concept that is now ubiquitous not only within the field of psychology, where it first emerged, but within many related disciplines (Maddux & Gosselin, 2012). The term was originally introduced by noted psychologist Albert Bandura (1977) and quickly caught the imagination of academics, as well as those in numerous fields who saw the benefit of applying this concept to their own professional perspectives.

Self-efficacy concerns people's beliefs about their personal capabilities, and how these beliefs influence their expectations about what they are attempting to accomplish, the belief that "I can make this happen." Bandura's (1977) scholarly definition, when he first introduced this construct, was that self-efficacy represents beliefs about the ability "to organize and execute the courses of action required producing given attainments" (p. 3). It involves the belief that one will be able to apply their skills to new and challenging circumstances, that they will be able to mobilize their resources to accomplish new goals. Certainly, interpersonal conflicts represent challenging circumstances that bring one to mediation. Moreover, self-efficacy in a given circumstance has powerful *motivational* properties in moving one toward the pursuit of particular goals. Meta-analyses, collating findings across many studies, have confirmed that efficacy beliefs contribute significantly to people's level of motivation (Bandura & Loche, 2003).

The importance of this concept to mediation is Bandura's (2006) recent claims that self-efficacy is *not* a global, immutable personality trait. That is, self-efficacy is specific to one's own, unique, circumstances, in which goals are essential, particularly in the face of problems that demand realistic solutions (Maddux & Gosselin, 2012). Thus, self-efficacy is highly relevant to those specific conditions that bring people to mediation, where the notion of empowerment is central. As Maddux and Gosselin cogently point out, self-efficacy theory suggests that "formal interventions should provide people with the skills and sense of efficacy for solving problems themselves" (p. 3). This is precisely the assumption that underlies the *inAccord* concept of empowerment.

However, in our own work we have moved beyond assumptions. That is, we are directly, through our research on the *inAccord* model of mediation, asking disputants about their personal *experience* of empowerment. In our exit survey, we ask disputes to respond, on a four-point scale, to the following types of questions: "I liked the fact that I personally had a lot of say in the negotiations;" "It was important to know that I had some control as we went through the mediation process"; "I appreciated the fact that I was partly in charge of what was happening throughout the various stages." We are currently collecting data on the responses of disputants to these questions, obtaining their own perceptions of the importance of empowerment, as they have moved through the mediation process. As a result, we can next link their perceptions of empowerment to their understanding of the stage-related skills, to whether they signed a Memorandum of Agreement, and to their self-reported satisfaction with the mediation process, assessed on our exit survey. That is, we can directly examine the efficacy or a sense of empowerment, fostered by the mediation intervention, as it affects the desired outcomes of the process. In this manner, we can directly apply the very powerful concept of self-efficacy that currently dominates many related fields, to our mediation model and efforts that emphasize empowerment. Moreover, as will become apparent in the next chapter, we have extended the concept of empowerment to our categorization of emotions, viewing some as empowering whereas others are viewed as disempowering.

The Need for a Systemic Change.

Paul Warren, Director of Old Dominion University's Certificate Program in Conflict Management, argues that mediator neutrality is a myth. Because mediators cling to this term, he believes little has been written to help guide mediators in dealing with the strong feelings that will invariably arise for them during disputes. He offers a broader definition of neutrality, couched in systems theory. According to Warren (2001), neutrality speaks to an emotional quality of calm within the mediator that is expressed in the sessions, to an awareness of the impact of the parties' emotionality on both sides of an issue and an awareness of the mediator's and parties' combined subjectivity of their notions about what "should" be. This is analogous to the claim that the mediator can be *in the conflict, but not of it.* The systems model assumes that no one can be truly impartial or neutral because each of us brings our own biases, reactivity, and experience to the mediation. This is similar to a concept of interactional mediation and the inclusion of the mediator affecting the outcome that is discussed by Lang and Taylor (2000). However, Warren (2001) does believe that perceptions of bias can be mitigated by employing the concepts of differentiation and self-regulation during the process of mediation, concepts which are addressed in the next section.

Differentiation and Self-Regulation

Differentiation, when focused on the mediation context rather than in its original definitions from therapy, can refer to a mediator's ability to remain connected but not reactive during a session. This is accomplished by consistently defining one's self within the system, and maintaining a self that is not subsumed by the conflict or the disputants. For example, if a mediator feels the emotional intensity in the room rising, she might say, "It is feeling very heated in here right now. How are you two feeling?" In this way, she is able to demonstrate a clear connection to the intensity, yet not react in a way that steals the show, or that makes her complicit with the emotional qualities. Instead, the mediator labels the emotions and reflects them back to the clients with an open-ended question such as "how is this process going for you?"

This is similar to the concept of reflective practice described by Lang and Taylor (2000). Taylor (2002) further describes the concept of differentiation, which originated in developmental psychology and family systems theory, and she then states that the concept applies to the mediation process as potentially affecting the abilities of the disputants to negotiate for themselves. The more the disputants, as well as the mediator, are able to be healthily differentiated, the more the mediation process can unfold as intended, with separate disputants who are able to make good choices for themselves and who are not manipulated or controlled by the other disputant. Moreover, this necessitates a well-differentiated mediator who is not codependent or unduly affected by the ploys and manipulations or emotional qualities of the disputants, but able to maintain the integrity of the meditational process.

Warren (2001) defines self-regulation as the degree to which mediators are able to track their personal reactions to the disputants and their conflict. This entails the development of a strong sense of mindfulness or self-observation. The mediator must first be able to realize if he or she is becoming affected by the dispute, and then have the capacity to separate themselves from the surrounding emotional climate. In our *inAccord* model, mediators are encouraged to assess their own emotional states and responses in order to better support their ability to maintain a differentiated, strong self. He or she must practice the skill of self-regulation, not allowing their emotions to dim or control their perceptions, therefore being able to provide a more consistently unbiased and neutral process for the disputants.

The *inAccord* model assists the mediator with the two mitigating concepts of differentiation and self-regulation as proscribed by Warren (2001). The *inAccord* survey instruments allow the mediator to track the understanding and satisfaction of the disputants during each stage of the process. This assists the mediator in remaining engaged during sessions but not reactive, as he or she can trust that the structure of the process will hold the emotional intensity in check. The *inAccord* survey instruments administered after each stage as well as the measurements of emotions pre-and post-mediation, help the mediator cultivate a professional sense of mindfulness and self-observation. This occurs because the mediator becomes not only a passive witness to the emotional disruptions, but an active participant in building a structure that prevents the emotions from negatively impacting settlement.

A Final Word on Impartiality

Some theorists and practitioners are beginning, as Warren does, to define neutrality as a difficult, if not impossible, achievement in mediation. However, there is still a pervasive belief that mediators can exhibit impartiality and even-handedness in mediation. Even this term of impartial mediator behavior is subject to debate when viewed in a broader context. Theories that often place mediator impartiality along a spectrum of expanded to strict neutrality seem to insist that mediators maintain a one-dimensional, pure impartiality. This may be the result of trying to retain impartiality as critical, while the ground slowly erodes under the concept of neutrality. If mediation loses both its pure stance of neutrality and impartiality, what legitimizing stance will replace them? In most cases, impartiality is presented as a mediator's attitude and behavior exemplified by fairness and objectivity. However, attitudes and behaviors are not one dimensional in their application to the many elements of mediation.

A mediator will find, at the very least, that impartiality can be applied in three distinct ways: (1) impartiality towards disputants, (2) impartiality towards what would be considered a usual and customary experience and what a reasonable person might do, and (3) impartiality towards whether the disputants sign or do not sign the MOA.

Suddenly, impartiality becomes a spectrum, which is subject to many variations depending on the theory that informs the mediator's practice. For example, an *inAccord* mediator could lose impartiality because of the value placed on reaching settlement. Using a more relational approach, a mediator might compromise impartiality when educating the clients on the *Touchstone Skills* and attempting to balance the power between clients. Using a more directive approach, a mediator could forfeit impartiality by forcing a collection of courtroom norms based on procedural justice concepts like equal time, careful analysis of the type of information being given, and pressing disputants to identify their strengths and weaknesses instead of facilitating collaboration among the parties. As can be seen in these examples, impartiality is a much more fluid concept as opposed to a strict moral code that a mediator must follow because it is based on interpretations made by the mediator as to what constitutes a fair and balanced settlement.

Chapter Four:
The Critical Role of Emotions

Chapter Overview

In this chapter, we will first address the role of emotions in the *inAccord* model. Critical to our approach is assessing the disputants' self-reported emotions relative to the conflict that brought them to mediation. We will describe the development of the *My Feeling* survey instrument to assess disputants' emotions. An important theme will be the identification of the disputants' emotions at the *outset* of mediation. Two categories of emotions have been identified, empowering versus disempowering emotions. These emotions will be described and are embedded in our surveys and will enable the mediator to determine which approach will best facilitate the mediation process. As described earlier, the issue of whether there is a *match* between disputants self-reported emotions or a *mismatch* will inform the mediator as to which approach to adopt. The assessment of disputants' emotions at the end of the mediation process will also be instructive if there are changes. If the disputants' emotions have moved from the more disempowering to the more empowering emotions, this will suggest that the mediation efforts have been successful. Finally, our approach to emotions will draw upon recent psychological theory that emphasizes the function of positive emotions, emotional competence, and the role of self-conscious emotions.

The Role of Emotions in the inAccord Model

A novel feature of the *inAccord* model is the role played by emotions. Emotions are *powerful forces* that disputants bring to the mediation table. One major new contribution of this model is the identification of emotions that are empowering as well as emotions conceptualized as disempowering, namely, negative affects that can disrupt or prolong the mediation process. Our expectations, when the *inAccord* model is effective, are that empowering emotions would increase in strength by the end of the process whereas disempowering emotions would *decrease* in strength. Our rationale is that calling attention to these two classes of emotions, given that the surveys are embedded in each phase of mediation, will heighten the transparency component, bringing greater clarity to the process. That is, disputants will become more aware of their emotional reactions, which will facilitate their active role in the process, leading to a greater sense of their empowerment.

An important feature of the model is that disputants report to themselves and the mediator the emotions at the outset of mediation, as well as at the end. In this model, when monitoring the disputants' feelings, we explore the match or mismatch of empowering versus disempowering emotions between the two disputants or parties. We endeavor to understand the following questions: Do they both report empowering emotions? Do they both report disempowering emotions? Or does one party report empowering emotions, whereas the other reports disempowering emotions? As indicated in earlier chapters, the particular emotions of each party dictate the intervention approach employed by the mediator. In this chapter, we will explore recent theorizing about the role of positive emotions, including the importance of what we will label *cognitive-emotion hybrids* such as hope and optimism, or discouragement and despair. The role of self-conscious emotions, such as humiliation, will also be highlighted.

Evolution of our Focus on Emotions

It is important to address the evolution of our focus on disputant's emotional reactions to the conflict. The first author (Ries) developed the list of emotions based on considerable experience both as a family clinician as well as a mediator. It became clear to her that certain emotions could be conceptualized as *empowering* whereas other emotions seemed to derail progress toward the resolution of conflicts and were thus viewed as *disempowering.* The goal of an intervention, in the face of conflict, should be to reduce these disempowering feelings and to enhance the more empowering or facilitative emotions. It was our hypothesis that the stages of mediation in the *inAccord* model and teaching the *Touchstone Skills*, as well other interpersonal competencies, would produce such an effect. Our early research supports this contention (see Chapter 7).

Unlike certain types of research that are *theory-driven*, this was not the approach we adopted. Theory-driven research, also called the *hypothetico-deductive* method, begins with theoretical assertions to then be documented through research. That is, *hypotheses,* derived from one's theory, are clearly specified. These dictate appropriate experiments, driving a data-analytic strategy, and conclusions, based on the results of such studies, are then *deduced.* These conclusions may or may not support the original theory. Textbooks on the scientific method often describe this strategy as moving from the *general* (i.e., theory-driven hypotheses) to the *particular* (i.e., specific experiments to verify or dispute the theory).

An alternative strategy has been called the *inductive* approach to research, which is what we employed. This approach has been described as reasoning from the *particular* to the *general*. The beginning point, the particulars, are natural *observations* in the real world, where one observes human behavior over numerous incidents that appear to represent a larger pattern where one ultimately draws an inference about a more general principle or conclusion. However, any such conclusions become hypotheses that must then be documented by empirical research.

Some of the major giants in the field of Psychology, namely Freud (1952) and Piaget (1960), adopted the more inductive approach. The nature of Freud's particular observations consisted of his clinical interventions in the lives of many patients which lead him to systematize these specific insights into more general conclusions. These, in turn, lead him to the construction of a more formal theory. An early example led him to a theory of the dynamics of clinical syndrome that he labeled Hysteria in women during the Victorian era. He eventually put forth an entire theory about the etiology of this disorder, including suggestions for its treatment.

His eventual theory about *defense mechanisms*, still much respected, evolved in much the same manner. After observing many patients who manifested these mechanisms, for example, denial, projection of blame, reaction formation, etc., he culled these common observations, these "particulars", into a general theory of defense mechanisms. Personality researchers, to follow, subjected these observations to more rigorous empirical studies, documenting their validity in how people cope with challenges in their daily life. Considerable subsequent discoveries have come from the keen observations of clinicians whose formulations were later subject to more intense scrutiny, through appropriate research designs and procedures.

Application of the Inductive Method to our Focus on Emotions

We have applied such an approach to our focus on emotions. As noted earlier, the first author (Ries), in the course of her extensive clinical and mediation experience, gradually developed an appreciation for particular emotions that were critical, in moving through conflict toward a resolution. These observations led to the list of emotions presented earlier. While there are many more emotion labels in the English language, including more neutral emotions, these appeared to be the primary affects that were most relevant to conflict resolution. In Ries' experience, it became useful to divide these into those emotions that were empowering such as understanding, optimism, and trust and those that were disempowering, such as anger, depression, and blame. However, these were tentative conclusions that necessitated a more rigorous empirical examination, leading to the construction of the *My Feelings* survey.

Here are some of the initial observations in Ries' earlier mediation work that led to the selection of the emotions that we are now researching.

Serenity
Understanding
Forgiveness
Optimism
Hopefulness
Contentment
Trust
Happiness

Discouragement
Jealousy
Anger
Depression
Insecurity
Despair
Blame
Humiliation

When a disputant feels highly disempowered as indicated by such emotions as depression, jealousy, anger, and discouragement, but is able, to move into the more empowering emotions of hopefulness or optimism through mediation, there is a good chance of obtaining a signed Memorandum of Agreement. It is important for the *inAccord* mediator to understand that anger, although viewed as a disempowering emotion, can be the life-giving emotion required to move towards agreement. To stifle this emotion may drive a disputant back down to despair. Anger is productive; it is an emotion that can indicate to the mediator and the other disputant when a value or boundary has been crossed. Some writers have termed the use of anger as negative motivation, which moves a person away from undesirable outcomes, as opposed to positive motivation, which moves them toward what they see as an advantage. Often, in mediation, we can help the disputant harness the negative motivation to avoid the delays inherent in legal proceedings and continued conflict in order to bring about room for negotiation and agreement.

In caucus, when a disputant begins in despair and moves up to anger, Ries has found they are heading in the right direction for settlement. What becomes important is that the disputant does not remain in anger, but begins to move up the scale in order to move into decision-making and problem-solving. On the other hand, if one disputant is in optimism or hopefulness and the other is in anger, the two are not an emotional match. They literally fail to understand each other and are unable to relate to the other's perspective while functioning in this emotional state, also called a mismatch.

When disputants are in emotional mismatch, it then becomes necessary to use the concepts of *Best Alternative to a Negotiated Agreement(BATNA); Worst Alternative to a Negotiated Agreement(WATNA); and Most Likely Alternative to a Negotiated Agreement(MLTNA)*. The mediator can use an understanding of these concepts to help frame questions that help emotionally mismatched disputants rethink their interests, needs and positions.

Best Alternative to a Negotiated Agreement: Using this concept, a mediator might ask questions such as, "What would you like to see come of today's mediation?" or "If you didn't get your exact desired agreement, what would be the next best agreement?"

Worst Alternative to a Negotiated Agreement: Using this concept, a mediator might ask questions such as, "What would be the worst thing that could come of today's mediation?" or "If you don't come to an agreement today, what will happen?"

Most Likely Alternative to a Negotiated Agreement: Using this concept, a mediator might ask a question such as, "What do you think is most likely to be the agreement today?"

These questioning techniques are used to move disputants out of disempowering emotions and help the mediator try to achieve a level of understanding. This does not mean agreement with the emotion, but rather that the mediator or disputant is conveying a sense of understanding about the emotional content of the communication. The mediator could convey that by saying something like, "I can see how you might have that emotion, considering that…".

In the *inAccord model,* the mediator is looking for an understanding of the emotional needs (reflecting underlying interests) of the disputant who is not empowered.

The Importance of Identifying Disputant Emotions at the Outset of Mediation

Central to our mediation model is the importance of identifying disputant emotions at the outset of the process. Typically, disputant emotions evoked by the conflict are running strong when they seek out mediation, particularly negative feelings. Some disputants are frustrated, others are angry; some have fallen into the depths of despair. Others may be more hopeful and optimistic, or wanting a reason to be so. It is critical that the mediator be sensitive, early in the process, to the emotions that each disputant brings to the mediation process, as well the mediator's own feelings, which can serve as a barometer or gauge of the emotional climate between the two.

Many mediators concur with regard to the importance of attending to the emotions early in the mediation process. Bolton (1979) was one of the first to make a distinction between the emotional and substantive aspects of a conflict. He observed that when feelings are strong, for example, extreme anger, distrust, defensiveness, scorn, resentment, fear, or rejection, it is usually a sound strategy to address the emotional aspects of the conflict first. Rational problem-solving will be ineffective if the mediator does not first acknowledge the disputants expressed or underlying emotions. Fischer and Ury (1991) similarly observe that in a particularly bitter dispute, emotions can derail the mediation process by bringing a negotiation to an impasse or an end. Thus, the skillful mediator needs to first acknowledge the disputants' feelings as legitimate. These feelings may need to be expressed constructively before effective communication can proceed.

Kals and Jiranek (2012) extend this thinking into the realm of "organizational justice." They observe that "The analysis of emotions is the silver bullet for the understanding and resolution of justice conflict" (p. 229). They cite, as examples, anger, resentment and indignation if employees feel their rights have been violated in the workplace, arguing that emotions are good indicators of the virulence of the conflict. Taylor (2002) describes the process of *emotional flooding,* when disputants re-experience past trauma in such a way as to be triggered emotionally by the current dilemma, and must work through the old feelings so as to not misconnect them to the feelings about the current dispute.

Although we concur with the general conclusion of those who stress the importance of identifying emotions early in the mediation process, the *inAccord* model moves beyond this observation, in several important respects. First, we attend not only to the more obvious negative emotions that disputants bring to mediation, but to the positive emotions as well, since the more positive feelings are those that we want to encourage through the mediation process itself. Second, we have categorized emotions into those that we label as empowering and those that are viewed as disempowering. This feature of the model can be particularly helpful to the mediator, in gauging what approach to employ.

Finally, unlike others who merely urge the identification of emotions early in the process, we actually assess them directly, through self-report instruments. While self-report assessment tools are often criticized within the psychological research community as being non-objective, this is precisely the point. Our model alerts the disputants to be aware of their subjective emotional experience. It is first and foremost the disputants' own perceptions of their subjective emotional states that give meaning to their experience, so that must be the starting point.

The Construction of the My Feelings Pre-Survey

The *inAccord* model is unique in that it asks disputants directly about their emotional reactions to the conflict through one of our first assessment instruments, the *My Feelings Pre-Survey*. We take the disputants' perspectives about their own emotions around the conflict seriously. This is central to concepts of transparency and empowerment. Granted, a sensitive mediator will use techniques to further probe into emotions that may not be fully realized. However, allowing and encouraging disputants to report on their own feelings supports their sense of empowerment, namely, that they are encouraged to take an active role in the process by sharing their own perceptions of their emotional state around the conflict.

Toward this goal, we crafted the *My Feelings* pre-survey assessment instrument that is first administered during Phase One. We have also observed that additional useful information is provided by directly asking disputants to identify their own feelings as they pertain to the conflict. The *My Feelings* pre survey identifies two clusters of emotions, those that, in the experience of the first author (Ries), can be labeled as empowering and those that can be labeled as *disempowering*.

Here, we provide the complete list of each category of emotions, where the disputant is asked to rate, on a four-point scale, the strength of eight empowering emotions and eight disempowering emotions. The eight empowering emotions are: (1) Serenity, (2) Understanding, (3) Forgiveness, (4) Optimism, (5) Hopefulness, (6) Contentment, (7) Trust, and (8) Happiness. The eight disempowering emotions that disputants rate are: (1) Discouragement, (2) Jealousy, (3) Anger, (4) Depression, (5) Insecurity, (6) Despair, (7) Blame, and (8) Humiliation. (The *My Feelings* survey is provided in Appendix A.)

As described above, where development of the emotional survey is presented, our working premise for use of the survey was that the strength of the empowering emotions would increase whereas the strength of the disempowering emotions would decrease as a function of this mediation process in the hands of skillful mediators. The changes in the level of these two emotion clusters are an essential component of our premise. Our findings, based on mediators acting as disputants, provided very compelling evidence for just such shifts in emotion levels (see Figure 7-1, in Chapter Seven). We are unaware of any other mediation model which directly assesses disputants' self-report of emotional states in the beginning stages of mediation process, or any other model of mediation which relates the disputant reports of emotional states linked to predictive outcomes in the mediation process. This may prove an important contribution for disputant outcomes using the *inAccord* model of mediation, contributing significantly to the fields of justice and mediation.

A more intriguing use of our data has led to our use of these ratings to inform mediators about how best to select an approach to the mediation process for given disputants. Given that there are always two disputants present at mediation, we asked the question of whether it might be important to determine whether there was a match between the types of emotions that each party reported, or whether there was a mismatch. By match, we refer to those parties who both report empowering emotions, or those who report disempowering emotions. They would seem to be on the same affective wavelength. In contrast, other disputants represent a mismatch, in that one party is high on empowering emotions whereas the other is reporting strong disempowering emotions. What are the implications of match versus mismatch?

As previously described above, the rationale for why match versus mismatch has implications for the approach to be selected by mediators is related to the issue of power imbalance. When there is an imbalance, when one party feels empowered emotionally, citing the more positive emotions, but the other party reports disempowering negative emotions, thereby leading them to a sense that have less actual power in the relationship, then different approaches are dictated for the mediator. The relationship between matches/mismatches and the power differential of the two parties are made clear. If there is a match, then the mediator proceeds with a more relational approach. In contrast, if one party is empowered emotionally and the other is not, the mediator selects a more directive approach to address the related imbalance in power.

In this chapter, we wish to address another novel, but as yet hypothetical, implication of our choice of empowering emotions versus disempowering emotions. We should ask the research question, "Within each cluster, are certain emotions likely to be more predictive of outcomes such as signing or not signing the Memorandum of Agreement, or reporting positive versus negative reactions to mediation on our exit survey?" We have yet to examine this possibility. The particular choice of the emotions in both the empowering and disempowering categories, first identified by the first author (Ries), were not merely grouped into these two emotion clusters. Rather, they were ordered within each cluster with regard to their predictability of the likelihood of successful outcomes. The *My Feelings* surveys will allow further research on this question and others over time. For example, consider two sub-clusters within each of the two overarching categories of the emotions, empowering versus disempowering.

With regard to the empowering emotions, in the clinical experience of Ries, the first four emotions, (serenity, understanding, forgiveness, and optimism) should produce more optimal outcomes, whether it be signing the agreement or reporting positive reactions as measured on our exit survey. Following this thinking, a mediator would attempt to move the disputants further toward these emotional reactions as they move forward in the process, in a sense helping them build more of what Salovey & Mayer (1990), refer to as emotional intelligence, which is "...the ability to monitor one's own and others' feelings and emotions, to discriminate among them and to use this information to guide one's thinking and actions (p. 189)." As the disputants build this intelligence through the *Touchstone Skills*, we expect they will begin to gain more perspective and ability to find creative and collaborative solutions to their conflict.

In terms of the disempowering emotions, Ries has conceptualized them as two possible sub-clusters, where the emotions of discouragement, jealousy, anger, and depression may be more workable than the negative emotions of insecurity, despair, blame, and humiliation. Other writers on emotion classification (Salovey & Mayer, 1990, Zinck, 2008) would agree with this premise referring to the latter emotions as self-referenced feelings as opposed to the former which are progress or goal related negative feelings. According to Zinck (2008), self-referenced feelings such as shame, pride and guilt are "usually conceptualized as essentially involving the subject herself" or, in another sense, they are feelings that are internalized. Feelings such as jealousy or anger, are not self-referenced, but are evoked by an external situation or person outside the self and, according to authors such as Salovey & Mayer, may be used to help one progress toward a goal.

Mediators can help disputants identify and work with disempowering emotions and progress toward common goals. Ries has observed that when a disputant reports emotions in the disempowering cluster of emotions, the mediator might be more able to move them toward more empowering emotions such as hopefulness and optimism, leading them to be more likely to sign the Memorandum of Agreement. Moreover, if in caucus a disputant begins with feelings of depression and the mediator can encourage the disputant to move toward anger, this is more likely to be a path toward a settlement. Anger, Ries contends, is important to understand since it can be a central emotional force that is necessary to move toward agreement, more so than debilitating emotions such as despair, blame, and humiliation. That is, anger can be productive when it alerts us to a situation or person that is dangerous or threatening in some manner.

Furlong (2005) offers a similar view of anger in what he terms the model of "moving beyond the conflict" (p.24). He acknowledges that anger can initially be destructive when it is linked to one party's venting, attacking, insulting or demeaning the other party. Anger in this form prevents one from being able to listen and appropriately hear the other party's perspective. However, Furlong points to a workable feature of anger in that it indicates that the party is taking the issues seriously, even though they may not yet take full responsibility for their part in the conflict. The task of the facilitator, then, is to help the parties move beyond anger into the next phase of what he terms "acceptance," namely the acknowledgement that one is part of the problem and therefore must participate in the solution or the resolution of the conflict.

In our future research, we can dissect just which emotions in each cluster of empowering and disempowering emotions are most associated with movement toward positive outcomes. We may even posit other cognitive-emotional hybrid categories, based on other research, which might lead to better outcomes in mediation. This is an intriguing area of future study that will not only inform our research results, but will have important implications for mediators and the disputants we wish to serve. The underlying goal is to determine how clusters and sub-clusters of emotions facilitate the mediation process.

Self-Conscious Emotions

Within the field of psychology, emotions have become much more central as key actors on the stage of human behavior. Emotions have finally been given their due, as legitimate constructs that play a vital role, in consort with cognitions. One category of emotions, receiving considerable recent attention, is that of "self-conscious" emotions (Harter, 2012, Lewis, 2008). Unlike the basic emotions such as fear, anger, and sadness, which often operate automatically in response to threat within one's environment, self-conscious emotions involve more cognitive reflection on the self. These emotions include shame, guilt, humiliation, and embarrassment. Harter (2012) has compared and contrasted the causes and consequences of each of these emotions, although humiliation is the emotion most critical to mediation.

Humiliation is particularly relevant to the issue of conflict. Lindner (2006) has provided an excellent treatment of the role of humiliation, and shares the recent perspective on the functional role of emotions. Unfortunately, the job description for negative emotions does not necessarily result in charitable outcomes. Such is the case with humiliation. Lindner (2006) observes that humiliation involves putting down, holding down, and rendering the other helpless to resist the debasement. When feelings of humiliation arise in global level conflict situations, where there are imbalances of power, rifts are created and trust is destroyed. In the worst case scenario, violence erupts destructively. Noted New York Times columnist Thomas Friedman in 2003 was quoted as reporting that "If I've learned one thing covering world affairs, it is this: The single most under-appreciated force in international relations is humiliation" (as reported in Lindner, 2006, p. 116). Lindner concludes that feelings of humiliation impact conflict malignantly when they are translated into violence.

It is noteworthy that in the selection of emotions to include in our *inAccord* survey on disputants' ratings of their own feelings, author Ries placed humiliation at the bottom of the hierarchy of negative emotions, reflecting her view that this was potentially one of the most destructive emotions that disputants can bring to mediation. Thus, mediators must be especially sensitive to defusing this emotion, helping disputants to ascend the emotion ladder into more constructive emotions that can facilitate the mediation process.

Lindner's perspective on humiliation dovetails with Harter's research. Harter (2012) became initially interested in the role of humiliation in the 12 high-profile cases of school shooters, who violently murdered and injured classmates randomly, with no concern for their lives. In each case, these white, middle-class teenage boys, who were relentlessly teased, taunted, and tortured by their more entitled classmates, eventually snapped and retaliated into violence. Although considerable recent attention has been devoted to the issue of bullying and victimization within the school culture, Harter's analysis is unique in that it places a negative emotion, namely humiliation, at the crux of the revenge scenario that we have now observed, repeatedly, in these high-profile school shooting incidents. The need for interactive justice, to right the wrong of humiliation, might well be the basis for drastic actions such as these.

Being bullied, as hundreds of children and adolescents experience daily in our schools and neighborhoods across the country, does not automatically trigger violence or revenge. Many suffer through the assaults without retaliation, oppression itself is not sufficient. What eventually triggers a violent reaction is a history of profound humiliation, an emotion that provokes retaliation in the most violent form, namely the killing of others. That the subsequent victims of these murders were not selected targets but the result of random shootings, highlights the irrationality and desperateness of these acts. Played out on a larger scale of countries where the oppressed are also humiliated, this emotion is truly a force to be recognized.

Lindner (2006) also considers other self-conscious emotions such as guilt and shame. Her analysis of guilt is similar to others' understanding of this emotion in that it is the most potentially constructive of the negative self-conscious emotions (see Harter, 2012). Guilt, in this author's analysis, drawing upon others' descriptions, is caused by specific transgressions or moral wrongdoings that violate one's own or others' ideals for the self. They can lead to a fear of public evaluation or exposure that threatens one's social status and identity. However, guilt has more positive consequences than shame or humiliation, in that it typically mobilizes the individual to engage in acts of confession, contrition, apologies, and efforts at reparation. That is, it can promote an attempt to restore relational bonds and to strengthen relationships.

Lindner (2006) concurs, pointing out that the feelings of guilt for omissions and transgressions, if acknowledged and remedied by apologies and forgiveness, can be a powerful and healing force in conflict. However, they need to be accompanied by candidness, humility, and warmth, if they are to be constructive in the mediation process. She concludes: "Guilt can best be borne to healing, if embedded in respectful restorative justice" (Lindner, 2006, p. 282).

Emotional Competence

There are several recent trends within the field of psychology that converge with the goals of mediation as taught through the *inAccord* model. The first theme that we find consistent with this model addresses the concept of "emotional competence" (Saarni et al., 2006). The term "competence" was primarily reserved for cognitive skills, athletic skills, as well as more circumscribed categories such as musical talents or mechanical abilities. However today, with the increasing importance of emotions to the field of psychology, interest in "emotional competence" has come to the fore. Developmental psychologists have identified a sequence of eight levels of emotional skills that are typically mastered in order, each skill building upon the previous set of emotional capabilities. Many of these acquisitions translate directly into the *inAccord* Model, where the convergence of thinking is notable. Mediators using this model could informally assess these levels to determine the disputants' separate levels of emotional competence.

Level 1. Here, the capacities involve an awareness of one's emotional states, including the possibility that one may experience multiple emotions (see Harter, 2012). At even more mature levels, there may emerge an appreciation for the fact that one might not always be consciously aware of one's emotions, due to unconscious dynamics or selective attention. Our *inAccord* model attempts to make disputants more aware of their emotions, first by asking them to report on their conflict-related emotions on the My Feelings Survey. A sensitive mediator should also be able to detect clues as to unconscious emotions that would need to be uncovered in order to facilitate the process of moving toward agreements.

Level 2. The individual must develop skills to discern others' emotions based upon situational and expressive clues that require some degree of cultural consensus as to their emotional meaning. Here again, these are precisely the skills that the *inAccord* model tries to instill, given the importance of understanding what the other party is feeling, as well, through dialogues that encourage perspective-taking.

Level 3. Another important component to emotional competence is the mastery of a culturally-relevant vocabulary of emotion terms, namely verbal facility with commonly-employed emotion terminology. In mediation, where dialogue is so critical, these skills are imperative.

Level 4. Emotional competence also makes reference to the capacity for empathic and sympathetic involvement in another's emotional experiences. This is at the heart of many of the skills that mediation attempts to foster.

Level 5. One must further develop skills in understanding that one's inner emotional state need not correspond to its outer expression, both in oneself and others. This theme speaks to our own emphasis on transparency and authenticity in that disputants are encouraged to get in touch with their innermost feelings, learning to label and then communicate them clearly and effectively in the negotiation process. Self-biases and self-deception, as we have discussed, can represent serious roadblocks.

Level 6. Emotional Competence also makes reference to the development of skills to cope adaptively with aversive emotions and distressing circumstances by using self-regulatory strategies that weaken the intensity or the temporal duration of negative emotional states that are disruptive (such as our list of disempowering emotions). What is needed are skills to strengthen those more positive, empowering emotions that can lead to more effective problem solving strategies. Clearly the conflicts that disputants bring to mediation represent distressing circumstances that are associated with aversive emotions and must be dealt with before effective problem solutions can be entertained.

Level 7. Individuals must come to realize that the nature of a relationship is largely defined by how emotions are communicated within that relationship, where ideally one displays genuineness in the expressive display of emotions. Moreover, there must be emotional reciprocity or symmetry within the relationship. Genuineness, of course, is analogous to authenticity, in our model. Symmetry is akin to our notion of a power balance in emotional states such that one party does not overwhelm the other with disempowering emotions. This will weaken the other person's power if there is a mismatch in which the other party becomes dominant, due to more empowering emotions that lead to a power imbalance.

Level 8. In this final and highest level, "emotional efficacy" is the designated goal. The individual at this level is very much in touch with his/her emotions and can understand, accept, and respect his/her emotional experiences. A person at this level develops a moral belief system about what constitutes the desirable emotional balance in a relationship, and strives to meet that goal. Here again we see a convergence between the concept of "emotional efficacy" and the principles that are encouraged in the *inAccord* Model, which is designed to empower individuals, in part through their emotional understanding, to reach higher goals in an efficacious manner.

Hope Theory as Applied to Mediation

There are other current trends within the field of psychology that relate to the issue of the role of emotions in mediation. One such application can be found in what has been labeled as "Hope Theory" (Snyder,1989, 1994). Snyder, a psychologist who became interested in the concept of hope, first conducted numerous open-ended interviews with individuals asking them about the role of hope in achieving their goals as well as what goes awry when goals are thwarted. It became apparent to him that hope was the other side of the excuse-making process (Snyder, 1989). The common thread in the literature had been that hope involves the perception or the belief that one's aspirations can realistically be achieved. Snyder's interviews revealed that there were two basic components that led him to his Theory of Hope. These involved the construct of *pathways,* namely psychological routes to pursue in order to reach one's goals and secondly, *agency,* the motivational component in hope theory, which is defined as the perceived ability to utilize pathways to reach one's desired goals.

Pathways require that people can organize their thoughts and behaviors in order to bring about desired future conditions in the form of goals. Toward this end, one must be able to generate various routes connecting the present to this imagined future. Ideally, individuals should be able to generate multiple pathways when encountering barriers to achieving their pursuits. Research has demonstrated that high-hope people are more effective at generating alternative pathways to their goals (Irving, Snyder, & Crowson, 1998.) However, not all individuals who come to mediation are high-hope people who can generate alternative strategies that they might pursue in resolving their conflict. Here is where a skilled mediator can be effective, in encouraging and empowering lower hope disputants to generate alternative solutions, guiding them through the process, introducing adaptive skills that allow them to move along the pathway to a negotiated agreement.

Agency is the perceived ability to utilize these pathways to reach desired goals; it involves self-referential thoughts about the ability to initiate and sustain movement along a pathway (Snyder, 1994.) Agency is critical to many goal pursuits, including conflict-resolution, and is crucial in situations where people become "blocked." In situations where there is unresolved conflict, a skilled mediator can serve as someone who can help disputants move beyond their experience of the psychological blockage that is interfering with their motivation to pursue relevant pathways. There is some conceptual overlap between Snyder's concept of *agency* and Bandura's construct of self-efficacy. Specifically, Bandura (1997) defines efficacy expectation as the situation-specific evaluation that an individual can carry out a particular course of action for a specific goal pursuit. Here, again, is a potential role for the mediator to facilitate the motivation of the disputants, to empower them toward the choice of possible alternatives in the conflict resolution process.

Hope is not necessarily or automatically successful, since it depends upon the level of hope and the extent to which the goals are realistic (Rand & Cheavens, 2009). These authors report findings revealing that hope flourishes when the probability of hoped-for goal attainment is at an intermediate level. That is, hope can be too expansive, too grandiose and often unrealistic, in which case meeting goals may be thwarted. At the opposite pole, hope can be too meager or constricted, limiting any movement toward achieving one's goal. The Goldilocks principle of "just right" applies here, in that an intermediate level of hope is likely to be more realistic, identifying goals that require a stretch, but are ultimately within one's grasp. This is another arena in which mediators can facilitate the process, by encouraging people to move toward goals that can actually be realized.

Within Hope Theory, cognitive, as opposed to emotional, processes are conceptualized as central. Emotions enter into the equation, although for Snyder and colleagues (see Snyder, et al., 2002), cognitions precede emotions; that is, positive emotions stem from perceived progress in effectively overcome obstacles. That is, thoughts about one's motivational state and the likelihood of particular outcomes give rise to emotions and not vice versa (Rand & Cheavens, 2009).

This leads to an important question: "Which comes first, a cognition or an emotion?" This theoretical question evokes memories of the controversy within the field of academic psychology in the 1980's that posed this same question and then led to research to find the answer. Two key players in this debate, Lazarus (1982) and Zajonc (1980) engaged in a heated exchange taking opposite sides of the issue. Lazarus, riding on the crest of the wave of the cognitive zeitgeist at the time, argued vehemently for the primacy of cognition, emphasizing that emotions are the products of cognitive activity. Lazarus argued that a person's cognitive appraisals of events and their perceived significance for well-being are necessary for the evocation of an emotion, they are always crucial to the elicitation of an emotion. Weiner's (1985) attribution theory is consistent with this viewpoint, in arguing that causal thoughts precede or change the experience; this should be critical to an understanding of emotions such as pride, pity, guilt, and anger. Weiner (1985) cites research documenting that specific thoughts give rise to particular emotions – according to this formulation, we think first, feel afterward, and these feelings are based on what we think.

Zajonc (1980) countered these arguments, suggesting that emotional reactions can occur without prior cognitions, that they do not necessarily require cognitive activity. In his seminal writing, he developed the axiom, "Preferences need no inferences." He makes the claim that affect (emotion) arises early in the process of registration and retrieval, and that it derives from a parallel, separate, independent system. He argued that affective reactions are inescapable; they cannot always be voluntarily controlled. Moreover, they seem to be irrevocable, in that humans are never wrong about what they like or dislike, but could be inaccurate about what they think. He concludes by observing that if preferences or emotions were nothing more than cognitive representations of object features, then the problems of predicting attitudes, decisions, aesthetic judgments, and first impressions would have been solved long ago. Often, he observes, affect or emotions are fairly impervious to cognitions, giving, as examples, falling in love or appreciating a work of art.

As the field of psychology has evolved, it has become clear that the inquiry into "which comes first, a cognition or an emotion," is a false dichotomy and bogus question. One can readily come up with examples of situations in which cognitions logically precede an emotional reaction. For example, from Weiner's attribution perspective, if someone is late for an engagement, that person's emotional reaction will depend upon an appraisal of the cause; was the person late because of a car accident (engendering emotions of empathy and pity) or was he/she late because there were irresistible President's Day sales at the mall that could not be passed up (engendering the other person's emotions of frustration and anger). You can also imagine situations in which a person has an initial emotional reaction, for example, Zajonc's (1980) contentions about first instantaneous impressions, whether it is encountering a new work of art, meeting a new person, or love at first sight, where emotional reactions clearly seem to predominate.

In the second author's research efforts (Harter, 1999, 2012), this controversy addressed the correlation between self-worth and depressed affect. Those who adhere to Lazarus' position would argue that the appraisal of oneself, a cognition, must precede the emotional reaction of depression, that is, I don't like myself as a person (thought) and then I get depressed (feeling). The alternative directionality of effects is also possible, that is, I get depressed about something that happened (feeling), and then I don't think of myself as a good person(thought). In work with adolescents (Harter, 1999), there were two distinct groups, those who endorsed the view a cognitive evaluation of the self precedes the emotional reaction of the depression, and a second group that acknowledged that an emotional state such as depression provoked a negative cognitive appraisal of the self. In the natural laboratory of obtaining responses to open-ended questions, we found that among adolescents, both directionalities exist, muting the academic arguments.

Changes within the broader field of the psychology of emotion also speak to the general role of emotions in human functioning. For many decades, a discussion of the role of emotions was to view emotions as dysfunctional or disorganizing, as disruptive and therefore maladaptive. In many texts, emotions were simply given scant attention, as a cursory look at the index of topics would reveal. The "new look" in emotion theory (Campos, Mumme, Kermoian, & Campos, 1994; Saarni, et al , 2006) makes a strong argument for the functional role of emotions. We have emotions because they help us. According to these authors, four general functional categories can be identified.

•Emotions have a protective value, as both Darwin (1965) and James (1890) cogently argued, since they prepare you for fight or flight.

•Emotions provide organizational and motivational functions, that is, an appropriate, intermediate level of anxiety or anger can help individuals to organize their behavior toward a particular goal.

•Emotions also act as signals to others in interpersonal communication. For example, sadness or depression may elicit an empathic reaction in significant others.

•Emotions are also signals to the *self*, and they may provide insights into one's motives, conscious or initially unconscious. They can provide clues as to what is important in life. They can also facilitate particular future actions, or dictate that the person refrain from a particular course of action. Emotions not expressed or not labeled can be displaced maladaptively.

How can this excursion into the changing views of the role of emotions be linked back to the issue of hope and the role of mediation? First and foremost, the role of hope and its relationship to emotions does not fall neatly into one of the two arguable positions of whether cognitions precede emotions versus emotions precede cognitions. In writing about Snyder's theory of hope, Rand and Cheavens (2009) describe how at any given point in the pursuit of a goal, a person may encounter stressors. A stressor or obstacle is defined as any impediment that could jeopardize a goal pursuit. Conflict within a marriage or a family can represent one such example. The stressors or conflict, in our example, generates emotions that feed back to influence pathways to solutions and a sense of agency, both of which direct the ongoing goal pursuit which may be resolution in the face of conflict. The resultant emotions are a function of how the stressor is appraised, as attributional theory would suggest.

Rand and Cheavens (2009) thoughtfully observe that high-hope individuals are more apt to experience concomitant positive emotions because they are more likely to see stressors as challenges to be overcome. In positing this link, they are essentially giving voice to the fact that emotional predilections in high-hope individuals are primary and functional. Those authors go on to point out those with higher hope should be better able to generate the best routes to accomplish their goals and have more motivation to use these desirable pathways or routes, resulting in increased success. Studies reveal that high-hope people do generate more strategies or pathways for effectively coping with stressors or conflicts and express a greater likelihood of using these strategies in the future, a major goal of the *inAccord* model. High-hope people also have an enhanced ability to take the perspective of others, a key component in the *inAccord* model of mediation. Interestingly, Rand and Cheavens (2009) also note that those with low hope are more likely to use avoidance as a coping strategy. In our own current work, we are also examining various coping strategies that we can now relate to disputants' self-report of the efficacy of mediation.

There are clear examples of how hope can function both as a cause as well as an effect, rendering the debate about which comes first, cognitions or emotions, as obsolete, at best, and meaningless, at worst.

The *inAccord* model adopted a functional perspective on emotions, and has articulated these functions. We identify emotions as links in the chain of mediation, sometimes preceding cognitions, sometimes acting as the result of cognitive appraisals. We do not fall in the trap of contending that one necessarily and always precedes the other. Toward our goals, as have been described earlier, we ask disputants at the outset, to indicate which emotions are most salient for them as they reflect on the conflict that brought them to mediation. They fill out a checklist of eight emotions that have been found to be empowering and a separate list of eight emotions judged to be disempowering based on the clinical experience of first author (Ries). We are anticipating that the emotions disputants bring to the conflict as they approach mediation are critical predictors of understanding and satisfaction with the stage goals, as well as with the outcomes of the mediation. Considering the dyad of disputants, an important concept is whether the emotions that they report "match" or are congruent, that is, both enter the process with either empowering emotions or disempowering emotions. Conversely, one disputant may report empowering emotions whereas the second party reports disempowering emotions, leading to a mismatch. This creates specific implications for both how the mediators proceed and how they select what approach to use, as has been described.

As a starting point, we take the emotions that disputants bring to the mediation process seriously; we place a great premium on the emotional states of each party. Perhaps even more to the point, we do not view these emotions as traits, as solidified and intractable. That is, we see them as malleable emotional states that can be impacted through the mediation process. It is for this reason that we reassess their emotional reaction at the very end of the process and find that they are altered as a result of the mediation intervention. Empowering emotions increase in strength and disempowering emotions decrease in strength.

Is hope a cognition or an emotion, and how is this relevant to the "feelings" we selected? Snyder's (1994) theory of hope identifies it as "cognition", an appraisal that is intimately related to positive emotions viewed as separate constructs. This perspective mirrors the thinking of the time, when Snyder first introduced his theory. Cognitions and emotions were conceptualized as separate entities, allowing for the examination of how they might be related, addressing the question of "which comes first" in the popular sequential models of the day. However, these dichotomies have fallen from grace, as newer thinking acknowledges that there can be what we label as *cognitive-emotion hybrids* that combine both appraisals and an affective reaction. We give the common term "bittersweet" as one example of how these combination hybrids work (Harter, 2012). It can be bittersweet when a loved one moves to another part of the country to pursue better educational or professional advantages; a friend or family member can be both happy for the new opportunity offered the person, but also sad that he or she is leaving. So is the concept bittersweet a cognition or an emotion? We would argue that it is both, that it is a hybrid. Many words in our English language would seem to connote such blends.

For this reason, our list, captured in the *My Feelings Pre-Survey*, represent a number of such terms, where it is difficult to disentangle the cognitive from the emotional component. For example, one such term is "optimism," closely linked to hope. Other such terms that we have concluded are "serenity," "trust", and "understanding." In our opinion, these represent hybrids of a cognition and an emotion that, in the clinical and mediation experience of the first author are important predictors of how disputants will react to the mediation intervention.

These terms have been added to more conventional emotions terms, such as happiness. Negative affective descriptors refer to what are considered to be as typical emotions (e.g., anger, depression, humiliation, jealousy) but also include what we are calling hybrids, for example, discouragement, blame, and insecurity. Our goal is not to dissect these hybrids into their cognitive or emotional components. Rather, from experience, we have knowledge, both from Ries' experience as well as our initial pilot studies, that the list we have compiled is quite effective in predicting disputants' gains as a result of the mediation process. Furthermore, we have documented, statistically, that the hybrid terms converge with the more conventional emotion labels to form clear, reliable clusters. Our intent is to continue to employ these clusters both as pre-test assessments and then post-test indicators where we can document change as a result of the mediation training.

Our concept of *cognitive-emotion hybrids* is consistent with the thinking of others in the field of mediation, although most do not invoke this concept specifically. However, they do include similar affective states in their list of emotions. For example, Hawkins (2002) includes terms such as optimism, serenity, and understanding under his category of emotions, just as we have independently placed them on our own list of empowering emotions. He includes despair and blame among the negative emotions, which we have placed on our list of disempowering feelings.

To return to the construct of hope, which we consider one of these cognition-emotion hybrids, the Theory of Hope (Snyder, 1994) specifies implications for intervention efforts, particularly those employing cognitive restructuring and behavior modification techniques. The strategies employed in these therapies provide insight into the pathways and motivation toward goal attainment that are specified in Hope Theory. Moreover, Hope Theory has been employed to develop novel and promising individual, as well as group, interventions. Mediation would be one such application of this theory, because the mediator can help disputants develop and take ownership of the pathways and strategies to resolve conflicts, as well as impact their motivation to do so. Hope, in this analysis, has been only one of the emotional hybrids that we have included in our survey. The same effects are observable for the other cognition-emotion constructs that define our *My Feelings* pre survey, lending support to the efficacy of the *inAccord* mediation model.

The Function of Positive Emotions

Hope theory has features in common with the Broaden-and-Build Theory of Positive Emotions (Frederickson, 1998). When emotions first entered the field of psychology as a legitimate topic of study, attention was primarily devoted to the function of *negative* affects (e.g., fear, anger, sadness). Positive emotions were somehow deemed less adaptive, from an evolutionary perspective, less relevant to survival. However, recently positive emotions have captured the attention of theorists (e.g., Frederickson, 1998; Cohn & Frederickson, 2009) who have offered a functional perspective on the role of such affects. Fredrickson and colleagues have put forth what is labeled as a Broaden-and-Build Theory of positive emotions.

The broadening function refers to the claim that positive feelings serve to widen the array of thoughts and actions available to the individual, they produce more flexible response tendencies and solutions to life's challenges. As a result of a broadened mind set, one has access to more personal coping resources, which, in turn, enhance the likelihood of success in the future. This broadening function makes the individual more receptive or open to new information and promotes enhanced creativity.

The broadening argument shares much in common with Isen's (2000) discussion of the role of positive affect in decision-making, as it can be applied to mediation. Isen observes that, "Positive affect has also been found to promote creativity and flexibility in problem solving and negotiation, as well as both efficiency and thoroughness in decision making and other indicators of improved thinking" (p.548). Isen cites numerous findings that have been found in a wide range of settings and populations. These skills are critical to the *inAccord* model.

According to the Build hypothesis of this theory, positive emotions first produce a broadened range of solutions that the individual can now build upon to construct enduring personal resources. This building function provides a source of agency for achieving important life goals. Findings from Cohn & Frederickson (2009) reveal that positive emotions are associated with the ability to develop a more long-range perspective that facilitates the purposeful development of plans and aspirations for the future. Thus, positive emotions can assist the individual in facing life's stressors, including interpersonal conflicts. To the extent that building resources provides one with a sense of agency, this function overlaps with the concepts of empowerment and self-efficacy, so central to the *inAccord* model of mediation.

The very skills, as defined by the Broaden-and-Build theory of positive emotions, are therefore at the core of the mediation process. For example, disputants in the *inAccord* model are taught the *Touchstone Skills* of communication including reflecting, reframing, and questioning which engage them in more positive solutions (broadening) and can become enduring personal resources (build) long after the mediation concludes.

Lindner (2006) also cites Frederickson's Theory of Positive Emotions, as it specifically applies to conflict resolution. She observes that what negative emotions are to threat, positive emotions are to opportunity. That is, while negative emotions narrow a person's thought-action decisions, positive affects broaden this pathway, promoting an expanded repertoire of potential solutions in the face of conflict.

The Broaden-and-Build Theory of positive emotions is particularly relevant to our approach to mediation, where two categories of disputant feelings are assessed at the outset. The first such category specifically names positive emotions that are considered to be empowering in that they facilitate the mediation process, including the active role of the participants.

In summary, while the particular emotions selected for the Survey items were drawn from the first author's clinical experience of mediation, we have adopted a broader approach to the concept of an emotion, as described in the chapter's section on hope. We have included in the emotions surveyed what we label as *cognitive-emotional hybrids* such as hopefulness, serenity, and contentment, which Frederickson and colleagues also cite as emotion constructs, in addition to traditional positive emotions (e.g., happy). We concur that positive emotions serve a critical function in the *inAccord* model.

Our second category of emotions we consider to be disempowering, namely negative affects (e.g., anger, jealousy, despair) that can derail an individual or prevent one from effectively engaging in those skills necessary for the successful resolution of a conflict Disempowering emotions, if too intense, can interfere with a disputant's ability to flexibly generate multiple solutions to conflicts, to one's mind set to entertain alternative strategies that might lead to a resolution. Only through this broadening function can a disputant then move on to the build function in which, through a sense of agency, one can construct personal resources that will allow him/her to develop realistic plans for the future.

PART TWO:

The *inAccord* Model in Practice

Chapter Five:
The *inAccord* Mediator

Chapter Overview

In *Justice, inAccord* is intended as a presentation of the *inAccord* model and related themes, a primary text for the *inAccord* Mediation course, and as a guide for facilitators, mediators, and arbitrators. The central functions of transparency and empowerment discussed in Chapter Three and the additional function of the role of emotions discussed in Chapter Four combine to create the foundation for the *inAccord* model of mediation. These functions must guide the mediator during each phase of the model and serve as benchmarks for how the mediation is progressing. In this section of the book, we translate these functions as well as other theories, concepts, and principles discussed in the previous chapters into actual practice. Here we address the "how to" of implementing the *inAccord* model.

This chapter covers the foundational skills that any mediator must have in order to be effective in facilitating the *inAccord* model. We begin with a discussion of the competency cycle and how it relates to the need for ongoing self-reflection in the maturity and development of any practicing professional. This is followed by a detailed description of four essential skills sets that are used throughout the *inAccord* model:

- Recognizing critical moments in mediation
- Building rapport with each disputant
- Employing the *Touchstone Skills* of reflecting, reframing, and questioning
- Conducting fair and impartial caucuses when needed

The chapter concludes by introducing pre-mediation protocols that offer a solid structure to help contain the inevitable intensity of any dispute.

Transformative Processes and the Cycle of Competence

It is important that those using the *inAccord* model understand not only the theory and processes of this profession but when and why to use specific interventions and techniques. Lang and Taylor (2000) referred to this as the Reflective Practitioner and the *inAccord* model encourages a similar self-awareness entitled the *Conscious Mediator*. Being conscious means we are aware of why we are taking a specific action or employing a specific technique. In order to prepare for mediation as a career, it is imperative that a mediator use an ongoing reflective learning process, such as journaling or peer supervision, to keep skills up to date and finely honed.

Transformative learning requires us to be aware of and change our frames of reference by critically reflecting on our assumptions and beliefs. This perspective allows us to consciously create and implement plans that bring about new ways of defining our shared reality. Reflecting and recording our experiences enables us to further develop, refine, and articulate observations about our internal learning process, which can deepen understanding of our own evolution of thinking and grasp of complex concepts and applications. A primary practice of reflection is to write down and review our words to reveal if they are true and accurate portrayals of how we are evolving. This view of a beginner's mind corresponds to the Competency Cycle diagrammed below. After the definitions of each component circle, we will offer the example of learning to play tennis to illustrate the competency cycle. We will then apply a sequence of stages to the realm of our *inAccord* model.

Cycle of Competency

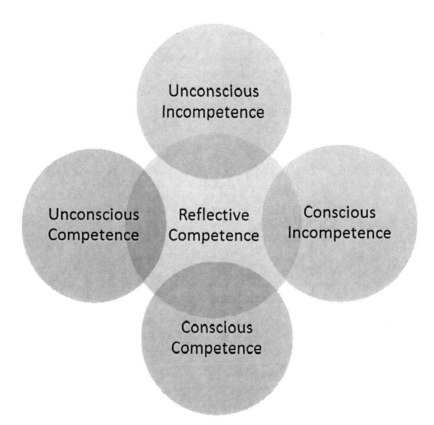

Unconscious Incompetence: This is the beginning stage at which *you don't know what you don't know.* You don't know the limits of the area of knowledge you seek to understand.

Conscious Incompetence: Though you don't understand or know how to do something, you recognize the deficit. This is the stage where *you know what you don't know.*

Conscious competence: You understand how to do something. However, demonstrating this requires a great deal of consciousness or concentration. *You know how to do it, but you have to think your way through it.*

Unconscious Competence: You have sufficient practice that it becomes "second nature" and can be performed with some mastery depending upon the situation.

Application to tennis. Picture yourself watching a high level tennis tournament. You watch how the professional players hit the ball and move around the court with ease. You think to yourself, this does not look that hard. I could play tennis like these players. You overestimate your capacity to play tennis and underestimate the skill levels of the players, in terms of their years of practice, and their commitment to the game. This is a state of *unconscious incompetence* where you are unaware of how difficult it is to actually perform a task and you overestimate your competence at being able to effectively perform the task.

Now picture yourself taking your first tennis lesson and discovering that the moves and strategy are much more complex than you first imagined. This is the state of *conscious incompetence* where you now understand that you don't know what you thought you knew. For example, you cannot exercise the timing required to throw the ball when serving. In addition, you find that you lack conscious control over new skills which have yet to be developed, noting that sometimes when you serve, the ball goes into the net, at other times it flies out of the court. Over time, and many years of lessons, you begin to become *consciously competent* and improve your serve, your ball placement, and your offensive and defensive strategies.

At the next stage of *unconscious competence,* the execution of the skills becomes "second nature" and you begin to perform them automatically. The psychological literature refers to this as "procedural memory" meaning that one does not have to consciously think about executing these skills because the memories are encoded in your body and are no longer processed at higher cognitive levels.

Note that this is a cycle. You move through the circles or stages in order, in a clockwise direction, and complete the cycle, but only up to a point. For example, in regards to the tennis metaphor, suppose you move to a higher level of play, with new, more talented and competitive players, where matches become more challenging. You suddenly recognize that your level needs to improve again and so you start at the level of unconscious incompetence, at the beginning of the wheel. It is important to understand that this is a natural, never-ending cycle of learning where success is measured by your willingness to apply reflection to each stage of any learning process you develop.

The *reflective competence* circle in the middle applies to every circle or stage. In the tennis example, at each stage, you would reflect on the various elements of your game, such as your performance during a particular set, how the entire match went, and what you would do differently in the future. *Reflective competence* is the main focus of the conscious mediator and it intersects with the other spheres to varying degrees depending upon the mediator and the mediation.

Application to mediation. The competency cycle and reflective practice is inherent in moving within competency stages in a communication process. Because mediation is such a dynamic process, you are uncovering and integrating information that you did not know and responding to it with the parties as you move through the cycle during each session. With this reflective competency, the mediator can adjust and intentionally select the mediation style or approach he or she feels is most appropriate (directive to relational) for the situation. This could also be viewed as a 'Chosen Conscious Competence' or an enhanced competency stage. Because a mediator is cycling through these areas throughout the mediation, he or she may land in any quadrant and require reflective competency to proceed.

Application to the inAccord model. Picture yourself watching a live mediation. You observe the mediator facilely employing the *Touchstone Skills* of reflecting, reframing, and questioning. You think to yourself, I could easily do that. So you take a course in the *inAccord* model of mediation. You begin to examine the various Phases and Stages of the process. You are now at the stage of *conscious incompetence.* You begin to grasp the fact that you know what you don't know. You do not yet have control of these new skills, you are not able to reflect, you are not listening carefully to the disputant's concerns, the emotional climate in the room is escalating, and you do not know how to intervene appropriately. At the next stage of conscious competence, you begin to effectively employ the phase and stage concepts and the accompanying surveys. You begin to gain greater mastery of the *Touchstone Skills.* At the final stage of *unconscious competence*, you intuitively utilize the various skills as if they were second nature.

While reflection occurs at every stage in the mediation process, every mediator should make time after the session to quietly reflect on what they might have done differently in the case. This is a time to reflect on whether the use of directive versus relational approaches and techniques were effective or why it might be helpful to shift from one to the other within a given mediation case. In this way, the conscious mediator makes appropriate adjustments when reconvening the mediation session. However, a mediator must be prepared for the fact that this need for reflection will start all over again with each new mediation case as the disputants bring their unique issues and personalities to bear on the resolution of the conflict. This is what makes the profession of mediation both exciting and challenging and the conscious mediator learns from both mistakes and successes in each mediation case.

Recognizing Critical Moments

A mediator's "people skills" will be called upon constantly in the course of a mediation session. He will be choosing interventions and actions minute-by-minute and each choice will accumulate to ultimately determine the success or failure of the mediation. Sound like a little bit of pressure? It is. How a mediator handles the pressure will largely be determined by his or her experience and by the set of skills he or she brings to the negotiations. Lang and Taylor (2000) refer to these high pressure times as critical moments. There are four factors that demonstrate the emergence of a critical moment:
- The moments require a response from the mediator.
- There are multiple responses available to apply to the situation based on the mediator's formulation and theoretical orientation.
- The mediator senses that a decision must be made quickly.
- The mediator senses that the moment seems pivotal and may determine the direction of everything that follows.

Ultimately, mediations are an accumulation of many critical moments that combine to create a successful settlement or a failed mediation. It is important to be alert to these pivotal moments in mediation because if they are missed, it may adversely affect the course of the entire process. During these critical moments, clients may be signaling, consciously or unconsciously, that there needs to be a shift in direction, focus, or approach. If the mediator responds to these moments with the *correct* interventions based on sound theory, it will *positively* impact the course of the negotiations.

A conscious mediator will know when she is experiencing a critical moment in mediation when she feels mired down, caught in a bind, or feels pressure to respond yet is aware that several responses are possible. There will be times when her clients ask her a question and she needs a moment to reflect. The mediator should not be afraid to suggest a break while she takes time to review the case notes and formulate a response. It is better to break for ten minutes than offer the wrong intervention. The mediator may even need to table the question in order to review it with a supervisor or outside expert. This allows her to move on to another issue and not hold up the entire process. Of course, there will be times when the mediator will not have the time to either break or table the issue. In these instances, it is important that the mediator takes a moment in the session to gather her thoughts before she responds. In this way, she may be demonstrating a behavior that the disputants might choose to emulate when they have choices to consider in the negotiations.

Increasing Self-Awareness

The conscious mediator will develop an increasing awareness of critical moments with each new case she mediates. At the beginning, her own inexperience and anxiety/excitement at mediating her first few cases will work against her ability to notice these critical moments. Yet, she possesses an internal barometer that will help her identify critical moments: her body. The mediator can begin to pay attention to how she responds physically to impasses, escalations, and stonewalling during sessions. Perhaps nausea will be the barometer, or an increasing tension in her neck and shoulders. She might find herself developing a nervous reaction like drumming her fingers or swinging her leg. These can be used to mark the moment when the conscious mediator senses a critical moment, sometimes long before her mind makes the connection.

Jumping Out of the System (JOOTS). Lang and Taylor (2000) outline three steps for the conscious mediator to take when a critical moment is identified:

1. The mediator acknowledges that the moment is occurring and reflects in action in order to make sense out of it.
2. The mediator offers her observation to the disputants. This alone may alter the moment by bringing it into conscious awareness to all parties in the room.
3. The mediator might offer the disputants three options: continue, change, or experiment with a new choice. This keeps the power of the mediation in their hands.

In Hakomi Therapy, founder Ron Kurtz (1997) talks about the moments in a session where the system of the client or clients seems to draw the practitioner in. At this moment, the practitioner begins to lose both his or her effectiveness and the power that is inherent in being an outside observer. This same process can be played out in a mediation session. A mediator may find himself becoming confused, losing his impartiality, or experiencing the feelings of one or both of the disputants. These are all signals to the mediator that he may have lost his footing and slipped into their system. Much like identifying a critical moment, the first step is his awareness that this process is occurring.

The next step is to initiate what Kurtz refers to as JOOTS or "jumping out of the system." This is much like following Lang and Taylor's second step: to name what is happening to everyone in the room. This often breaks open a critical moment for discussion, much like breaking a spell. Mediators walk a fine line of leaning in to the interactive process in order to effectively guide the clients through, yet they must take care not to lean in so far that they become part of the interactive system between the clients. Being in the system is like being too close to a blackboard: the mediator is writing down ideas but may be too close to make sense of what he is writing. He simply will not be able to see with the same clarity and objectivity. Of course, when a conflict is particularly heated this is not an easy balance to maintain.

Building Rapport

We begin the essential skill sets of a mediator with the practical procedures involved in establishing understanding and rapport with the disputants. Rapport is that intangible feeling a person has when they sense they are connected with another person in some manner, whether through common interests or shared values. When we feel rapport with another person, we often feel aligned or in agreement about something. Some people have a natural ability to create rapport; however, for most people it is a communication skill that takes practice until a state of unconscious competency is reached.

The conscious mediator builds rapport like a sturdy bridge between themselves and the disputants. The more time and care the mediator spends building rapport, the stronger the relationship will be when the intensity builds and there is a need to negotiate and problem-solve an issue. That initial contact where the mediator builds rapport will be goodwill the mediator needs to draw on during difficult times. Here are some fundamental steps to building rapport:

- Use reflective listening skills to accurately hear what the other is saying.
- Make empathic statements, that demonstrate an understanding of their situation and needs.
- Ask questions about their views, the problems they see, or the reservations they have. Be sure these questions are open-ended, which means they are phrased to elicit more than a simple "yes" or "no".
- A mediator might find things in common to strike up a brief conversation about them and both build trust and ease tension.
- The mediator should look the person in the eye and use their name during the conversation.
- Be prepared for any cultural difference that may exist. For instance, in some cultures too much eye contact may be perceived as threatening.

Rapport Starts with Pacing. Pacing is a term that means meeting a person where they are by either matching some part of their ongoing experience or by reflecting something they know to be true. For instance, when a mediator reflects back to a person that they seem excited as they sit on the edge of their chair, the mediator is pacing with them. If the mediator has guessed correctly, the disputant will often feel met and begin to open up more. The easiest way to pace is to ask questions such as, "What is going on for you right now?" or "What do you need at this moment?" or "How can I be of help to you?" In short, pacing involves looking for ways to connect with others.

Checking Assumptions. As a mediator paces the other person, he must constantly check his pacing for accuracy. Nothing is more annoying, and therefore destructive to rapport, than reflecting someone's experience inaccurately. This does not mean the mediator cannot make a mistake here and there. But, we are not mind readers and therefore need to check out our assumptions. The mediator can also do this by monitoring the disputants' body language. Sometimes, he will notice a closing of their body or a slight movement away from if he is not accurately pacing them. Part of negotiation is being able to lead the other party into collaboration and navigate the give and take of joint problem solving. Before the mediator can lead, though, he or she must have convinced the other party that he or she can follow them which is the essence of pacing.

When you begin to practice pacing, be aware of the fine line between simply parroting the other and the true art of moving in rhythm with someone. Practice pacing gradually in no-risk situations or tactfully with someone you'll never see again. As we move into a discussion of the *Touchstone Skills*, you will see how building rapport integrates into the three skills of reflecting, reframing, and questioning.

The Touchstone Skills for Communication

There is a Native American proverb that says, "Tell me a fact and I'll learn. Tell me a truth, and I'll believe. But tell me a story and it will live in my heart forever. " People come to mediation to tell their story, and it is a vital part of the mediation process to allow them to do so and then, hopefully, transform it, as noted by Winslade and Monk (2000) and Bush and Folger (1994). The mediator must, therefore, possess superior communication skills that help each party tell their story in the most articulate, representative, and truthful manner possible. This involves the use of the *Touchstone Skills* that help frame the essential storytelling phase, both by the mediator and by the participants, and help guide the discussions and negotiations throughout the entire process. These *Touchstone Skills* are: Reflecting, Reframing, and Questioning.

Reflecting

There are many wonderful books and methods available that teach people how to communicate more effectively. Mediators Without Borders builds on the communication classic, *People Skills* by Robert Bolton (1979), and suggests this book as a complement to the *inAccord* mediation education. Additional helpful information about communication used during mediation is available in Taylor (2002), where she describes the five important mediator communication techniques of reward, restatement, redirection, reflection, and reframing. More information is also available in the work of McKinney, Kimsey and Fuller (1995), and in Folger, Poole and Stutman (2005).

According to an occupational survey developed by Gordon (1970), 70% of all our waking moments are spent in communication and, amazingly, 45% of all this time spent in communication is devoted entirely to listening. Imagine then, how critical it is that we learn to listen well. Yet, most of us are poor listeners, and it has a consistently negative effect on all of our relationships. We begin to learn how to be ineffective at listening at a very early age. We learn it from our parents, teachers, relatives, and friends; therefore, it is critical that anyone interested in conflict resolution begin learning how to listen with understanding and acceptance. Mediators need a higher level of intuitive recognition, ability to problem-solve and knowledge of face-saving in order to be effective. Using the *inAccord* model, they also teach a beginning level of these skills to the disputants as part of the learning that occurs during the mediation effort.

Deutsch (2006) concurs, observing that with the mediator's guidance, disputants must learn reflecting skills and responsive communication which includes taking the perspective of the other, recognizing and accepting the other's needs as well as one's own. Moreover, he also identifies *self-reflection* about how one is handling the immediate conflict as necessary to the success of mediation, requiring that one prevent old habits and emotional hotspots from making one regress to less constructive modes of conflict resolution. He also asks that disputants reflect on the particular *framework* of the conflict resolution model that is being employed by the mediator. Such awareness is facilitated by the very transparency of the *inAccord* model, as highlighted in the surveys that disputants complete at each stage of the process.

Reflecting is a fundamental communication skill that takes time to learn to use effectively. In a reflecting response, the listener restates the content of what the speaker has communicated, verbatim. Just as a mirror reflects an image, the *Touchstone Skills* of reflecting echoes back the exact words of the speaker disputant. The mediator ensures the exactness of the reflection by making it clear to the speaker that the intention is to create understanding by mirroring back their words in totality. Many times, the disputants will talk rapidly under stress and repeat phrases unknowingly. The simple process of the mediator reflecting back the words helps the speaker slow down. More importantly, the reflection of key phrases enables the speaker to stop repeating in an attempt to underscore the importance of the phrase. In effect, once they feel someone has actually heard them, they can move on to another point or stop and deepen their stated issue.

In a similar vein, Deutsch (2006) urges that in the heat of conflict, the disputant must appreciate the fact that each party at the outset of mediation is highly likely to experience strong emotions. The emotions evoked may be anxiety, anger, rage, fear, depression, humiliation, withdrawal, and so on. Ideally, in reflecting such feelings, a disputant can come to label not only his or her own emotions but those of the other party. Consistent with our own approach of identifying and encouraging positive *empowering emotions,* Deutsch suggests that feelings of *hope* and *optimism* be nurtured, two emotions on our emotion survey that mediation seeks to foster.

Advanced Reflecting. This is a higher-order communication skill that involves a brief restatement of the main themes that the disputant expressed over a longer period of conversation than would be covered by the more basic skills. This is a skill that is used quite often in mediation when there are conflicts of needs, or where problem solving is required. Additionally, it can be used as a way of translating the disputants' words into more readily understood themes and issues for the both the listener and the speaker. For instance, a mediator might restate a parent's detailed complaint with the other parent in a divorce as, "Let me try to summarize some of what you are saying into key points and please let me know if I miss anything. It seems like your main concerns are the inconsistent transfer of your children on the weekends, the amount of exercise and good nutrition they are receiving at your ex-husband's house, and how late they are reporting they are staying up at night." The following introductory sentences are good ways to introduce a summary reflection:

- "One theme you keep coming back to seems to be. . ."
- "Let's recap the ground we have covered so far . . ."
- "I've been thinking about what you've said. I see something that may be a pattern and I'd like to check it out. You . . ."
- "As I've been listening to you, your main concern seems to be . . . "

Why reflecting works in mediation. When disputants first begin to learn reflective listening skills they often feel that the method is too structured, mechanical, and unnatural. This is true of most new skills learned in mediation. Anytime a mediator or disputant learns a new skill, it feels awkward for a time. It takes months to incorporate these *Touchstone Skills* into a style that is natural to a disputant's unique personality and talents. The mediator can help alleviate any anxiety the disputants might have about using reflective listening by modeling this technique and reminding the disputants that they do not have to be perfect and these skills will not only serve them in mediation but in other areas of their lives as well.

Reframing. When a verbal exchange occurs, mediators must accurately gauge the situation in order to respond effectively. In the case of communication, this would entail listening carefully and then responding by framing the disputant's words. *Framing* is posing or labeling the problem appropriately so it can be solved. It is how the issue or conflict is defined. More importantly, it is the process of stating/framing the issues in a clear, direct way that evokes a receptive, constructive response. Framing can also be used to create a structure for a process. In mediation, the mediator will often begin a case by stating, "The purpose of this mediation is to help you arrive at a mutually agreeable solution to your dispute." This creates a framework for the ongoing progression of the case.

Reframing, on the other hand, is the process of changing how a disputant conceptualizes their or their adversary's attitudes, behaviors, issues or interests. It is the skill of restating the structure of a situation in a way that accurately reflects the content, yet is easier for the other to access. In reframing, the gold nuggets are the interests, the data, and the previously missed information. The insults of personal attacks, escalating statements, condescending put-downs, ambiguity and overgeneralizations are eliminated when reframing is done appropriately. Reframing often accomplishes the same objectives as reflecting. The mediator reflects back the content of the disputant's message, usually in a way that makes the message more easily heard by the other party. This process usually begins with a framing statement, such as, "It seems . . ."

A central goal of reframing is to help disputants change *positions* into *interests*. Disputants often come to conflict with a belief, a resolve that they know what has happened and that only one solution will work. All of their thoughts and emotions may be channeled into the position they take, the story they have come to believe as truth. Underneath a position lies the interest. An interest is what the disputant is really looking for. It is what will bring true satisfaction to the party. The *Touchstone Skill* of reframing can help parties move from their positions to their true, underlying interests.

Let's use a statement from a workplace dispute to illustrate this skill. Alex, a young hire at a tech company, is in a dispute with a middle manager at the company. He made the following statement during stage 2 of the mediation process, "Chris is the most obstinate person I have ever met. I think she wants me gone so she can continue to run our division like a family, where she is the all-powerful mother, instead of like a business poised for success." The mediator stops Alex at this point and reframes the statement as follows, "It appears you feel Chris is unwilling to collaborate with you and may want you out of the company. You also seem to want her to work for the success of the business. Is that right, Alex?" Note how the mediator eliminated the toxic language of "obstinate" while still honoring the intent of the statement. Additionally, she reconstructed the last sentence by taking out the characterization of her as an "all-powerful mother" and reframed it into a focus on his desire that Chris care, as he does, about the success of the company.

Deutsch's (2006) analysis complements these observations, describing constructive conflict resolution: "At the heart of this process is reframing the conflict as a mutual problem to be resolved (or solved) through joint cooperative efforts" (p. 32). Reframe is a joint activity that should help to further foster a cooperative orientation even if the goals of the two parties are initially at odds. Reframing, according to Deutsch, has inherent within it the assumption that whatever resolution is achieved, it is acceptable to each party and considered to be *just* by both, that is, that the result is a win-win situation.

Questioning. Most disputants learn to ask close-ended questions that are seeking a "yes" or "no" response. These questions are valuable when the disputant or mediator is attempting to verify a fact or to keep a conversation from opening up into a larger discussion. However, in mediation, questioning becomes more artful as the mediator and parties seek to draw out shared interests and common ground. Open-ended questioning can be used to uncover more complex answers or to open up dialogue in a non-threatening way. The following list contains examples of probing questions designed to sometimes gently, sometimes assertively, tease out the details of a party's story instead of peppering them with a series of close-ended retorts. In a very contentious divorce case, a mediator used probing questions to keep the couple from verbally berating one another. He did so by intervening with the following questions:

- Help me understand what you think is important about keeping the house, Ellen?
- David, what do you want in this instance?
- Are you agreeing with what David is saying or do you have a different understanding?
- Ellen, what would a civil divorce look like to you?
- What does it mean to you, David?
- What would help you feel comfortable with this conversation?

In another instance, a mediator is helping two managers debate the use of flex time:

- Richard, please take a moment to educate me about what you mean by flex time?
- Shandra, I heard you offer a potential solution, are you saying you might agree to flex time in some instances?
- Help me out with something. What would it take for you to feel comfortable with rethinking the company's flex time policy?
- You've told me what doesn't work for you Richard, now what would make you more comfortable with this idea?
- I'm confused. Do you want flex time for everyone or just for designated employees?
- How would you each find the information you need to make this decision?
- If time is a consideration, what needs to be done for you to feel comfortable?
- If things don't go your way today, what do you foresee doing? [Drawing out their Best Alternative To a Negotiated Agreement in caucus]

The Use of Caucuses

An intervention available to the mediator during critical moments is the use of caucuses or private meetings. Sometimes, the parties, especially if they have an on-going working relationship, need to get comfortable confronting each other and their issues in a constructive manner. The caucus is the mediator's opportunity to understand the underlying needs and interests of the parties. Caucus may be useful when:

- Destructive interruptions are not gracefully managed in the session. It may be a time to check out the motivation of the party and find out what one disputant is trying to achieve by constantly or aggressively interrupting the other disputant.
- The power imbalance needs some adjustment. This can be accomplished by helping a disputant understand that his/her use of power is preventing the progression of the mediation.
- Managing strong emotions. If a disputant is overly weepy or angry, it may be good to check out the source or the intensity of the emotion in private versus having the disputant try to figure it out in the session.
- Information is not readily being shared that the mediator believes is crucial to the mediation.
- Coaching a disputant may help them in their communication with each other, their approach, and their analysis of the situation.

The caucus is also useful when parties:
- Need a break
- Need encouragement to explore options
- Need to think through options
- Need encouragement to be flexible and to create options

The mediator's objectives in the caucus include:
- To discover more about each party's needs
- To see the "facts" through their eyes

- To find out what each party might do if mediation fails
- To find areas of negotiation
- To find trade-offs
- To reduce emotional blow-ups in joint sessions
- To keep the parties on track

Steps to Conducting a Caucus. If a caucus is to be used, all parties must have the same opportunity in order to avoid the appearance of some type of favoritism. The mediator decides who will go first; the other is escorted to a comfortable, quiet place, out of sight and hearing range of the mediator. The mediator is then free to coach the disputant to raise a difficult issue, to encourage the disputant to offer an apology, and to explore why the communication may have gotten stuck. Before returning to the session, the mediator determines with each disputant, what information is strictly confidential. The mediator does not come back to the session to report, but rather to continue to facilitate the party's discussion of the issues and options. The mediator may have a formal caucusing process that relies on a series of steps such as:

1.Restate Confidentiality Agreement

This step reminds the disputant that any information they share during a caucus is completely confidential and will only be shared in the joint session if the disputant releases the mediator to do so.

2.Use the *Touchstone Skills* of Questioning

The mediator might begin by saying, *"Start wherever you want."* Or, *"What do you need to tell me that you cannot say in the joint session?"* They may use the reflecting and clarifying questions to summarize an understanding of the conflict.

3.Keep an Accurate Record of Proceedings

The mediator should let the disputants know they will be taking notes and encourage them to do the same. Sometimes note-taking by the disputants can cut down on the amount of interruptions they make. In addition, the mediator can use notes at a later time to model respectful listening. This is done by referring to the notes and checking out their accuracy with the disputants. This communicates that the mediator is both listening and respecting their needs by seeking clarification.

4. Monitor Cognitive Interpretations and Errors

Mediation includes monitoring disputants' cognitive interpretations throughout the process. This can be accomplished by asking how they view the other disputant's interests and positions. Often, in joint sessions, the atmosphere is too intense to support accurate listening by the disputants. They will hear through the lens of stress, anger, and, ultimately, fear. For example, during a joint session, one disputant may state an interest with a good deal of intensity. The other disputant may react internally to the intensity and begin to react to the disputant stating the interest. They may say to themselves: "Here he goes again, trying to get his way." Or, "I will not be bullied by him anymore."

All this internal talk is making it very difficult for this person to hear the other person at all, let alone hear them accurately. More importantly, this person is reacting, not to the statement of interests, but to the internal dialogue that is happening while the other person is speaking. In the caucus, the mediator's job will be to identify when the person has misinterpreted the other. The mediator can refer to notes taken during the session and remind them of what was actually said. This is a delicate process because many people do not understand how they could have gotten it so wrong and they may be defensive. This is a good time for the mediator to remind them that we all engage in misinterpretation countless times every day.

5. How to Intervene When Appropriate *(in caucus)*

A private caucus provides opportunities for the mediator to make brief interventions that help move the party from seemingly fixed positions. These interventions include:

Confrontation. Sometimes the mediator will need to confront a party about a certain behavior that is destructive to the mediation process. The mediator may use data or feedback to let the party know how he or she is coming across to the other party. It is good to remember that confrontation is an advanced communication skill and must be used delicately.

Evaluation of Strengths and Weaknesses. This is an area where the mediator can easily cross the line and become too directive. However, as the facilitator, there will be times when the parties must be encouraged to gauge the strengths and weakness of any one proposal. This can be aided by using probing questions to elicit the pros and cons of what they are proposing.

Identifying Competing Interests. A caucus is a good forum for identifying contradictory interests that one party might have.

Summarize Often. This is a great way to move discussions into concise findings while constantly seeking clarification and verifying accuracy. This can be accomplished through statements such as: *"Let me check out what I have so far from what you have said."* Or, *"There seem to be three or four key needs that you have expressed. Let me see if I understand them correctly."* At this point, a mediator might try floating some possible solutions by asking "what if" questions. For instance, the mediator might ask a disputant that refuses to deal with an abusive adversary: *"What if he found a way to control his anger. Would that make a difference to you?"* If the disputant responds positively, the mediator may have just found a way through an impasse, provided the other disputant is willing to tone down his anger and abuse. There are three things to bear in mind before proposing possible solutions:

- Focus on small steps, not on large final solutions.
- Focus on concrete behavior. For example, the mediator might rephrase the questions above and ask: *"What if he stopped criticizing you in front of me and the other parties?"*
- Focus on steps that honor the interests of the disputant who is in the caucus and not the interests of all the disputants.

6. Effectively Close the Caucus

The mediator should end the caucus by reminding the disputants of the confidentiality of the meeting, invite them to make any other statements they may have left out, and ask them what message, if any, they would the mediator to communicate to the other side. It is important to use this process with each party in the dispute. After the mediator has completed the first series of caucuses, he can determine whether to convene a joint session or continue with more private meetings.

Problems with using caucus. The mediator must guard against:

- Becoming an advocate for one party or one solution other
- Letting the caucus go too long, thereby disenfranchising the party who is waiting
- Overusing this tool so the mediation becomes too fragmented
- Loss of accuracy in knowing what information is strictly confidential and what is not
- Ethical dilemmas such as finding out something that ethically compromises the process

The use of caucus can be a powerful tool if the timing and the strategy are well thought out. It can also energize a mediation case if a time-out for clearing the head (including the mediator's head) is indicated.

Pre-Mediation Protocols

There are elements of logistics and protocols used in preparing for a mediation that can have a positive impact on the progression of the process. These include careful attention to the physical setting and arrangement of the mediation and caucusing rooms, a checklist of what to include in the opening statement of the mediation session, and forms and surveys that are clearly defined for the disputants at the outset of their mediation process.

Mediation Location. The physical location of mediation can have a significant effect on the proceedings and contribute to the very success or failure of the process. One obvious consideration is to ensure that the mediation location does not grant one party undue influence or power. This can be mitigated by choosing a neutral location. If a mediator is mediating a personal dispute, the use of the mediator's own private office offers the best neutral grounds. If the dispute takes place in an organization, efforts should be made to bring the parties out of the workplace and into a neutral location, preferably the mediator's office. However, sometimes issues of time and the proximity to supporting documents and persons may make moving the dispute to a neutral location difficult. In these instances, the mediator must try to locate a place within the organization that is not perceived as the prime territory of either party. A neutral conference room might be appropriate in this case.

Rooms for Caucusing. It is the duty of a mediator to make sure that privacy is protected. Slaikeu (1996) cautions that the most important physical requirement of mediation is a private room that ensures complete *confidentiality.* This means that the room must prevent outsiders from hearing any conversations taking place inside. There must be a prepared place for break-out private meetings, out of earshot of the other parties. This could mean a caucus that takes place in a private room, during a walk around the block, or over the telephone. The most important aspect of caucus is the protection of the parties' rights to privacy, especially during delicate negotiations. One method that many use to maintain confidentiality is the use of "white noise" machines that interfere with sound coming from the office or from the surrounding corridors. These relatively inexpensive devices can be effective to maintain privacy in all the conversations.

Physical Arrangement of Mediation. Once the location is chosen, care should be given to the internal physical space of the setting: the size and shape of the negotiating table (preferably round), the seating arrangement, placement of physical objects such as a flip chart, the amount of space allowed between the parties, and the space for private and public interactions.

It will be difficult to create the perfect location and physical arrangement in the mediations you plan. A mediator should use his or her personal level of comfort as a guide and be sure to obtain feedback from others as they design their mediation space.

Mediator's Statement Checklist. It's coming up to one o'clock and a mediator has a new case beginning at one-thirty. This may be the first face-to-face contact the mediator has had with either party; therefore, the manner in which the mediator prepares for and executes this *critical* moment will establish the tone for the entire mediation. The first goal in beginning mediation is to create a sense of safety, credibility, and openness for the disputants. Secondly, they should be adequately prepared for what to *expect,* what is and is not permissible, and understand the important concepts of neutrality, impartiality, and confidentiality. There are certain key elements that the mediator should cover in this opening statement, each designed to educate, inform, and ensure that disputants understand the process.

1. Welcome and Introductions

When a mediator welcomes the parties to the office and the process of mediation, it is important to acknowledge their *willingness* to try to reach their own agreement. The mediator begins by addressing the parties by name and introducing himself by name. If he chooses to use a social or professional title such as Dr. or Mr., he will be setting a more formal tone. If he prefers a more casual tone, he might ask them to address him by his first name and perhaps ask them each how they would like to be addressed. Their response might provide more information about their position and power. Many mediators take time to say how long they have been mediating and a offer brief overview of their education. The mediator can end this step by asking them how they feel at this point and if they have any questions.

2. Explain the inAccord Model

The mediator may have mailed them this information earlier or perhaps spoken to them individually on the phone. However, it is psychologically important for the disputants to hear this topic (even if it is for the second time) in front of each other and the mediator. At this point, the mediator will hand them a printout of the overview of the *inAccord* Three Phases with the 4 Stages identified in Phase Two.

3. Define Role as Mediator

This is a good time to for the mediator to address both the tasks he will perform as a mediator and the ones he will not perform. If he is a therapist as well as a mediator he can state clearly that he will not be providing any therapy. If he is an attorney, it is critical to let them know that he will not be offering any legal advice. If he is a mental health worker he will not be addressing mental health issues. The mediator's role is to facilitate the *inAccord* model.

This is a good time for the mediator to let the disputants know the mediator's availability between sessions and what his limitations are. While he defines his role as a mediator, he can cover the topics of impartiality and neutrality. It is vital that the mediator communicate to all disputants that on issues of substance he will act with impartiality and that he is neutral in his relationship to all parties involved. This is also a good time to set a limit about the acceptance of emails and *phone* calls from either party.

4. Describe the Steps Taken in the First Session

It is important that the mediator let the disputants know what they can expect in terms of next steps. They can be referred back to the *inAccord* model for the 4 stages of the mediation process handout. At this point the mediator can offer a brief explain of the issue identification, the Touchstone Skillsets, option generation and the final MOA so they can begin to feel the collaborative nature of the process. This is the time to briefly explain the use of private meetings during the negotiations. It is enough to say that caucus is used to allow people to fill out the surveys, to get a handle on intense emotions, explore broader options, or gain perspective. The mediator should be sure to mention that these separate meetings are confidential unless the disputant in caucus chooses otherwise.

5. Define Confidentiality and Any Duty to Report

Confidentiality is one of the hallmarks of mediation, and it applies to both verbal and written disclosures. Confidentiality can help the disputants feel free to talk openly about interests, feelings, concerns, and even fallback positions. It is important that they are reminded that caucuses are confidential and are not shared with the absent party unless the mediator is otherwise instructed by the party. There are major exceptions to confidentiality that are common to all professions in most countries. These include threats to life and limb and reported abuse of the elderly and children.

6. Explain the Logistics

This includes information such as length of sessions, timing of breaks, and estimated time of the bargaining process. This is a good time to gain permission from the clients to take notes during the session reminding them that these notes are confidential.

7. Describe Behavioral Expectations

Most mediation guidelines include ground rule procedures to handle interruptions, the role of witnesses and the media, desired communication between the parties, and negotiation behaviors. Some mediators have quite elaborate guidelines as part of their written agreements to mediate. The *inAccord* model uses the caucus in Stage 2, to set the ground rule of the use of the *Touchstone Skills* as the communication set to be used by the mediator and the disputants throughout the mediation process.

8. *Concluding Remarks*

At the end of the opening statement, it is always a good idea to ask the parties if they have any questions or need clarification on some issue. Lack of understanding at the beginning might adversely affect the mediation down the road. The mediator's concluding remarks should be focused on gaining a commitment from all parties to move ahead with mediation. This may be simply stated as a question: "*It appears that you understand the mediation process and are prepared to move ahead and bargain with one another in good faith in order to reach a settlement.*"

9. *Introduce Necessary Mediation Documents*

Once the opening statement has concluded and any lingering questions answered, it is time to go over the documents that need to be signed in order to continue. These documents include the fee agreement, an agreement to mediate, any releases of information necessary in order to speak to outside sources, and the Phase One survey instruments.

Mediation Agreements. The mediation agreement is a contract for service with the disputants. It is a very important document as it sets out the terms and scope of services and it addresses confidentiality and its exceptions. Many mediators also define expectations of their clients in a mediation agreement that they want the client to agree to in writing.

One of the most important boundaries established early in mediation is the fee contract for services. Often it is better to have a separate agreement outlining payment to ensure that it is understood and agreed to by all the disputants. This agreement should define clearly what percentage each party will pay for the mediation itself, who will pay for various aspects of data collection if any, and who will pay for outside experts should they be necessary. Withholding payment to a mediator can be a tactic used by some disputants as a power play or to stall the negotiations. One way to avoid this problem is to contract for a retainer up front. For example, a mediator may require a divorcing couple to each contribute a portion of the expected costs to retain her services and she may ask that this always be kept at that amount. It can be very difficult to collect payment after settlement, especially from a disgruntled party. This agreement also establishes the mediator as a credible authority and protects her from the liability of trying to collect fees later. Samples of the pre-mediation documents can be found in the appendix after the survey instruments.

It is important to remember that the professional practice of mediation is a journey not a goal and as such it is important that a mediator be open to change and unexpected discoveries. As a professional, it is imperative to keep abreast of changes in the field and new research as it emerges. This can be accomplished by joining professional associations, taking continuing education courses to expand knowledge, and networking with colleagues to share best practices. Human interaction and conflict are fascinating fields of study that impact how mediation practice will change over the years and the impact of these fields and others can make the journey one of continued surprise and stimulating mystery.

Chapter Six:
Facilitation of the *inAccord* Phases and Stages

The Three Phases of inAccord

This chapter provides a more detailed overview of the *inAccord* phases and stages for the inAccord mediator or facilitator. We begin by reviewing the *inAccord* model and then expanding on the techniques used in each of the four stages in phase two of the process. Table 1 is reproduced here to help with a review of the model and to serve as a visual guide through the phases, stages, and use of the survey instruments along the way.

In Phase One, labeled as *pre-mediation assessment*, the disputants submit their agreements to mediate, fee agreements, and any releases of information that might be necessary. The mediator will have already shared the *inAccord* process. Three surveys are administered in Phase One. First, the mediator uses a survey to assess the disputants' typical conflict styles. The second survey measures disputant feelings or emotions about the conflict they are bringing to the mediation. The final survey administered in Phase One quantifies their expectations about saving time, money and the relationship.

Table 1 illustrates that Phase Two, labeled as the *4 stage intervention*, is the heart of the mediation intervention, and marks the phase where the mediator becomes more active in service of the process. In this phase, the mediator facilitates each disputant's understanding of the *inAccord* process and each disputant's satisfaction level during the progression of each of the four stages as the mediation progresses.

In Phase Three, post mediation outcomes are assessed by providing disputants the *My Feelings Survey* again. An additional *Exit Survey* is also administered in order to fully assess the learning and usefulness of the process for the conflict. The *Exit Survey* also attempts to assess the core values of the model and whether the participants felt the mediator was fair and impartial.

Table 1: Overview of Phases and Associated Surveys to assess the inAccord Model

PHASE ONE Pre-Facilitation Assessment	PHASE TWO 4 Stage Intervention Scores	PHASE THREE Post-Facilitation Outcomes
Conflict Styles Survey* -Avoidance - Competition -Compromise -Accommodation -Collaboration *My Feelings* Pre Survey* -Empowering Feelings -Disempowering Feelings *My Expectations* Scale* -Saving money -Saving time -Saving the relationship	*Stage 1*: Sharing of Perspectives: Issues, Positions, and Interest Identification**(caucus; review touchstone skill sets) - Understanding - Satisfaction *Stage 2*: Developing the Agenda and Option Generation** -Understanding -Satisfaction *Stage 3*: Joint Solution Statements: Testing the Agreements in Principle** -Understanding -Satisfaction *Stage 4*: Crafting the MOA* -Understanding -Satisfaction	*Signed versus did not sign* *Exit Survey*** - inAccord Model successful, party satisfied -Can understand, implement inAccord Model -Mediator fair/impartial -Process transparent -Process empowering *My Feelings* Post Survey* -Empowering Feelings -Disempowering Feelings *My Expectations* Scale* -Saved money -Saved time -Saved the relationship

*Mediator evaluates disputant responses to survey
**Mediator completes a parallel version of this survey

Phase One:Pre-Mediation Assessment

Using the Conflict Styles survey tool, the disputants are first asked to identify their conflict styles. In this survey administered at the outset, we emphasize to disputants that people have different styles of dealing with conflict, that there is no right or wrong style, and that how people react to and cope with conflict can differ according to different situations in their lives. Thus, we use the five different conflict styles noted by the Thomas-Kilmann questionnaire (1974), as well as five different contexts in which conflict might arise. The styles we have selected overlap with those of Thomas-Kilmann as well as Wilmont and Hocker (1978); however, our interest in these styles involves the disputants' perceptions of the conflict style they used as opposed to an interpretation by the mediator or other outside expert. The five different conflict styles we refer to are:

(a) *Avoidance* (avoiding or refusing to engage in conflict),
(b) *Competition* (becoming competitive in that one feels that it is important to obtain their personal goals),
(c) *Compromise* (trying to find some middle ground, although this give and take does not fully meet either party's goals completely),
(d) *Accommodation* (giving in to another's wishes, sacrificing one's own goals to minimize conflict) and,
(e) *Collaboration* (where one prefers to work cooperatively with the other party until a mutually agreeable solution is found).

Deutsch (2006) has argued cogently that before disputants can acquire the actual skills explicit to conflict resolution, they must first become aware of their pre-existing orientations to *conflict* and how they typically respond in conflict situations. These pre-existing orientations are precisely what we have labeled as conflict styles. To facilitate disputants' awareness and identification of their particular styles of dealing with conflict, we specifically ask them about the five orientations described above, providing brief descriptions that are captured in the parenthetical statements. This survey, like all of our surveys, can help the disputants, as well as mediators, become aware of parties' particular styles of handling conflict, which are likely to vary across different domains in their lives.

We are particularly interested, not only in the disputant's perspectives of their own styles within their personal lives, but how these styles may differ in various situations such as family of origin, workplace, home, and recreation. People can often show different strategies and responses to conflict when in different contexts. How one responds to conflict with one's mother is not necessarily how one would deal with one's boss or neighbor. It is our assumption that differentiating the styles across these situations will provide a more meaningful approach in understanding how it relates to the particular conflict that brought them to mediation. For example, in the case of a workplace dispute, it would be important to differentiate between the conflict styles the disputants identify as using at work as opposed to the style they identify as using at home. In this sense, we do not rely on a single conflict style label but acknowledge that styles may change according to the situation. Our survey tool asks disputants to indicate which of these styles they demonstrate in five different contexts or situations, which they utilize most often. The contexts we ask about are:

(a) Growing up in their family of origin,
(b) In their home life right now,
(c) When spending time with friends,
(d) During recreation or play, and
(e) When conflict occurs at work.

Depending upon the nature of the conflict that disputants bring to mediation, some of these contexts may be more relevant than others. For example, if a disputant reports that his typical style in a workplace conflict is competitive and the conflict that has brought him to the table involves a work dispute, then he may need to learn more collaborative skills through the mediation process. If the disputant and mediator realize that this competitive style is exacerbating the conflict, this may be important information for resolution and contribute to the growth and knowledge of the disputant. In contrast, if the conflict occurs in a marriage, then information about their conflict style in *that* context will be useful. So, for example, if a disputant's style in such a conflict situation is avoidance, that is, avoiding or refusing to engage in conflict, such a conflict style may interfere with the disputant's ability to use the *Touchstone Skills* of reflecting, reframing and questioning to open oneself up to understanding the perspective of the other party. However, if both disputants and mediator were made aware of the conflict styles that disputants naturally bring to mediation, this may help to move the process along more productivity. In this way the use of the conflict styles survey tool can be part of the broader learning that is enabled by our model.

We are also interested in people's emotional reactions to the conflict that brought them to mediation. We know emotions can be powerful forces in people's lives and relationships, as well as during the activation of the dispute. As we have noted, some emotions are more helpful than others in resolving or managing the conflict at hand, while others are less relevant and potentially destructive to the process. They are each derived from the perceptions that the disputants bring into the mediation context and mediators can benefit from learning whether disputants report emotions that are more empowering or emotions that are disempowering, because the disempowering emotions might make it more difficult for people to move forward in the process. For this reason, we employ the *My Feelings* survey at the beginning and end of the mediation process to accurately gauge disputants' emotional states.

To reiterate, the *inAccord* mediation model begins with the mediator informing the parties about the process they will be following and includes administering the *Conflict Styles* survey to both disputants before they enter the mediation session. Next, the mediator administers the *My Feelings Pre-Survey* instrument to both disputants. It is preferable to administer these surveys when disputants first arrive at the mediation in order to have a more immediate measurement of their emotional states. Once completed, the mediator evaluates the disputants' responses for concordance in terms of the degree to which each disputant feels empowered or disempowered about the conflict.

This evaluation guides the mediator in choosing whether to use a more *directive* or *relational* approach.

Applying the Approaches. First author Ries conducted a mediation case of two members of a nonprofit board whose continued animosity was rendering the entire board ineffective. Ries first administered the conflict styles and found that the two members had markedly different approaches to dealing with conflict. One member was highly competitive in his style and, in his words, envisioned his working relationships as survival of the fittest. The other board member, on the other hand, was avoidant and tended to meld himself into more of a team mentality. He believed that if everyone worked together for the common good, the organization would succeed. Used alone, this survey might have indicated that the mediator would need to employ a more directive approach with the disputants; however, the *My Feelings* survey demonstrated that both members were in an emotional state of empowerment. Ries shared this information and explained to the disputants that she would be using a more *relational* approach and the rationale for doing so. This rationale included the need to have a workable, indeed a collaborative, relationship at the monthly board meetings.

In the case example described, both parties were expressing empowering emotions; however, there are two other possible combinations of emotions. Both parties could be reporting disempowering emotions or there could be a mismatch where one party reports empowering emotions and the other reports disempowering emotions. In the case of a mismatch, then a more *directive* approach is indicated, as discussed below.

Phase Two: Stages of the Mediation Process

Phase Two includes the 4 stages of the mediation process wherein the mediator teaches the necessary *Touchstone Skills* in Stage 1, that can help guide the disputants more effectively through the mediation process. During these stages, the mediator is assessing disputants' understanding of the concepts at each stage as well as the degree to which they are satisfied with the mediation experience and what they have learned or mastered. The four stages include:

Stage 1: Sharing of Perspectives/Issues, Positions, and Interest Identification

Stage 2: Agenda Setting, Option Generation

Stage 3: Joint Solution Statement, Testing the Agreements in Principle

Stage 4: Crafting the Final Memorandum of Agreement

In Phase One, the completed *Pre-Feelings Mediator* survey (see appendix) guides the Mediator in choosing whether to use a more directive or relational approach throughout the mediation. Once completed, the mediator fills out a form to note the degree to which each disputant feels empowered or disempowered about the particular conflict. If both disputants are empowered or both are disempowered, the mediator will fill this out in his or her survey and chose a more relational approach, meaning both disputants will remain at the same table in the same room throughout most of the mediation. However, if one disputant is empowered and the other disputant is disempowered, meaning there is a mismatch of emotions, a more directive approach will be chosen. This means the mediator will, after the Sharing of Perspectives in the same room at the same time in Stage 1, talk with the disputants separately, either at separate times or in separate rooms.

Stage 1: Sharing of Perspectives. This stage begins with each disputant sharing his or her story with the other disputant in front of the mediator in a joint session (at the same table in the same room), stating his or her vantage point or interpretation of the conflict. Again, in many cases this may be the first time disputants are hearing each other's views in a room together. In the *inAccord* model, Stage 1 is always completed in joint session. If the directive approach is chosen due to a mismatch of emotions in the *Pre- Feelings* surveys, Stage 2 will take place in separate rooms with the mediator as witness and shuttle negotiator. At this initial Stage 1 and in the Mediator Opening Statement, the mediator asks for agreement with some ground rules for the dialogue. During the Sharing of Perspectives in Stage 1, the mediator extrapolates the *issues* (the reasons they are seeking mediation), each disputant's position (what each disputant would like to see happen), and underlying interests (why each disputant is taking the position he/she is taking), and lists these on a board for the disputants to approve prior to moving on to Stage 2.

In the case of a workplace dispute, a mediator decided to ask the disputant whose *My Feelings* survey was slightly less empowering to share their perspective of the conflict first for twenty minutes and then asked the next disputant to share for an additional twenty minutes, without interruption from the other. Each disputant was given a pad and paper to write down any questions, in order to not interrupt the party sharing their perspective. It is important to maintain balance and impartiality in the process; therefore, the disputant who shared their perspective second, will be the first to have a private meeting or caucus, following Stage 1. This helps ensure that there is equality in both the time that each person shares and in who goes first and last.

The sharing of perspectives for a set time is not a dialogue but a monologue where the other disputant is instructed to remain silent and respectful during the sharing. The mediator will be helping guide the disputant who is speaking by using the *Touchstone Skills* of *reflecting* content where needed, by *reframing* negative statements, and by asking open-ended *questions*. These skills will be taught to the disputants in the first caucus, either privately or in joint session, following Stage 1 to empower the disputants and allow for a transparent and effective dialogue. The disputants are each informed that these *Touchstone Skills* will be used throughout the 4 Stages of the mediation. Once all the issues, positions, and interests have been written out on the board, the mediator will break into the first caucus and begin to teach the disputants the *Touchstone Skills* of reflecting (asking the party to repeat the words of the mediator verbatim, as a model to work with the other party, to make sure of the accuracy of the story being told or the point being made), *reframing* (creating a picture or frame that is more palatable to hear and removing inflammatory language), and *questioning* (asking open ended questions for clearer understanding of the other parties underlying interests, such as "help me understand" versus a "why" question).

A mediator in an emotional divorce case used this first caucus after Stage 1 to teach the *Touchstone Skill* of reflecting by focusing on less

136

emotionally charged content that was not part of the actual dispute. For example, she had the two disputants practice reflecting by using stories outside of their marriage. To bring down the tension, the mediator asked the disputant to repeat after her: "I like peanut butter sandwiches", the disputant reflected "You like peanut butter sandwiches". The mediator said "yes, I like peanut butter sandwiches and sometimes I like extra butter on my peanut butter sandwiches". The disputant reflected back "You like peanut butter sandwiches, and sometimes you put extra butter on your peanut butter sandwiches". The mediator responded "Yes, I like peanut butter sandwiches, sometimes I add extra butter, and sometimes I cut off the crust." The disputant reflected "you like peanut butter sandwiches, sometimes you add extra butter, and sometime you cut off the crust". "Perfect reflection" replied the mediator, "now do that exact reflecting technique with the other disputant when we return into session together, using their exact statements. You may find that once they feel you actually hear what they are saying, they will not continue to repeat themselves." This teaching of the *Touchstone Skills* is followed by administering the *inAccord* Stage 1 survey instrument, which captures disputants' understanding of and satisfaction with Stage 1. The survey tool captures this information from the perspective of both the mediator and the two disputants.

Stage 2: Agenda Setting and Option Generation. In this stage, each party shares his or her vision for the future and is challenged to listen to the goals of the other party, which may include goals opposite to their own. These goals frame the agenda for negotiation. There may be fundamental value differences at this stage, yet disputants must agree to a willingness to use the *Touchstone Skills* of reflecting, reframing, and questioning each other. It is important that the disputants understand that it is acceptable for their stories to differ as their perspectives are unique. It is important in Stage 2, to direct the disputants to look to the future without arguing over who is right and who is wrong. They must be encouraged to move beyond right and wrong and find a way to move forward despite their different perspectives on the past. Only in this way will they be successful in finding a resolution.

The mediator helps the disputants' identify common threads of important overarching values, such as respect, and common interests. Each time the disputants are met with diverging concepts, they are reminded of the convergence of the higher principles that guide their process (their overarching values and common interests) as they set their agenda and generate options. In a workplace example it may be the ongoing success of the company. In a family, a higher overarching value may be the best interest of the children. In a country it could be a common interest of peaceful relations with one another.

This stage begins after the parties have successfully moved from their positions to an awareness of the need for options. At this point, they can begin generating these options using one or both of the following strategies:

- Beginning with General Issues and Moving to Specifics
- Beginning with Specific Issues and Moving to Generalities

The following case study will illustrate the concepts in this section.

Case Study: The Easement

Dave lives in his dream home in the mountains of Colorado. There is an easement through his property to the Anderson cabin, which is used only a couple times a year. For the first three years, Dave enjoyed his relationship with the Andersons who always made sure the gates were closed and that they did not disturb Dave at home. This September, Dave left on a two-week bicycle trip across the state. When Dave returned, he found his gates open and rushed up to the house expecting the worst. The house was undisturbed but the out buildings were tampered with. When Dave entered the old horse stable, he found cigarettes, beer cans, and trash in the arena. The guesthouse was even worse. There were several windows broken, the refrigerator was dumped over, and the food pantry had been completely trashed. There was food everywhere. Dave was furious and asked neighbors if they saw anything strange while he was away. Ben, the neighbor next door, said he saw the Anderson boys using the easement several times to access their parent's property on the other side of Dave's house. One night, he said many cars came and went as if there was a party at the cabin on the Anderson property. Dave called the Andersons and said that he expected payment for the damages to his property.

The Anderson boys had used their parent's cabin while Dave was out of town and admitted to crossing the easement several times. However, they were adamant that they did not enter any of Dave's buildings, nor did they leave the gates open. The Andersons had never had this kind of trouble with the previous owners. They were quite upset with Dave's accusations. Mr. Anderson has agreed to attend mediation with Dave to resolve this dispute.

In this case, the disputants divided an issue into smaller, more manageable components. This helps the disputants break down more complex and multi-faceted issues, especially those that are threatening to prevent settlement. There are two ways for a mediator to help disputants divide an issue:

1. Suggest that a larger issue be defined in more narrow terms.

Dave was very angry and could only talk about someone having to pay dearly for the damages. The mediator helped define the issue as a more specific need to have some compensation for the damages.

2. Ask the parties to take an issue and split it into component sub-issues.

Dave's main issue was that he expected payment from the Andersons for damage to his property. The mediator suggested that Dave itemize the damage into two sub-categories: the stable and the guesthouse. This was helpful later when it was determined that two separate parties caused the damage to the two structures.

Another approach is to ask the disputants to define or create a bargaining formula or principles that will guide the generation of options. Unlike the previous breaking down of the issue into smaller parts, this requires the parties to agree on more broadly defined issues. This is used when the disputants may have more agreement on broad principles than they do on specific issues. In this case, Dave and Mr. Anderson agreed that the negotiations would always be focused on maintaining a good relationship between their respective households. This helped temper the discussions and create a collaborative atmosphere at the outset.

Methods of Option Generation. The parties can deepen the collaborative process by agreeing to a framework within which to create options for resolution. These include:

Open Discussion. This is simply an informal discussion of the parties' interests. If there is low conflict, it may be the only process necessary. If they are having trouble with creative ideas, move them in to a brainstorming session.

Brainstorming. This can be used effectively in low to mid-level conflict. The mediator begins by offering rules for brainstorming:

- Please withhold any judgment, criticism, or evaluation of ideas.
- Be as wild and outlandish as you want to be.
- We are looking for quantity in this process, not quality.
- Feel free to build on other ideas.
- All of your ideas will have equal worth.
- Do not interrupt to offer feedback.
- If they are new to this process, the mediator directs them to brainstorm for a few minutes on something unrelated like how to create new features for cars or how to create new gadgets for their homes.

The mediator begins this session by asking for as many ideas as possible and records each of them for discussion later. The following suggestions can keep the process flowing:

- Ask for outside-the-box (radical) suggestions.
- Keep offering them positive feedback about their ideas.
- Keep it going fast so there is less time for criticism and analysis.
- Use "we" instead of individual names to keep them more bonded.
- When the process lulls, take a short break and have them come back for another session.

Facilitated Generation. This can be used for mid- to high-level conflict as the mediator becomes more active. The mediator frames an issue as a problem and then asks a "how" question. For example, in an employee dispute the mediator might say, "How can Joe still have his creative process in the office space he shares with Kim while still keeping the office orderly enough for Kim to function positively within?" (Joint Solution Statement) Each disputant is asked to respond to this question, one at a time. The mediator keeps track of all the ideas, no matter how controversial or improbable. As in brainstorming, the disputants are asked to abstain from offering judgment or analysis of the ideas. The mediator encourages parties to build on one another's suggestions.

Single-text Negotiation (becomes the groundwork for the MOA). This is a helpful tool in any conflict regardless of the level of intensity; however, it is a necessary tool in *directive* mediation where the mediator is performing shuttle negotiations between the parties. Using the single text approach, the disputants work with one document. The document may be developed by the mediator after hearing all concerns in the dispute. The document is then taken to all the disputants who begin to make improvements and revisions that make it progressively more acceptable to all concerned.

Generation Refinement Techniques. Once the mediator has established an exhaustive list of possible options, it is time to begin identifying the realistic options and how to address each one. There are several techniques that the mediator presents at this time including:

1. Establish process for discussing options. Once the issues have been identified, the parties can choose a process for refinement that may include:

- Establishing larger agreements in principle that will guide the discussions. For instance, divorcing parents may decide that every option is considered in "the best interest of the children".
- Parties can decide if the mediator has permission to help move past impasse by adding potential issues to the current ones.
- Parties will decide whether to tackle issues from most difficult to least, least difficult to most, or alternate between the two.
- Sometimes, it helps to begin with a less charged issue in order to build early confidence in the collaborative process.

2. Seek to link potential trades of interests. This process is used after any of the processes above, to begin to refine the generation process. In this process, the parties and mediator begin to identify interests that may be connected and then begin discussing trades that

each party may be willing to make. For example, one party may want more money in a dispute and the other needs more time. The mediator can begin to help them see a link between these interests that may involve a trade of money for time or vice versa.

3. Bite sizing issues. Some issues may seem overwhelming or too complex for parties to tackle. In this instance, the mediator might direct the parties to break the issue down into components that could be negotiated independently. This can help during option generation when parties become entrenched in positions over a large issue.

4. Outside feedback. Some issues may require outside experts or resources in order to shed new light on the dispute. This is best used when the mediator suggests this option as a way to move the process forward. Outside experts might offer model agreements from other similar disputes, make a presentation to all the parties on solutions that have been successful with others, or provide necessary technical knowledge. For example, when deciding how to value a business operation, an outside expert would be required to establish that value. In some instances, the outside feedback may consist of the mediator offering an article or outside resource for the disputants to examine during a recess between sessions.

A workplace example can illustrate this concept. One disputant in a contentious workplace dispute remarked that the only solution was for one of them to go. The other employee, in response, retorted that he would be staying and she better get used to it. The mediator was able to reframe these statements and open the discussion for a more collaborative solution. She did so by asking them "Let's say you both stay for a while. What would need to change for each of you to make that feasible?" As the conversation deepened between the two, a series of common and divergent interests began to emerge. As they did, the mediator clarified their positions into overarching common interests that would hopefully evolve into the words for the first paragraph in a Memorandum of Agreement.

The mediator in this case used this beginning conversation to create a list of underlying interests on a flip chart. This sparked a more detailed discussion of options as the disputants were able to see the details behind the positions and interests that might be shared. Once each disputant agreed that the list of interests was complete, the mediator set the stage for how to create potential options for compromise among interests that were both common and competing. To build an early success at collaboration, the mediator asked each of them to choose how they would like to come up with an agenda and list of options. She let them choose among various options such as brainstorming, alternating between tackling difficult and easy interests, or beginning with a few common agreements to build goodwill.

At the end of this stage, the disputants can expect to have an agenda for the next stages and a list of potential options for resolving the conflict. This document is saved for discussion in the next stage where they revisit overarching common goals and identify joint solutions and agreements in principle. At the conclusion of Stage 2, the mediator has a choice. If the approach is directive, based on the mismatch of emotions, a private meeting is held with each of the disputants to administer the *inAccord* survey instruments for Stage 2 and capture each disputant's understanding and satisfaction with this stage of the model (from the perspective of each party and the mediator). This also may be achieved in joint session, using a more relational approach, based on both disputants feeling empowered or both feeling disempowered, a match of emotions based on their individual *Pre-Feelings* Survey and the *Mediators Pre Feeling* Survey indicator.

Stage 3: Joint Solution Statement: Testing the Agreements in Principle. At this point, the mediator asks both disputants, "What would it look like if this conflict were resolved?" As we discussed, this sets up the common values, translating into the first paragraph of the Memorandum of Agreement and fast-forwards the disputants to a future time when the dispute is resolved or managed. This begins the Agreements in Principle or Stage 3 of the mediation. A typical first line may read something like this, "In the spirit of resolving (the issue or conflict) and moving forward in a spirit of collaboration (joint overarching solutions), Disputant A and Disputant B agree to the following terms..." which are then specified. This list is taken from the potential options generated in Stage 2. In a case of two managers arguing over the viability of instituting flex time where employees could pick their own start and stop times as long as they worked an eight hour day, they were able to generate an option of keeping the flex time schedule preferred by one of them, while incorporating the more resistant manager's idea of instituting a review process that tracks employee productivity.

This step of Testing the Agreements in Principle involves discussing any assumptions, and clarifying agreements for each of the issues. It is an appropriate time to address and answer the specifics of who, what, when, where, and how as components to the agreement. For instance, this is where the manager may discuss options for flex time, including if such a process can be worked into the company budget. In addition, the discussion can involve who will conduct the quarterly reviews, how the reviews will be measured, and what corrections would be deemed appropriate. This is also an appropriate time for the mediator to assist with a SWOT Analysis (Strengths, Weaknesses, Opportunities, or Threats) for each of the options that are transformed into agreements in principle. For our example, if the managers decided to go ahead with quarterly reviews of the flex policy, they would examine the strength of having quarterly reviews such as creating a predictable time frame, what potential weaknesses it might create such as not allowing enough time for data collection, opportunities it might bring forward such as increased productivity, and any threats that might make it unfeasible. At the end of this progression, the *inAccord* Stage 3 survey instrument is administered to the disputants and the Mediator completes parallel forms for each of the disputants. This may be done in caucus, or together at the table, depending on the approach used by the Mediator.

Uncovering and Examining Parties' Hidden Interests. Negotiation can be seen as a bargaining "game" in which each side holds certain interests in their hand that they want to have satisfied. Because Western culture, in particular, is focused on competition and win/lose, many times parties will hold on to certain "cards" or interests in an attempt to win more ground during the negotiations. This can be frustrating for a mediator who is trying to guide a collaborative process among parties who may come into the mediation as if they were entering into a poker game. Nevertheless, identifying these hidden cards is the beginnings of helping disputants find their way to a win/win settlement. Moore (2003) identifies four broad reasons for hidden interests in mediation:

Parties Are Not Aware of All of Their Interests. Sometimes a party is not aware of, or misperceives, their interests in a case. This could be the result of external factors such as advice from attorneys or friends and traditional ideas about what a settlement process entails. They might be predisposed to struggle over positions and not know the difference between positions and interests. It is the mediator's job to help the parties recognize that the cards they hold should be interest, not position, based. For instance, an employee may present that he is frustrated over his lack of advancement at work. However, the mediator asks clarifying questions and the employee finds that what he really wants is a raise not a promotion. This allows the negotiations to stay focused on the underlying interest of higher pay rather than advancement.

Disputants Intentionally Hide Certain Interests. This is a natural process of negotiation as disputants withhold certain interests, usually for one of two reasons. First, they may hope that by keeping certain interests hidden they might increase their gains or outcomes. Or, they may hide certain interests in hope of using them later to leverage the greatest number of concessions from their "opponent." It is up to the mediator to constantly watch for these tendencies and maintain an overall atmosphere of collaboration, regardless of the competitive nature of one or more parties. In a divorce dispute, one disputant may hide that they really do not want the house any longer (even though they are demanding it) in an attempt to see if they can get that asset and sell it. It is up to the mediator to find the underlying interest (the money from a sale) and bring that into the conversation.

Disputants Confuse Interests with Positions. When emotions begin to heat up during a negotiation, one or more of the disputants may begin to drift away from interests and back to hardline positions. This is a defensive reaction to increasing stress in the bargaining process. It is as if one party has left the negotiations and retreated behind their original fortresses (positions.) The mediator must find ways to keep the emotional heat turned down and use specific interventions to maintain enough safety to prevent retreat by any party.

Disputants are Unaware of Procedures for Exploring Interests. It is rare to find a mediation in which all of the disputants are aware of the procedures for discovering and discussing hidden interests. If they believe that there is not an avenue to uncover the other disputant's' interests, it may produce an insurmountable obstacle for settlement.

Case Study: Half a House

Bill bought a house from a couple, Mike and Susan; however, the couple failed to disclose that a piece of the property actually was owned by the local city and not by the owner of the parcel. When Bill went to enlarge his house, he found that it was partially built on a city right-of-way; therefore, he could not obtain the permit to begin construction. The local zoning official told him that he only owned half of his house and he better get a lawyer. Bill called one immediately. The process began to follow the usual legal channels with each side hiring competing lawyers. Then a mutual friend suggested that the two sides hire a mediator. The realtor who sold the property and was named in the legal action agreed to attend the mediation with the two parties. When the parties arrived for mediation, they were accustomed to an attorney admonishing them to keep quiet and let him do the talking. There was a great deal of information that each party held tightly in their hands and it was up to the mediator to move them away from positions of right and wrong to issues of specific interests.

Moving from Bluffs to Framing a Joint Problem. Disputants will not necessarily be candid simply because they have chosen to enter into mediation. Certainly, laying the important pre-negotiation groundwork and presenting a comprehensive and clear opening statement will pave the way for more honest and open negotiations. However, most of us have an association of negotiating as a card game, and a big part of playing cards is knowing how and when to bluff. Bluffing is simply saying that you have interests that you actually do not have, or implying you will do something when you do not intend to do it. Bluffing is a very common occurrence in mediation; therefore, it is a good idea to know how to uncover it, recognize it, and help the party drop the bluff.

The Art of Bluffing. If a bluff is going to work, it has to appear to be credible. This means the disputant that is bluffing has some perceived authority, capacity, or will to carry out an action in order to get a particular interest met. This bluff seldom gets called in a joint session for fear of what might happen if the weaker disputant challenges an already tough player to show his or her cards. It is up to the mediator to take the party into a caucus to ascertain the disputant's true intentions. If the mediator finds the disputant is indeed bluffing, there are two strategies to employ in the caucus:

1.*Persuasion.* First the mediator must assess with the disputant if there will be any long-term effects on the relationship between the disputants if the bluff goes unchallenged. The mediator should also help the disputant assess the potential cost to all the disputants if the mediator sets a precedent of leaving the bluff unchallenged. In this instance, the mediator has used persuasion to influence the behavior of the disputant. Once the disputant is cognizant of the negative effects the bluff may have on the outcome of the bargaining, they may choose to withdraw the bluff.

2.*Rationalization.* Moore (2003) defines a rationalization as a "logical and plausible argument for a shift in position or approach" (p. 261). As an example, let us say that Bill, the owner who unknowingly bought half a house, refuses to pay for any of the mediation costs. His argument is: why should he since he was the one who was cheated. The realtor does not want to pay because she feels the couple who listed the house did not disclose the zoning problems to her either. The couple who sold the house claim they simply cannot afford to pay for the entire mediation after the previous legal bills.

The mediator senses some bluffing by all the parties and decides to take them each into private caucus. In the caucus with Bill, the mediator discovers that he is more committed to sharing the costs than having the process go back to litigation. The realtor is more interested in protecting her reputation and appearing to be an advocate for the couple who listed with her than refusing to pay any money for mediation. The couple actually might be willing to pay half the cost if the realtor and Bill split the difference. A perfect ending to this would be if all the parties returned to a joint session and explained their shift in position in terms of their interests. If one or all are afraid of losing face, the mediator could intervene and, with permission, summarize each party's rationalization.

Interest Acceptance and Agreement. Once the disputants have identified their issues and interests, they must organize them into three possible divisions:

1. Mutually Exclusive Interests

These are the interests that cannot be satisfied without canceling out the satisfaction of another's interests. In the Half a House case, the parties identified several interests that canceled out the interests of the other party. The realtor desired a speedy resolution and wanted Bill to rescind the house deal and give it back to her to resell; but Bill loves the house and does not want to give it up. These interests are incompatible.

2. Compatible Interests

These are the interests of both disputants that do not exclude or may be similar to the other disputant's interests. Bill's desire to hold on to the house was compatible with Mike and Susan's need not to get the house back because they used the closing money to purchase their next home. These disputants have a common interest in keeping their respective houses.

3. Mixed Interests

This is simply an acknowledgement by the disputants that there are some compatible interests and some competing needs between the two disputants. This indicates that, although not all needs will be met, there is a possibility to trade off certain interests in order to reach resolution.

Framing Joint Solutions. The mediator concludes this stage of the process by creating a statement that frames the joint problems. This statement should include the interests of all of the parties illustrated in one comprehensive statement. The purpose of this stage is to engage the disputants in a collaborative process of framing the many issues of the dispute in a way that identifies all the interests that the disputants seek to satisfy. This statement can be used as a guiding document for the negotiations. In the Half a House case study, a framing statement might be:

How can Bill keep his house, be able to remodel his home, gain ownership of the entire parcel from the city, and temporarily find a place for he and his fiancé' to live? At the same time, how can Mike and Susan keep ownership of their new house and not be driven to file for bankruptcy over the mounting legal bills? Finally, how can the realtor protect her professional reputation in the community and accurately answer questions from the state real estate commission?

This statement should include all of the parties' interests. The purpose is to bundle all of these competing and compatible needs into one written document so the parties can quickly see that their needs are respected, even if they eventually are not met by the settlement. Now the parties can explore the interests in more detail and begin to generate options for settlement.

Final Bargaining. Bennett and Hermann (1996) have developed a categorization of mediator moves for impasses. These entail the mediator influencing the parties' perspectives, the available resources, and/or the overall procedures of the mediation through specific interventions.

Influence the Parties' Perspectives (Private Caucus). Using this strategy, the mediator will attempt to influence the manner in which parties perceive information, choices made by both sides, and how they see one another.

- When you begin the caucus, ask the party, "How is the process going for you?"
- Ask the parties what they will do if there is no agreement and what their BATNA (Best Alternative to a Negotiated Settlement) might be.
- Ask the parties what the economic, social, time, and emotional consequences of this impasse might be.
- Take them back through their stated interests and needs and ask them if the current stalemate is satisfying them.
- Take them back through the history of concessions to date, noting the gives and takes.

- Ask them what standards of fairness they are using and ask if there might be others available to them that would end the impasse.
- Have the parties identify the roadblocks and come up with solutions to help them get unstuck.
- Use tools such as reframing to help them shift their perspective.
- Use role reversal and ask them to describe the other person's perspective.
- Practice moving beyond the impasses with the mediator taking on the role of the other party in the discussions.

Bring in New Elements. Using this strategy, a mediator will bring in new elements to bear on the disputants' situation in hopes that they will influence the dynamics, the extent of possibilities, and the perspective of the conflict.

- Ask for a second opinion from another mediator.
- Bring in an outside expert such as an attorney, appraiser, or accountant.
- Refer the impasse elements on to arbitration.
- Enlist therapeutic help from professionals, peers, support groups or other professionals.
- Offer solutions that have worked for other mediation parties in the past.
- Offer the parties problem-solving homework assignments to take home and work on when the pressure is less intense.
- Bring in witnesses or other advocates.
- Use techniques such as brainstorming to develop additional options to the impasse.

Influencing the Procedure. In this case, the mediator will introduce moves intended to change some element of the process of interaction between the disputants.

- Switch the negotiations to another issue and table the impasse for later discussion.
- Return to the mediation agreement, restating the parties' commitment and the ground rules for the process.
- Use private caucuses to help parties move beyond impasses.

- Try out trial periods for certain offers or proposals.
- Adjourn the negotiations for a brief walk or stretch to break the tension.
- Switch the meeting to a different time and/or place.
- Rearrange the seating in the room.
- Break for lunch.
- Arrange the next meeting as a telephone conference or Skype call.
- Have attorneys or other advocates in the room as witnesses.

Stage 4: Crafting the final Memorandum of Agreement. In this stage, the mediator begins with the opening paragraph of the Joint Solution Statement that was developed by the disputants in the previous stage. It is then appropriate for the mediator to alternate the points of agreement from person to person, for balance and equality of process, until agreements have been reached that will satisfy all the concerns and issues presented, and which will frame the set of agreements each person is willing to follow. In the workplace example from earlier in the chapter, the flex option became part of the joint solution statement for insertion into the MOA in the following manner, "In the spirit of working collaboratively for the success of our company, we agree to allow the current flex time policy to remain in effective and track employee productivity quarterly. Alterations to the flex time will then be considered for adjustment on a case by case basis." Details of how this will be instituted should be included after this statement. For instance, it should state, if possible, who conducts the reviews, who decides the budget, and what the process and corrections entail. This is followed by the signature of the now former disputants to the Memorandum of Agreement.

In mediation the final contract is referred to as a Memorandum of Agreement or Agreement, or simply an MOA. This agreement carefully and concisely sets forth the negotiated solution and/or agreements to the dispute. The MOA can stand as a contract or can be submitted to the court to become an order of the court. This is why it is helpful to have a single text agreement from the onset of the mediation so everything is well documented. In this way, parties can continually review the document to ensure it mirrors their interests and the overall collaborative process. If a single text is used throughout the process, it can be easily used as the body of the final MOA. The creation of the MOA often coincides with any final bargaining that takes place near the conclusion of the resolution process. Again, a single text agreement can remind the parties of the historical flow of the decision making process during the entire span of the negotiations.

Implementation of an agreement refers to the procedural steps the parties and mediator devise to put the agreement into action and end the dispute. If the action plan is weak, the entire settlement might collapse. Therefore, the mediator must help the parties create efficient, reasonable, effective, and durable procedures for implementing the agreement. These are the "who, what, when, and where" factors that must be clear, complete, practical, and measurable for each term specified in the agreement.

Generally, the MOA should be written in a balanced way that demonstrates the rights and responsibilities that each of the parties has contributed to the settlement agreement. It is important that the mediator take the parties through the entire MOA very carefully to confirm agreement before finalizing the MOA. This provides greater assurance that there will not be misunderstandings later that threaten compliance to the MOA. Parties should consult with their attorneys and any other expert professionals as they deem appropriate regarding the MOA. It is advisable for beginning mediators to have their first few MOAs reviewed by a more seasoned mediator to ensure clarity and completeness. Our Mediators Without Borders Society provides for-fee supervised coaching for student and professional practitioners both online and via telephone or SKYPE.

The Elements of Written Contracts. The basic elements of a written contract are:
1. The name or kind of contract
2. The parties to the contract, date, and place of agreement
3. Recitals that detail the relationship of the parties and describe the contract's functions
4. Promise clause describing the exchange the parties are agreeing to make

5. Closing verbiage and signatures

Additional contract factors might include:

- Clarity of the clauses: This refers to writing the clauses in such a way that they are not open to multiple interpretations or misinterpretations.
- Degree of detail in the clauses: This refers to the having precise terms to describe the settlement. Usually, in high conflict cases, there will be more attention to detailing the clauses.
- Balance of concessions: The written agreement should identify what is to be exchanged in clear terms and be constructed in a way that does not appear one-sided. This can be accomplished by alternating exchanges instead of listing one party's exchanges followed by the others.
- Positive attitude and perspective: The document should be written with a positive statement that acknowledges the cooperation among the parties and their dedication to compliance.

The Importance of Creating a Durable MOA. It is critical to draft the agreement concisely for the following reasons:

- To clearly document what was agreed to for future reference.
- To make sure that the words used embody the intent of the parties.
- To ensure there are no ambiguities or misstated provisions can result in future conflict.
- To prevent a badly drafted document from becoming an invitation to litigation.
- To create an understandable document for people not in the room during the negotiations who may need to refer to the implemented terms of the agreement.
- A well-drafted document reflects well on the drafter.
- A well-drafted document reflects well on the profession.

Considerations for drafting good MOA's:

- Before mediation, the mediator should know enough about the legal aspects of the case so that he or she can be an effective mediator and agreement writer.

- The mediator should have a complete understanding of the disputants' interests.
- As parties hone in on agreement, the mediator should ask detailed and specific questions to make sure that the agreement is meeting their expressed and underlying interests.
- The mediator should ask what-if questions to flesh out whether agreement is truly workable.
- The mediator should flesh out dates, times, type of payment, specific payment plans, accountability measures, and consequences for non-compliance.
- In a transactional contract, the mediator should make sure the disputants determine what closure will look like, including developing and negotiating criteria for compliance.
- The mediator should develop a monitoring and enforcement plan.
- The mediator should identify what will happen if the MOA is breached.
- The mediator should identify and address the conditions that might necessitate a modification of the MOA.
- The mediator should identify any limitations or exceptions to the MOA.
- The mediator should tell parties to review the draft MOA carefully for accuracy and completeness.
- The mediator should strongly encourage the parties to have their attorneys or union representatives review draft MOA's prior to signing.

Phase Three: Post-Mediation Outcomes

The most critical objective index of the effectiveness of the *inAccord* model is whether the disputants sign the Memorandum of Agreement. This is important because signing not only symbolically resolves the dispute but also indicates the success of the mediation itself. However, the mere act of signing does not reveal the particular reasons why people chose to sign or not sign. It was essential as a second outcome to measure the disputants' perceptions of the

154

mediation process once they had completed the four stages in Phase Two. That is why we felt it important to assess the disputants' evaluation of issues such as how helpful, effective, informative, fair or impartial the process was for them and the extent to which they are satisfied. These measurements are contained in the Exit Survey (see Appendix).

Having these outcome data from each disputant as well as the mediator helps us to better understand what is essential in the *inAccord* model. As can be seen on Table 1 the mediator also rates the disputants' outcomes on the Exit Survey with regard to their satisfaction with the mediation process, their view as to its success, as well as their understanding of key concepts. They also rate the mediator in terms of his or her neutrality or impartiality. In this manner, we can determine whether the disputants' rating of these outcomes or the mediator's judgments of the disputants' ratings better predict the objective outcome of the signing of the MOA. The survey instruments and related findings are discussed in more detail in Chapter Seven.

As a third outcome, we assessed the disputants' perceptions of their emotions through our *My Feelings* post survey. Disputants rated the strength of these same emotions that were included in the *My Feelings* pre survey. The pre and post-test design helps us determine whether or not the empowering and disempowering emotions have changed over the course of the mediation. These findings are reported in Chapter Seven on the importance of research evaluation. The mediator examines the disputants' final emotion ratings in order to once again evaluate whether there is a match or mismatch, namely whether disputants are in the same quadrant (both in empowering or both in disempowering emotions) or whether there is a mismatch (one disputant reports stronger empowering emotions while the other disputant reports stronger disempowering emotions.) Based on this information, the mediator decides which approach was more appropriate for the case, directive or relational.

A fourth and final outcome survey measures the extent to which disputants' initial expectations were realized as a result of the mediation. We examine whether the disputants felt that their goals of saving money, time, and the relationship were met by the end of the mediation process. These findings will be reported in the following chapter on the importance of research evaluation for empirical confirmation of our model.

PART THREE:
Research and International Applications

Chapter Seven:
A Preliminary Research Evaluation of
the *inAccord* Model

Chapter Overview

This chapter begins by emphasizing the importance of evaluating the efficacy of mediation practices, through appropriate research designs and implementations. Toward this goal, the authors have developed a three-phase model of the mediation process. In Phase One, we first evaluate the self-report of the disputant emotions as well as their conflict styles. We present findings from a first study in which we asses both empowering and disempowering emotions at the outset of mediation and then assess the strength of these emotions after the mediation has been completed. In Phase Two, we administer surveys that assess disputants' understanding of the mediation skills being taught, as well as their satisfaction with the process. In Phase Three, our surveys assess disputants' reflections on the outcomes of the mediation. For example, we ask about their satisfaction with the process, whether their expectations were fulfilled and whether they felt the mediator was neutral and impartial. We report our findings for each of these phases as well as suggestions on future research. An essential feature of our future work will be not only to assess the disputants' perceptions of the process but the mediator's evaluation of how the mediation proceeded toward intended outcomes.

Research Evaluating the Effectiveness of the inAccord Model

Much of the previous evidence for the effectiveness of the *inAccord* Model comes from the extensive clinical experience of the first author (Ries) who has employed these mediation techniques with clients whose conflicts often involved marital discord or disputes within the family. In addition, she has applied the *inAccord* principles to disputants within institutions or organizations, such as conflicts between employers and employees. Most recently, she has taken these principles and associated mediation techniques to Romania where cases commonly center on property rights, inheritance, and commercial disputes.

Although the accumulating evidence through these mediation interventions provides a powerful demonstration of its efficacy on a case by case basis, we are moving toward a more systematic, empirical documentation of the *inAccord* effectiveness, employing appropriate research designs and statistical techniques with sufficiently large disputant samples. For this first edition, we will describe a smaller sample and build on this in subsequent editions.

Our first study included a sample group of 58 trainees in a three-day program that provided an overview of the *inAccord* model of mediation. The trainees were presented with actual case studies based upon real conflicts or disputes that typically bring people to the mediation table. After they were provided with a detailed description of the conflict, trainees engaged in role-playing, going through all phases of the process as if they were actual disputants. When Ries provided the initial training, she modeled it as a process parallel to how a mediator using the *inAccord* methodology would handle an actual mediation case. At the start of the training, participants were introduced to the framework for the course. The learners then proceeded through the phases of the mediation including the requisite skills at four stages. They also completed all of the survey instruments. Similarly, novice mediators playing the role of disputants follow the same exact protocol. By experiencing what the disputants might think and feel during the process, the learners in our model are able to better understand what works. In this way trainees are mock disputants engaging in experiences comparable to real disputants, and can therefore learn firsthand what a disputant might find helpful, might feel, and might agree to do.

One might question whether, as trainees who have sought to learn about the mediation process, this may constitute a biased sample, in that they may be motivated to view the training program favorably. This is a legitimate question. This is meant to be a "learn by experience" part of a training exercise. We used this mock experience to help design our surveys assessing each phase. After they were developed using sample learning groups, these surveys were employed with actual disputants who sought to pursue mediation to help them resolve the conflicts or disputes in their own life. At the time of this writing we have 20 cases of actual disputant pairs, which would be construed as too small a sample size for meaningful statistical analysis. Therefore, we are currently continuing to collect many more samples until we reach an adequate size for standard statistical measurement. Our goal is to measure the exact mediator interventions that are most useful. To that end, we are continuing our research, adding many important factors that will determine the adaptability of the model to different constituencies.

An examination of the protocols of the actual disputants to date has revealed that their responses on our surveys are quite congruent with our original sample of trainees who were role-playing. This has given us confidence in the application of our research model. While there may be a positivity "bias" in a trainee sample, there may be a somewhat different bias in those seeking mediation as actual disputants. That is, most people come to mediation, much as they do to therapy, with some level of hope or conviction that the process will work for them, they are somewhat eager and trusting, which is why they commit to time and money. So, do they come to mediation with a bias to benefit? We have chosen not to think of either mock disputants or real disputants as being biased. Rather, individuals in both groups generally come with a hopeful expectation that the process will serve their needs, whether they are a trainee or a client, wanting either to learn about conflict resolution skills as a professional or to resolve the conflicts in their own lives.

We have divided our research evaluation into three phases or components that parallel the mediation process itself. The evaluation tools, which are questionnaires and surveys completed by both the mediator and the disputants, are very naturally embedded directly into the mediation process and mark progress from one phase to another. In this manner, the research protocol mirrors a principle at the heart of the *inAccord* model – the concept of transparency.

The first phase, Phase One, addresses an analysis of the feelings or emotions that disputants report at the outset. Phase Two addresses the heart of the intervention; the surveys provide an analysis of disputants' understanding of the skills that define the four stages of the mediation process. Phase Three focuses on an assessment of outcomes; the tools include whether disputants sign or do not sign a Memorandum of Agreement (MOA). In addition, exit questions address a number of dimensions, including:

- disputants' evaluation of whether the mediation was a success
- how well each disputant felt that the mediation met their specific expectations
- each disputant's ability to now understand and implement the goals of the *inAccord* model
- perceptions of the fairness and impartiality of the mediator

Additionally, disputants completed a *My Feelings* post survey to determine whether the strength of the empowering and disempowering emotions shifted as a function of the mediation process itself.

A major goal of the mediation intervention is that the disputants have a thorough understanding of the process, which facilitates a sense of empowerment by following the transparency principle. The introduction of surveys or questionnaires, naturally embedded at each phase of the process, ideally enhances the disputants' awareness and comprehension of their emotions, and the requisite skills needed to negotiate and resolve the conflict. Moreover, as part of our exit survey during the final phase, we ask disputants to report on whether they felt that the process actually promoted transparency as well as whether it engendered a sense of empowerment with regard to their active participation in the stage-related negotiations.

Phase One: Empowering and Disempowering Feelings

In Phase One, we assess feelings that are culturally relevant in the United States, emotions that parties report in response to the conflict situation. Feelings or emotions can be powerful forces in people's lives and relationships. Some emotions may be more adaptive than others in the mediation process. We have identified two classes of emotions, those that we have labeled empowering and those that are disempowering. Examples of empowering emotions are optimistic, happy, hopeful, contented, and forgiving. Disempowering emotions include depression, despair, anger, blame, and humiliation. We focus on these emotions because they are identified by the first author (Ries) as those most commonly occurring in the cases she has mediated over the years. In our subsequent work in different countries (e.g. Romania, the EU, and the Niger Delta) it will be critical to determine which emotions are relevant to each culture. This analysis will refer to the work of researchers such as Shaver, Wu, and Schwartz (1992) for studies on cross-cultural emotions.

Our goal in asking both parties about their personal feelings in Phase One, prior to the introduction of the mediation skills to be mastered, is to sensitize both disputants and mediators to the importance of the emotions that are expressed when people face a conflict. We are, in effect, normalizing the fact that it is natural for people to experience strong feelings when they are in conflict. For some, these emotions are empowering, for others their feelings can serve to be disempowering. After reviewing the *My Feeling* pre surveys, the mediator shares with each disputant where they fall in terms of their empowering and disempowering emotions. The mediator explains that if there is a match with the other disputant in terms of empowering and disempowering emotions, a relational approach to mediation is advised. However, if there is a mismatch between the two disputants, the mediator will explain why a more directive approach is appropriate.

We first developed a survey tool entitled *My Feelings* pre survey. Eight empowering and eight disempowering emotions were presented, each of which disputants rated in terms of the frequency with which they were experiencing them during this conflict. Measurement of these feelings was on a four-point scale: Most of the time, Some of the time, Not that often, and Hardly ever. It scored the strength of the feeling on a 4-point scale, where a high number meant that an emotion is high in strength. We selected a 4-point scale rather than a 5- or 7-point scale because it did not have middle point (e.g., between "some of the time" and "not that often"). Such mid-point choices allow the respondent to "hedge" and not really commit to clear positive or negative emotions, so we avoided this. The second author (Harter) has amply documented the effectiveness of this type of question format after years of developing instruments now in widespread use in this country and abroad (Harter, 1999, 2012). Considerable past psychological research (see Cowan, 2001) has demonstrated that the inclusion of too many points on a scale, (for example, ten choices rather that four) is not desirable because people cannot cognitively discriminate between that many options, their judgments are not reliable. From our feelings survey, two scores are obtained, the average of the eight empowering feelings and the average of the eight disempowering emotions. This provides a baseline for each disputant.

The combination of eight emotion items within each cluster forms a single score for each. Before combining items in this manner, a researcher should first demonstrate that the items in each cluster "hang together," each as an interpretable or meaningful construct (i.e., a cluster of empowering versus a cluster of disempowering emotions). Ideally we would want people who have high scores (4 or 3) on some of the emotions in a given cluster to have similarly high scores (4 or 3) on all of the emotion items in that cluster. In like fashion, we would want those scoring low on certain emotions in a given cluster (scores of 1 or 2) to report low scores on all emotions in that cluster. We applied this strategy to our findings.

For those familiar with statistics, we can compute an actual numerical index of *internal consistency reliability*, meaning that within a given cluster (thus the label "internal"), item scores are consistent with one another. The term reliable means that the scale can literally be trusted if the index to be calculated is sufficiently high. These values can range from 0 to 1 (with all values within these two end-points) where a 0 would mean that there is absolutely no consistency in scores within a cluster to a high of 1, which would indicate that there was perfect consistency. To clarify, perfect consistency would mean that each respondent in the group gave the exact same rating to all items within the cluster, whether it was a high, mid-range, or low score. Rarely, with samples of real participants, would we find that ideal outcome. In principle and practice, therefore, values in the upper range of .8 to .9 are considered to reflect excellent internal consistency and reliability. In our sample, the value for the empowerment cluster was .84 and for the disempowerment cluster it was .81, when the *My Feelings* survey was administered at the outset, attesting to the extremely high reliability of the two emotion cluster scores.

This survey is not only administered during Phase One but also in Phase Three, after the four stages of mediation are completed. In Phase Three, the items describing the different emotions are identical. However, the instructions ask the disputants to reflect on how they are feeling "now that you have completed the mediation process." Thus, the response choices are Very much, Pretty much, Not Very much, Not at all. (The reliabilities for Phase Three were .86 for the empowering cluster and .91, for the disempowering cluster, values that are staggeringly high!) By administering the *My Feelings* survey both before and after the actual mediation process, we can examine the possibility that these two classes of emotions may change as a result of the training. Ideally, the strength of empowering emotions should increase, whereas the strength of the disempowering feelings should decline in strength. (The complete survey instruments for Phase One and Phase Three are included in Appendix A.)

Based on the scores of the mock disputant trainees, the findings clearly reveal the predicted pattern (see Figure 7-1). Participation in the intervening mediation training process, mastering the skills at each stage, has a dramatic impact on these emotions for the sample as a whole. As Figure 1 documents, in Phase One, both classes of emotions are rated at the midpoint of the four-point scale, 2.5. As a function of the mediation skill training, there are major changes for both empowering and disempowering emotions. Empowering emotions, initially at a level of 2.4 increase considerably, to a high of 3.5, at Phase Three, a major shift on a four-point scale. Disempowering emotions show the opposite pattern, they decrease dramatically from 2.6 during the pretest to a low of 1.8. Both of these differences are highly statistically significant. This is the first demonstration of the efficacy of the *inAccord* model.

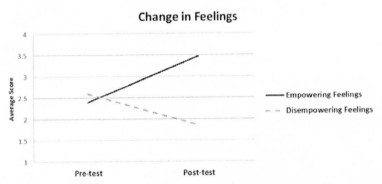

Figure 7-1. Changes in the strength of empowering and disempowering emotions between Phase One and Phase Three

Implications for outcomes. Figure 7-1 presents the average changes in empowering and disempowering emotions for the sample as a whole. However, there are also individual differences in the frequency with which these feelings are experienced. That is, individuals differ in how much they experience both empowering and disempowering emotions. This raises the question of whether these individual differences in the perceived frequency of emotions of both types are related to the outcomes assessed in the exit survey administered in Phase Three. We asked whether those individuals who report more empowering feelings also indicate that they experience more positive outcomes and also if those who report more disempowering feelings also experience less positive outcomes. The results provide a resounding "yes" to both questions.

First, the more people experienced empowering emotions, (a) the more they also reported that the *inAccord* mediation was successful and (b) the more they felt that the *inAccord* mediation met or realized their expectations. Second, and conversely, those people who experienced disempowering feelings at the beginning reported that (a) the *inAccord* mediation was less successful, they were less satisfied, and (b) the less they felt that the *inAccord* mediation met or realized their expectations. Thus, as one hopes to observe, individual differences in emotions directly impact the outcomes of the mediation.

Future Research. With larger samples from data currently coming in, we will be able to examine the emotion data from a different perspective. We will look at the issue of a match-versus-mismatch in the emotions experienced by each disputant. By match, we mean that both disputants score similarly (for example, both are high on either empowering or disempowering emotions, or both are low on both classes of emotions). A mismatch is exemplified by one disputant reporting high empowering feelings whereas the other disputant reports low empowering emotions. In another example, a mismatch would represent one disputant reporting high disempowering feelings, whereas the second disputant endorses low disempowering emotions. In Chapter Four on the role of emotions, we explored the implications of match-versus-mismatch for the mediator's choice of approaches.

Phase Two: Stage Understanding

Phase Two is at the heart of the mediation process, during which the parties are guided through the *Touchstone Skills* of reflection, reframe, and questioning techniques. The four stages are discussed in detail in Chapter Six. Our assessment first addressed the disputant's understanding of the *Touchstone Skills*. A brief summary description of these stages, including the specific skill to be mastered, follows along with two sample questions from each survey. Once again, we use a four-point scale.

Stage 1 involves the sharing of perspectives/issues, positions, and identification of interests. The particular skill is to differentiate the respective issues, positions, and interests.

Sample questions on the survey used in this phase include:

1) How well do you understand your underlying *interests* in the dispute?

Very well   Pretty well   Not very well   Not at all well

2) How well do you do you understand the *other disputant's underlying interests* in the dispute?

Very well   Pretty well   Not very well   Not at all well

Stage 2 addresses *the agenda setting and option generation.*
Parties were educated in caucus at the end of Stage 1in the three communication skills, reflecting, reframing, and questioning. Sample questions include:

1) How well do you understand the *reflecting and questioning techniques* for clarifying your issues?
Very well   Pretty well   Not very well   Not at all well

2) How well can you now *reframe hurtful statements?*
Very well   Pretty well   Not very well   Not at all well

Stage 3 addresses the *joint solution statements: Testing the Agreements in Principle.*
The skills involve the identification of common causes and higher ground. Sample questions include:

1) How well did the skills of reflective listening and reframing help you to clarify the options?
Very well   Pretty well   Not very well   Not at all well

2) How well are you now able to create a Joint Solution Statement that represents your interests?
Very well   Pretty well   Not very well   Not at all well

Stage 4 is defined by the crafting the MOA. Skills involve addressing the details of who, what, when, and where in the final Memorandum of Agreement. Sample questions include:

1) How well do you understand the terms of the final Memorandum of Agreement?
Very well   Pretty well   Not very well   Not at all well

2) How well do you understand the compromises you made in order to arrive at an agreement?
Very well   Pretty well   Not very well   Not at all well

Satisfaction with Stage Understanding

In addition to the assessment of the disputant's understanding of the skills and concepts presented at each stage, we were also interested in how satisfied disputants were with their understanding of skills, at each of the four stages. A sample question for each stage follows.

Stage 1:

How **Satisfied** were you with the process of sharing your perspectives and identifying your issues, positions, and interests?

Very satisfied   Somewhat   Not very   Not at all

Stage 2:

How **Satisfied** were you with the *list of issues identified for the agenda?*

Very satisfied   Somewhat   Not very   Not at all

Stage 3:

How satisfied were you with the *Joint Solution Statement agreed upon?*

Very satisfied   Somewhat   Not very   Not at all

Stage 4:

How satisfied are you with the skills you learned to help you resolve future conflicts?

Very satisfied   Somewhat   Not very   Not at all

Findings for Stage Understanding and Satisfaction

The overall findings for the entire group are presented in Figure 7-2. They reveal that disputants reported extremely high levels of *understanding* the various stage principles. Secondly, (see Figure 7-3), they were highly satisfied with the mediation at all four stages. Finally, and importantly, participants' understanding of the specific stage concepts, skills, and principles was highly related to one outcome from the exit interview, namely their overall ability to understand and implement the *inAccord* model. As predicted, the more disputants understood the specific stage concepts in the Phase Two training, the more they reported their general ability to understand and apply the tenets of the *inAccord* model, during Phase Three. A major goal is that the disputants should have a complete understanding of the mediation skills they are being taught. Our experience has shown that the introduction of questionnaires at each stage enhances their comprehension and also impacts their satisfaction with the process, which facilitates a sense of empowerment. The research findings, revealing high levels of both understanding as well as satisfaction, provide further evidence as to the effectiveness of the model. The two graphs, one for level of understanding (Figure 7-2) and one for satisfaction with the process (Figure 7-3) are presented on the following page.

Stage Understanding

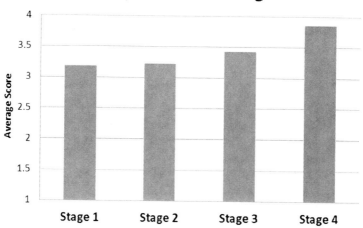

Figure 7-2. Level of understanding at each stage of Phase Two

Stage Satisfaction

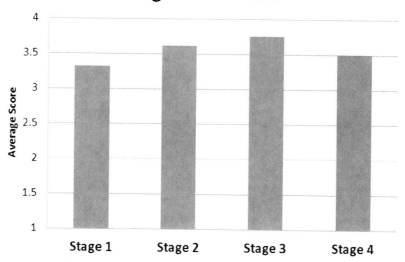

Figure 7-3. Level of satisfaction at each stage of Phase Two

Phase Three: Outcomes Evaluating the Success of the Mediation Process

In the final Phase Three, we sought to evaluate the outcomes employing two criteria that reflected the success of the mediation (see Table 1). Of course, a critical outcome, perhaps the single most important objective index of the success (or failure) of the mediation process, is whether the parties sign the Memorandum of Agreement. In the initial sample, the vast majority of disputants signed this memorandum. However, we need to go beyond just a head count of how many signed and did not sign, because this provides little understanding of the reasons underlying their choice. Thus, as a second outcome, we felt that it was essential to reveal the disputant's perceptions of the mediation process once they had completed the four stages in Phase Two.

Toward this objective, we constructed an *exit survey* addressing disputants' perceptions of a range of possible outcomes. We felt that assessing the disputants' perceptions of the process might elucidate why some parties would sign the Memorandum of Agreement and others would not. The exit survey consisted of 15 possible outcomes that disputants could endorse along another four-point scale (see the complete instrument in Appendix A). Of particular interest from a research perspective was whether the 15 items could be reduced to a smaller number of meaningful clusters. Employing factor-analytic statistical techniques, we determined that four factors or clusters of items could be meaningfully interpreted and so labeled. These four clusters defined subscales as follows:

The *first* subscale consisted of items that reflected the extent to which the mediation was deemed successful overall, leading to disputant satisfaction. We labeled this label this cluster the *inAccord*

Model Successful, with Disputant Satisfied.

Sample items were:
(1) How ***Successful*** was the mediation process for you?
Very Successful Pretty Successful Not that Successful Not at all

  (2) How ***Satisfied*** were you with the *inAccord* conflict resolution process?
Very satisfied   Somewhat Satisfied Not Very Not at all

The second subscale consisted of items reflecting the degree to which the disputant's specific expectations were met or realized. We labeled this cluster *Specific Expectations Realized.* Sample items were:

  (1) To what extent were your expectations about *monetary savings* ***Realized*** as a result of the *inAccord* conflict resolution process?
Fully Realized Partially Not really Realized   Not at all

  (2) To what extent were your expectations about *asset/resource savings* ***Realized*** as a result of the *inAccord* conflict resolution process?
Fully Realized Partially Not really Realized   Not at all

The third subscale contained items that measured the disputant's ability to comprehend and implement the *inAccord* principles. Thus, it was labeled *Ability to understand and implement inAccord conflict model.* Sample items were:

  (1) As a result of the inAccord Conflict Analysis model, how ***Effective*** do you feel about your ability to manage conflict?
Very Effective Pretty Effective Not Very Not at all

  (2) As a result of the inAccord Conflict Analysis, how much are you better ***Able*** to prevent destructive and negative responses to conflict?
Very Able Pretty Able Not really Able Not at all Able

The fourth subscale revealed perceptions of whether the mediator was fair and impartial, thus labeled as *Mediator Fair and Impartial.* Sample items were:

(1) To what extent was the mediator **Fair** *(meaning, appearing neutral and not biased)*?
Very Fair   Pretty Fair   Not that Fair   Not at all Fair

(2) To what extent was the mediator **Impartial***?*
Very Impartial Pretty Impartial Not that Impartial Not at all

Findings of Outcomes on the Exit Survey

The average scores for the sample on each of the four clusters or subscales, presented in Figure 7-4 Scores were quite high, above three on the four-point scale. Three of the four cluster scores were at 3.5 or slightly above. This pattern reveals that disputants rated the outcomes as extremely favorable along a number of dimensions. They: (a) were satisfied in that they found the *inAccord* model highly successful in resolving conflict, (b) felt that their specific expectations were met, (c) acknowledged their understanding of the *inAccord* Model principles, including their ability to implement them in future conflict situations, (d) believed the mediator to be fair and impartial. The *exit survey* provides additional evidence for the effectiveness of the *inAccord* model of mediation. (For the purpose of clarity and consistency, it should be noted that the three items on the second factor measuring the extent to which disputants felt that their specific expectations were met or realized, have now been moved to the end of the outcome measures, as reflected in Table 1.)

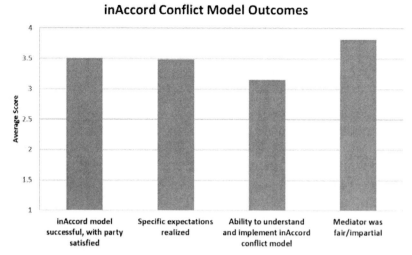

Figure 7-4. Perceived outcomes from the exit survey at Phase Three

These data brought up several questions and answers:

(1) How did signers vs. non-signers score on the exit survey? Did that discriminate them at all?

Most definitely on the subscale that measured how successful they felt the training had been/how satisfied they were, overall, with the process. Those who signed had an average score of 3.53 compared to a significantly lower score for the non-signers, who were less satisfied, who felt the program was less successful. The average for non-signers was only 3.17, a significant difference on a sensitive four-point scale.

(2) How might signers versus non-signers differ on their understanding of specific stages in the mediation process, might this provide a clue?

The findings clearly revealed that the two groups differed significantly in their Stage 3 understanding, which involved the comprehension of *Joint Solutions.* This constitutes a very interpretable finding given that this is the stage during which preliminary solutions are crafted, leading to the Memorandum of Agreement in Stage 4.

Thus, the more disputants feel that the skills they have acquired allow them to advance toward a joint solution, the more likely they are to sign.

(3) Moving to the front of the model, how would data from the *My Feelings* survey shed light on why some emotions would be reported by nonsigners at the end of the mediation process, compared to signers?

Here, we found that for the non-signers, in contrast to signers, disempowering feelings increased in strength between Phase One at the outset and Phase Three, where outcomes were assessed. That is, those who would become nonsigners became more negative, emotionally, as a result of the process, which may, in turn, have led to them to decline signing the Memorandum of Agreement.

(4) Finally, independent of the issues of whether disputants signed, their understanding of the specific stage concepts was highly related to the third outcome from the exit interview, namely, their overall ability to understand and implement the *inAccord* model. The more participating disputants understood the specific stage concepts in the mediation during Phase Two, the more they reported their general ability to understand and apply the tenets of the *inAccord* Model.

Conclusions from our Initial Research

We believe that the *inAccord* model applied to mediation may improve the consistency and delivery for disputants. Disputants will understand more clearly the phases, stages, and the *Touchstone Skills*. This will provide a research-validated procedure for determining the efficacy of these phases, stages, and skills directly taught to the disputants within their mediation services. Our research findings have first demonstrated the importance of two types of emotions, empowering feelings and disempowering feelings. Empowering sentiments (e.g., hope, optimism) increase in strength as a function of the mediation skill training, whereas disempowering feelings (anger, blame, depression) decrease in strength. Moreover, individuals who report more empowering feelings also indicate that they experience more positive outcomes (e.g., satisfaction, ability to implement *inAccord* problem-solving strategies when faced with conflict). Those disputants who report more disempowering emotions at the beginning experience less positive outcomes.

An understanding of the skills imparted by mediators is at the heart of the *inAccord* process. No longer do we have to guess or wonder if the parties in a dispute comprehend what we are trying to "teach." We can know immediately what they understand and, more importantly, what they do not understand. Another implication is that in each mediation phase, we can pause the forward progress until each of the parties are able to catch up to an appropriate understanding of skills, which is necessary to the success of the conflict resolution process. Moreover, because the skills learned at each stage of the mediation process are based on empowerment, even if parties leave the process early, they may still walk away with skills that give them an increasing ability to face their next conflict more effectively.

Finally, our results from the learners of the process who were disputants have documented the efficacy of the *inAccord* mediation model by illuminating important outcomes in the process. The participants in this first study reported very favorable outcomes in the form of satisfaction with the mediation, which they judged to be effective. They felt that their goals were met, and that they acquired general skills that would aid them in future conflict situations. Our overall pattern of findings is consistent with the current climate in the field of psychology, where emotions and cognitions together prove to be the best indicators of a desired outcome following an intervention.

Future Research

As described earlier in our book and at the outset of this section on our research, two key concepts in the *inAccord* model are transparency and empowerment. However, we do not simply want to assume that these critical components of the model are operative. Rather, from a research perspective, it behooves us to actively demonstrate that disputants feel that the process has been characterized by transparency and also that they have had a sense of empowerment in moving through the four stages. Toward this goal, we designed items measuring both transparency and empowerment, embedding them in the exit survey.

Items measuring transparency asked disputants about whether the process was made very clear to them, whether the clarity of the process was very helpful in guiding them to a decision, and whether they had a good understanding of what was expected at each stage of the mediation (see items 3, 9, 16 of the *Exit Survey* in Appendix A).

Items measuring empowerment asked disputants about whether they liked the fact that they were personally involved in the negotiations, about how important it was to them that they had some control as they went through the mediation process, and whether they appreciated the fact that they were partly in charge of what was happening throughout the various stages (see items 5, 10, 17 of the *Exit Survey* in Appendix A).

In our current administration of our surveys to actual disputants who have decided to come to the mediation table, we are administering these two subscales, measuring transparency and empowerment. In this manner, we can directly determine the extent to which, in their opinion, they felt that the process was transparent, as intended, and whether they felt empowered by the mediator, to take an active role in the process. We look forward to analyzing these data, an important next step in documenting the validity and the effectiveness of the *inAccord* mediation process.

Conflict Styles

In addition to the inclusion of these new survey subscales in the exit survey, we have developed another new survey to be administered at the outset of the process, one that asks disputants to reflect on their personal style of dealing with conflict. Obviously, actual disputants come to mediation because they are experiencing conflict at some level. However, parties bring with them a history of dealing with conflict, which we assume is a natural experience in the lives of all human beings. When conflict becomes excessive or unbearable, certain individuals seek out mediation. We asked what their typical style was when faced with conflict. Learning about individuals' perceptions of their typical conflict style may provide mediators with some barometer as to how to approach disputants, in order to maximize the effectiveness of mediation.

Next, we emphasize to disputants that people have different styles of conflict, that there is no right or wrong style, and that how people react to and cope with conflict can differ according to different situations in their lives. As noted earlier, we identified the five different conflict styles listed on the Thomas-Kilmann Survey (1974), which Thomas and Kilmann based on earlier conflict style categories created by Blake and Mouton in 1964. Our conflict styles survey adds five different contexts in which conflict might arise.

Our new survey asks disputants to indicate which of these styles they utilize in five different contexts or situations which they encounter most often. The contexts include conflicts with family of origin, current family, at work, with friends, and in recreational activities. Depending upon the nature of the conflict that disputants bring to mediation, some of these contexts may be more relevant than others.

Surveying Mediators

We have now developed parallel sets of surveys to be completed by the mediators themselves (see Appendix B). For example, during Phase One, when we ask disputants about their emotions (on the *My Feelings* survey), it is important to discern whether they are high on empowering emotions, disempowering emotions, or low on each of these emotion clusters. Mediators themselves cannot make this judgment, given that it is the subjective experience of the disputant. However, it is important for the mediator, who has access to disputant surveys at each phase, to appreciate the emotions of each disputant in the dispute, namely, whether they are predominantly empowering or disempowering. Moreover, as discussed earlier in our book, the extent to which the disputants represent a match of emotions (they both report empowering emotions or, alternatively, they both report disempowering emotions) or whether they represent a mismatch (one reports empowering emotions whereas the other acknowledges primarily disempowering emotions), will dictate the mediator's particular approach to mediation for given disputants.

The mediator surveys for Phase Two serve a different function. Recall that in Phase Two, there are four sequential stages during which the disputant reports on how well they understand the skill sets being taught. *The Touchstone Skills* sets of reflecting, reframe, and questioning were administered in caucus at the end of Stage 1. Here, the mediator can make their own independent judgments as to the extent to which the disputant has mastered the requisite skills at each stage. It will be imperative to examine the congruence of disputant and mediator ratings about the level of understanding that disputants display. Furthermore, it will be vital to determine whether the disputants' perception of their skill is a better predictor of outcomes, compared to the mediator's perceptions.

We have also developed a new *Exit Survey for Mediators*, to be filled out in Phase Three, where we assess the outcomes of the mediation. Recall that the disputants complete an exit survey reviewing four different perceived outcomes: (a) disputant was satisfied, felt mediation was successful, (b) disputant felt that their specific expectations were met or realized, (c) disputant felt that they understood and could implement the *inAccord* conflict model, and (d) disputant felt that the mediator was fair and impartial.

We have now created a new survey tool whereby we ask the mediator to evaluate each disputant, Disputant A and Disputant B, on these same four dimensions. In this manner, we can address which is more predictive of the parties' willingness to sign a Memorandum of Agreement, the parties' ratings or the mediators' ratings, or if the two sets of scores diverge or converge.

In conclusion, the addition of new instruments will open up novel and exciting strategies for analyzing the incoming survey data. As a result, we will be able to address new research questions, several of which have been described. Our research study is a work in progress, as we continue to develop our thinking and refine our instruments accordingly.

Chapter Eight:
The Mediators without Borders ADR Center Model and its Global Implications

Chapter Overview

As we described earlier in our book, it is not enough to simply point out that justice is not alive and well for most people. More importantly, we must turn our efforts to remedy the systemic problems that engender or maintain these disputes, such as: How do we create thriving systems of justice within our communities, and, more importantly, how do we maintain them as viable options for all, even when populations or individuals cannot afford private services or complex procedural justice infrastructures? The concepts of people taking control of their solutions, and the perspective of "deep democracy" as a global response, call out for ways to resolve these disputes in more tenable and efficient ways.

Arny Mindell (1992) developed the term deep democracy which has evolved into a philosophical approach that builds on conventional democracy's goal to include all individuals in the political process. This approach takes it a step further by seeking to foster a deeper level of dialogue and inclusiveness that makes space for all people as well as for their styles of communication, competing views, tensions, and feelings. The *inAccord* model aligns deeply with Mindell's philosophy, by promoting a space in the resolution of conflict where all actors not only take part in the process, but where their competing needs, interests, tensions, and beliefs are valued and given expression. Our unique focus on the role of emotions provides a greater outlet for this diverse meeting of disputants by teaching them the *Touchstone Skills* which encourage a deeper dialogue. In addition, our emphasis on measuring understanding and satisfaction at each stage of the mediation process helps ensure that each person is given time to express any obstacles to their free and unfettered participation in the *inAccord* model.

In this chapter, we turn to the ways in which we might deliver the *inAccord* model of mediation to appropriate audiences with the greatest number of people, and therefore make the greatest social impact. Here we are presenting the vision of Mediators Without Borders (MwB) and the web of globally-networked Alternative Dispute Resolution (ADR) Centers which can help to bring the *inAccord* mediation model to a broader audience. With expanded solutions for those who experience injustice, these ADR Centers can also collect the data necessary to measure the efficacy of the *inAccord* model, providing feedback and cross-cultural verification through research comparing different populations and cultures, and adaptations that might make this model more culturally appropriate for certain societies and cultures. Here we will discuss the ways in which the use of the ADR Center initiative in different global regions reflects the concepts of transparency, empowerment, and the role of emotions imbedded in the model, as well as identify and discuss impediments to this model when delivering it to and with other cultures as participants and social systems.

Description of ADR Center Initiative

This book has as a basic premise the global need for a more comprehensive, research-based approach to conflict resolution education and services, as well as a firm belief that the world is poised to embrace and to perpetuate peaceful means of resolving conflict such as our model. It is our hope that the *inAccord* model, and the theoretical foundations behind it, will contribute positively to this current and future global need.

Mediators Without Borders was founded as an educational company to provide mediation training, which we hope will serve to help with the large social task articulated above. As a business entity, we are interested in delivering our unique *inAccord* model as a specialized product to a national and international market. Our delivery system dictates the expanding ADR Center model of education and services that is beginning to be established throughout the United States and abroad, currently in Romania, the broader EU, and Nigeria.

As of this writing, the Mediators Without Borders ADR Centers are planned at specific sites around the world, and will be linked both physically and virtually through technology to our central business and research team in Colorado. Our research team is led by second author, professor emerita at the University of Denver.

We designed the web of conflict resolution learning and mediation ADR Centers on the foundational concept of economic sustainability. The ADR Center model serves a multi-layered function of operating as a location for multiple purposes, including: (1) teaching the *inAccord* model to social leaders and potential ADR practitioners, (2) conducting research using the *inAccord* survey instruments to provide feedback, and (3) providing local citizens with conflict resolution services using the *inAccord* model.

It is our vision that this network of educational ADR Centers will help create local solutions to conflict. By being connected to our organization, the local area can then archive these cases and their outcomes, which then can be used as resources for other ADR Centers dealing with similar issues. In this sense, an ADR Center in the Niger Delta that is successfully dealing with the tensions of an inequitable distribution of wealth and resources case might offer assistance to another ADR Center, half-way around the world in a village in Peru which is also struggling with inequitable resource issues, but in their own local context. This assistance could be offered in as simple a manner as a letter, email, or phone call, or through more advanced technology such as virtual classrooms, and web-based communication between ADR Centers and among practitioners. The hope is that the learning of what methods work to bring resolution to one area can inform and guide the process in another area due to the linkage through this organization.

Mediators Without Borders International University of Professional Studies

As a natural outgrowth of both the training of mediators and facilitators and the ADR Center initiative, Mediators Without Borders is in active creation of an international university of professional studies that will focus on three areas of research and scholarship: leadership, management, and ADR studies. The first track of study will include leadership with an emphasis on entrepreneurship, ethics, sustainability, and ADR. This track will include specializations in private sector leadership, NGO leadership, and public sector leadership. The second track of study will focus on management strategies with an overlap of leadership and ethics study, ADR, and team building and organizational development. The third track will focus on students who wish to complete a masters and/or doctoral program in Alternative Dispute Resolution. This track will focus on direct practice skills of facilitation, mediation, arbitration, and advanced specialization areas such as construction, family, workplace, and public policy conflict resolution.

The decision to create a professional studies program as opposed to creating an international peace and conflict resolution masters and doctoral program, is based, in part, upon the analysis of IPCR – International Peace and Conflict Resolution programs that was conducted by the United States Institute of Peace (Carstarphen, Zelizer, Harris, & Smith, 2010). This analysis revealed a disconnect between academic programs that teach peace and the organizations who seek to employ graduates who have conflict resolution skills. The authors note that, "Graduate-level academic institutions are not adequately preparing students for careers in international peace and conflict management" (p. 1). The study underscores the fact that overseas experience is the most valuable asset that employers want in their new hires. In addition, they want their new employees to have basic skills in fundraising, project management, writing and computer literacy, grant writing, and research skills.

This analysis, and the lack of research that has been noted in this field, prompted Mediators Without Borders to focus on a professional, career-focused masters and doctoral program where students can learn both theory and practical skills related to the tracks they choose. For instance, a student focused on working in NGOs would need to have classes in fundraising, grant writing, and project management as well as the direct practice skills of facilitation and conflict resolution. A student who chooses the public sector track of leadership or management would need specialized classes in public policy, good governance, and democratization as well as the practice skills of ADR.

The ADR Center initiative will provide our students with the ability to gain overseas experience through work/study apprenticeships in the ADR Centers and in the regional planning in various countries such as Romania, Nigeria, Bulgaria, Greece, France, and Hungary. The *inAccord* model and ongoing research studies will provide ample opportunity for our students to join in existing studies as well as have a hand in establishing new studies as the ADR Center initiative expands to more countries. Mediators Without Borders will always work to establish strong and enduring relationships with governments, NGOs, and other businesses because we recognize great value in bridging the gaps between private and public sector organizations who work for peace.

Bridging Corporate and Non-Profit Organizations

As an example of the types of problems in providing on-going conflict resolution services, a noted church leader in Denver, Reverend Heidi McGuiness, remarked at an MwB strategy meeting that from her experience in working with aid societies in the Sudan she was sensing the frustration of many in the global helping community with the transiency of non-governmental organizations, commonly referred to as NGOs. The frustration centered on the fact that these well-meaning groups came over to offer food and medical supplies and then, either because of increased violence or collapse of funding, left the area just as the locals were becoming dependent on their services. She recalled touring an area of war-torn Sudan where the guide pointed to numerous empty buildings, stating, "That is where the Presbyterians used to be, and that is where the Methodists used to be, and that is where a medical aid group used to be." The Reverend, who was well versed in the tribulations of this impoverished country, sensed the growing despair in the people as their hopes were raised and then dashed by each subsequent exodus. This is an understandable phenomenon as many aid workers graciously and bravely volunteer in the most disadvantaged areas, only to be forced out by funding cuts or unsafe conditions. This is why any model that wishes to be successful must train the local population and provide a sustainable system that locals can operate after the initial help to build it has left. This is the concept that MwB wishes to promote when setting up our conflict resolution training and service provision ADR Centers. We train those who will stay to maintain the operations of the ADR Centers.

NGO's are not the only organizations that "befriend, then end", or the only organizations to have their own internal conflicts that need to be resolved. International corporations have their own pitfalls. We find for-profit corporations answering to shareholders who want to see their stocks increase in value. Most of these shareholders are not involved in the actual workings of the companies in which they invest. There is a "disconnect" between the share indexes of stocks and how the company is actually making these increased earnings. Sometimes, this disconnect leads to disastrous results, as shareholders turn a blind eye toward corporate crimes, such as human rights violations, environmental tragedies, and gross economic inequities in the countries where they do business. A more sustainable approach is to have an effective conflict resolution mechanism attached to and used by the corporation that provides services when conflicts arise, whether those are between the corporation and the country where it is doing business, or within the organization itself.

Not surprisingly, corporations and NGOs have eyed one another cautiously, losing many golden opportunities to collaborate in solutions that could not only work for the rights of indigenous populations, but actually increase the corporation's bottom line of profits. We consider the need for a complimentary system of conflict resolution in these areas as a hybrid style of business between for-profit corporations and nonprofit aid groups. We are doing this through the establishment of free-standing ADR Centers, training cadres of mediation providers, and offering dispute resolution services to local communities.

Local Directors of ADR Centers

Many peace initiatives are delivered in safe havens away from the disruption of the armed conflict that is being deliberated. This isolation and insular approach can work against sustainability if the decisions that are made from afar do not create workable, physical solutions in those nations that are dealing directly with the social or political or armed conflict. In many cases, peace initiatives are often delivered "after the fact," when a conflict has escalated to a highly destructive level, while tensions are still high and the potential for harm is still great, but before the reconciliation phase of the conflict cycle described by Kreisberg (1998) has started. Conflict resolution communication that engages local communities at the earliest point and lowest level possible will create an intervention that is more preventative than reactive, and is therefore, more sustainable in the long run. We believe that our ADR Center model can serve in this capacity.

Mediators Without Borders has a bold plan for its ADR Center model, yet implementation will rely on careful measurement of the successes and challenges of each of the following initiatives:

1. Establish a physical and virtual ADR Center presence that can withstand disruptions, natural and man-made (ADR Centers in Nigeria and Romania are underway)
2. Establish the ADR Centers as centers of research to gather information that reputable organizations and citizens can use to facilitate worthy projects and local initiatives
3. Insure, by working with the local administrators in different countries, that our model and research surveys are culturally appropriate
4. Create alternative dispute resolution education and service techniques that will intervene with a conflict at the earliest point and lowest level possible

5. Use and teach the *Touchstone Skills* with our clients, ADR Center directors, at the international level, and with our advisors, investors, and colleagues
6. Engage local corporations in alternative dispute resolution solutions as a means that best serves their interests and the interests of the local communities within which they operate
7. Create a strong web of ADR Centers such that any one strand that breaks or is removed can be maintained by the strength of the global community of ADR Centers
8. Link the ADR Centers to our research team in Colorado, with accessible data to help people around the world conduct research and engage in networking with others working toward conflict resolution as a part of sustainable peace

Sustainability

The phrase "economic sustainability" stems from a United Nations paper, the Brundtland Report (United Nations General Assembly, 1987), which defines sustainable development as development which meets the needs of the present without compromising the ability of future generations to meet their own needs. Too often, global initiatives, no matter how well-meaning, lack the continuity to have a lasting influence in a nation or region. Many well-intentioned initiatives to broker peace fail to create sustainable solutions. Individual nations and communities must have broad commitment to any solution for their unique issues of conflict. They must feel respected, included, and have a decisive voice in the building of sustainable peace. With this in mind, the Mediators Without Borders ADR Centers are each collaborative partnerships with active participation and ownership from citizens within each country.

Transparency in the ADR Center Model

In our earlier discussion of the central theme of transparency, we stated that transparency means making the covert overt, shedding the mediator's role as the expert in the parties' dispute. This theme underscores the manner in which the ADR Center model is introduced in local communities. Local ownership and control ensures that the American team that heads Mediators Without Borders does not enter into other regions without invitation, and that the original team from MwB have culturally sensitive participants who do not come as experts as much as offering technical assistance to the local promoters and builders. The introduction of a Mediators Without Border ADR Center will exemplify the concept of making the covert overt by means of transparent policies, tuition rates for trainings that are fairly set, and a research model for the provision of mediation and conflict resolution services that will continually measure its application in diverse cultural environments.

Our earlier discussion of the use of transparency in mediation through a continual cycle can also be applied to the ADR Center teams in the following ways:

- Remaining focused on the interests, understanding, and satisfaction of the ADR Center Directors and corporate team.
- Encouraging all parties to communicate from a transparent stance based on increased self-awareness, increased awareness of the perspective of the "other", who are the ADR Center Directors and staff, by maintaining a goal of reaching an equitable business arrangement for all concerned.
- Empowering the ADR Center Directors and leadership team to find their unique voice in running of the business, by brainstorming options without judgment, by learning skills that will increase self-confidence, and by engendering a compassion that comes from learning to walk in another person's shoes.
- Reflecting on the process at certain points in order to make necessary adjustments to the process itself, such as the content and business policies used to create a successful, mutually satisfying partnership. It should be noted that the value placed on transparency in the *inAccord* model may not always be reflected in other cultures. Thus, one must be particularly sensitive to cultural variations in such concepts, rather than assuming that our own value structure necessarily applies to other countries.

Transparency, Neutrality and Impartiality

John Donovan of National Public Radio interviewed Michael Kocher, vice president of International Programs of the International Rescue Committee as part of a larger dialogue on the increased dangers to aid workers around the world. The conversation moved to a discussion of neutrality and impartiality when workers were entering foreign territories. The director made a very compelling distinction between his organization's stance on impartiality and that of neutrality. "Impartiality is being non-discriminatory. We hold it very dear. We're impartial in providing assistance without discriminating as to ethnic origin, gender, nationality, political opinion, race, religion." However, the director was adamant that this did not translate to neutrality, because his organization had very firm beliefs of anti-violence, women's rights, equality, and freedom. While they were impartial in regard to their service delivery, they were not neutral because they operated from a clear set of principles and beliefs which they carried into their work. As he stated, "You know, we're not neutral to genocide, the killing of civilians, sexual violation, forced migration. So that is a distinction to keep in mind just in the language we use" (Donovan, 2012).

The *inAccord* model supports the notion that impartiality must be a cornerstone of our business model, in our business practices as well as in the delivery of services from ADR Centers. However, we agree with the concept that neutrality cannot be as singularly defined, and that it may be important to approach situations, both in the business sphere and in the provision of conflict resolution training and services, where we maintain integrity of the concepts that lie under our practices, and therefore are not strictly neutral. Certainly, MwB holds to similar beliefs as described above, and supports values and maintains an active bias against the use of coercion, manipulation, and violence in interpersonal and inter-group disputes. This is why this model of conflict resolution makes a case for distinguishing between interest-based disputes and rights-based disputes, which are both employed where appropriate, as explained earlier in the book.

Empowerment in the ADR Center Model

Empowerment of disputants is a central theme of the *inAccord* model, and this theme is also embedded in the creation of the ADR Center model. Rappaport (1987) believed that ". . . the aim of empowerment should be to enhance the possibilities for people to control their own lives" (p. 119). Our business model echoes this as a guiding value, in the way in which we attempt to set up and maintain ADR Centers under local control and by invitation. The emphasis on local ownership of ADR Centers extends the empowerment model beyond the mediator and disputants doing the ostensible work of the ADR Center, to include the staff and directors who oversee the day-to-day business of managing a Mediators Without Borders ADR Center. Potential owners of ADR Centers are selected based on intrinsic skills, including empowerment as a concept, as well as their ability to deliver a marketing strategy for their region. We believe this planning process empowers them by providing a central element of self-efficacy, "the skills for solving problems themselves" (Maddux and Gosselin, 2012, p. 3).

Of equal importance is the manner in which local direction of ADR Centers contributes to the collective efficacy of the leadership team, ADR Center directors, and international staff. By learning to work together effectively to accomplish shared goals, we empower each other. As Bandura (1977) notes, collective efficacy influences shared motivation, planning and decision-making, the effective use of group resources, and persistence in pursuing goals. This concept is a core value we bring that supports and matches the work being done in the ADR Center. When ADR Center owners and staff begin to identify with a larger socially-responsible business such as Mediators Without Borders, we believe they will unite and feel more motivated and confident in tackling issues of injustice and conflict in their local communities.

A response to social equity is one call to bring the ADR Center model to the country of Romania. An impassioned Romanian citizen reached out to Mediators Without Borders to begin establishing ADR Centers in Constanta and Botosani, in his desire for more accessible and affordable conflict resolution alternatives for the land disputes of the area. We believe the ADR Center initiative we are starting there will help our Romanian friends experience personal and social change through the *inAccord* education and service model. As Whitmore (1988) notes, a sense of empowerment will enable people to act upon organizations and institutions within their communities which directly affect their lives, and MwB believes this concept will permeate the area by the development of ADR Centers in Romania.

Challenges Ahead for the ADR Center Initiative

We recognize there are very real challenges ahead as we begin the delivery of *inAccord* services in this country as well as around the world. We want to address some of these challenges and offer a rationale for how our model might either ameliorate the impediment to resolution, or serve specific cultures in a more limited way. These challenges or impediments include intractable frames, which could be defined as the inability to change the way in which the conflict is viewed by one or more of those affected, and the existence of identity-based conflict, which Rothman (1997) describes as deeply- held beliefs about oneself and one's core identity.

Other barriers to conflict resolution can include self-verification (Swann, 1996), people's tendency to want others to verify their perceptions of themselves, even when these evaluations of self are negative. Such a stance precludes a productive reframing of the issues. In addition, false-self behavior, the antithesis of authenticity, can also be a hindrance to mediation, as will be discussed. These challenges, and many not discussed here, exist for any individual or organization desiring to carry their message or model of conflict resolution to other countries and cultures. There may even be barriers to resolution we have yet to discover as we take this *inAccord* model to other nations, where the expression of feelings, which is so central to our model, may not be culturally appropriate. We believe it is imperative that any of us who dare to venture into these realms also design a system of measurement or checks and balances to consistently monitor effectiveness as we apply this model to other places and conflict structures.

We have identified several of these potential barriers or limitations to the use of the *inAccord* mediation model, and/or to the ADR Center-based model for training and providing services, for larger-scale socio-political conflicts, intractable disputes, identity-based disputes, and other potential problems not currently addressed by our current models. For instance, in Romania, there are ongoing conflicts from the rapid transition of the government from a brutal dictatorship to a nascent democracy. It takes our team more time to understand and assess who the decision makers are in the local governments and extra sensitivity to move carefully through a society with many lingering resentments and fragmented power structures. By being aware of these in advance, and by listening to the data and the local constituencies, the provision of our business and mediation model may help change these barriers.

Intractable Conflicts

On the global level of conflict resolution, where conflicts typically erupt across and within nations, the stakes for management or resolution of the conflict can be higher and the challenges can be more complex. These conflicts can lead to physical confrontations, uprisings, bloodshed, and war. There may be particular impediments of greater magnitude that are not encountered in disputes with interpersonal or intragroup conflicts. There are many seemingly intractable dynamics that influence the passionate frames that these disputants within a country bring to their conflict issues. According to Gray (2004), frames of perceiving the dispute can, in global or international disputes, be vastly different in the minds of two or more disputants. These disputants may be less willing to reframe the issues in ways that lead to resolution as they hold tenaciously to their point of view, resulting in a hopeless deadlock and maintenance of the conflict.

Gray (2004) contends that reframing usually does not occur easily, particularly for parties mired in longstanding, adversarial relationships where there is no real commitment to reversing conflict intractability. If neither disputant wishes change, it is difficult for even a skilled mediator to penetrate the barriers. Thus, intense commitment to one's frame or worldview prevents the reframing process, and could potentially prevent parties from accepting an agreement that might represent a compromise for all involved. Gray believes that some of the most difficult frames are those that appear to be frozen in time. One enduring example of these types of conflicts exists between the Palestinians and the Israelis that have persisted for centuries, frustrating even the more skilled and patient mediators in the process.

Gray's point about the intractable current frame a disputant holds is critical to our thinking with our *inAccord* model. It bring up a series of questions that may inform or be the center piece of future research: Rather than seeking a common frame, or even encourage a reframe, could a mediator frame a particular issues as an agreement to disagree? Would this in itself bring about a new willingness to manage rather than resolve the conflict? In this sense, might the mutual acceptance of disagreement of each of the frames becomes the re-frame? Might this mutual acceptance free the disputants from the powerful force of this issue of the conflict to attend to secondary issues?

On the other hand, intractable frames may call for a completely different approach to the conflict than can be offered through mediation. Pruitt and Olczak caution that mediation and negotiation are not panaceas for conflict resolution as issues of noncompliance and noncooperation may reflect that there is "insufficient motivation to escape the conflict" (cited in Bunker, 1995, p.68). Whether it is a result of the conflict not having enough of what they refer to as "ripeness" or there is simply insufficient trust, attempts to force a mediation model onto these situations would not be appropriate. This is not to negate the potential value of mediation or negotiation in such situations. However, we argue that any attempts to initiate mediation or negotiation should be carefully monitored through research design and study. This is our intent with our prudent and measured delivery of the *inAccord* model and research component to other countries.

Identity-Based Conflict.

Another particular type of impediment to the resolution of a larger scale national or international conflict has been described as "identity-based conflict," a term initially introduced by Rothman (1997). Identity-based conflict denotes ongoing struggles between groups that are intransigent and impervious to resolution, because they are deeply rooted in the underlying human needs and values that together constitute people's social and personal identities. During these conflicts, the very issue of "who I am as a person", or "who we are as a nation or region" is threatened, leading to a stronger need to withhold agreement to otherwise viable options. Rothman (1997) has articulated a four-stage process through which identity conflicts that threaten one's dignity and selfhood may be successfully resolved which he labels as: Antagonism, Resonance, Invention, and Action.

According to Rothman, Antagonism surfaces at the beginning of a dispute, in that festering angst and anger are now up for discussion. Initially, during this first stage, there is a negative, adversarial framing of the content of the conflict, an "Us" versus "Them" mentality. Other writers such as Berreby (2005) have tried to explain further the function and meaning of this sorting into Us/Not Us. Rothman aptly observes, "Conflict is often a powerful axis around which life stories are told" (p. 34). At Rothman's next stage of Resonance, reframing begins with a new narrative about the needs of each disputant. There is a focus on the why of who wants what, which provides an effective way to reframe the conflict as a vehicle for learning, growth, and cooperative action.

Reframing, in Rothman's stages, clarifies the needs and values that have been threatened on both sides, leading to the realization that "we are in this together." Such reframing requires honest introspection, shifting from blame and counter blame to a more internal attribution, for example, the acknowledgement that "I am afraid" rather than "you are aggressive." Both parties, through dialogue in the presence of a mediator, must come to take responsibility for their role in the conflict. Both parties ideally develop a new awareness of their own imperfections, promoting a less self-righteous or judgmental battle, in favor of more tolerance for the failings of the other side, as well. This process requires the type of transparency that is articulated in our *inAccord* model.

If reframing is successful, if parties can express what Rothman terms "analytic empathy," cognitively understanding the other's position, then the process can move to the next stage of Invention. Analytic empathy proceeds when both parties honestly identify their underlying needs, as well as hopes and fears. According to Rothman, during his third stage of intervention, brainstorming can lead to mutually acceptable, creative, and integrative options for addressing the central and underlying aspects of the conflict. The focus is on cooperatively resolving the conflict. Through collaboration, rather than competitive tactics, the parties learn that not only are they in this together but that "we can get out of this together." Rothman describes a number of cooperative problem-solving techniques to facilitate the invention of potential solutions.

Rothman's fourth and final stage is one of Action, building upon the preceding three stages. Joint agendas are established, fleshing out what should be done, and why, by whom, and how. Through cooperation, tangible solutions are identified and acted upon. There is a consolidation into specific plans for action. Throughout these four stages, disputants are guided by a mediator, although the focus is on how the disputants themselves can actively resolve the conflict, consistent with the *inAccord* model. Rothman ends his treatise with an application to negotiation among nations, adapting his principles to peace building in Jerusalem.

As Fischer (2001) points out, when group identities and the needs that underlie them are threatened or frustrated, intractable conflict is also inevitable. Such intractability, according to Rothman, stems from the more abstract and interpretive dynamics of history, psychology cultural, values, and belief of one's particular identity group. Thus, hostile interactions are often based on deep-seated racial, ethnic, religious, and cultural hatred that have persisted over long periods of time with sporadic outbreaks of violence. While these hatreds and prejudices may be amenable to change, since they are often socially learned and therefore can be un-learned, there are indicators from brain science that some of the response to the perception may be built in to our brains and physiology based on a triggering of our perception of threat, and therefore be less amenable to change (Berreby, 2005).

The challenge for mediators is that these deep-rooted social and political conflicts are not based on interests that can easily be negotiated or settled, in contrast to more superficial or circumscribed disputes; rather, they are based on non-negotiable needs that are resistant to conflict analysis and resolution. Rothman (1997) has cogently pointed out that if conflicts are based on these personal identity-based issues that define ones core self, rather than on interest- or resource-based conflicts, the negotiation efforts, even with a skillful mediator may be doomed to failure. However, his caveat is that "Identity conflicts require that special efforts be made to ensure accurate analysis, definition, and amelioration precisely because such conflicts are not tangible" (p. 12). Even these comments pose serious challenges for the mediator.

Fischer (2001) traces these themes through an extremely thoughtful and thorough analysis of how such identity processes have played out in the painful conflicts between the Greek-Cypriot and the Turkish-Cypriot communities, which has lasted for decades. These disputes have been resistant to many forms of intervention including litigation, negotiation, arbitration, power tactics, but to no avail. Thus, global conflict that, in particular, involves *identity issues that define the self,* are particularly challenging for today's mediator.

Shultz (Bunker, 1995) adopts a similar perspective to Rothman in applying how the principles of identity-based conflicts can derail the attempts to bring conflict resolution and peace. She points to the fact that often fierce identity issues are countered by fear and enemy images that are foisted on the other party. She analyzes the lengthy history of various Mideast peace process initiatives that have not been successful over the decades. The identity focus leads to fears that identity needs will be neglected or negated in a conflict settlement, and that compromise will be personally threatening, for example, "I could lose my sense of self which I thought was relatively safe and secure". She concludes that mediators need to be particularly sensitive to these identity issues, noting that power-based negotiations are insufficient.

Perhaps, no other continent faces the dilemma of identity-based conflicts more than Africa, where tribal conflict and loyalties stretch back across countless generations. Mediators Without Borders has been working for over three years to bring the ADR Center initiative to the Niger Delta region. This process has been marked by abrupt starts and stops as we patiently seek ways to effectively introduce this model into a region with many overlapping and complex conflicts. We have found that in such areas where issues of tribal identity collide with a fragile and nascent democracy, a long-term perspective is essential. This is in stark contrast to Romania, where the process of bringing the ADR Center initiative was so sudden we had to work diligently to slow it down. We have accepted that the process will unfold much more slowly in the Niger Delta and need to honor each area's need to understand that the adoption of a new model for justice systems and conflict resolution may come at different paces in areas where there are generational impediments, or where the climate is not yet ready to move from active conflict to the reconciliation phase of the conflict cycle outlined by Kreisberg (1998).

This exploration of social and cultural differences also brings into question our model's reliance on a settled agreement as a measure of success. It may be that our research study into diverse communities illustrates that this will not be an adequate measure in all cases. In Western cultures, which have resort to procedural law, something is not considered binding and final unless or until it is reduced to paper with signatures and dates, but other cultures do not have this tradition, and may not value it in the same way. In some cultures, one's handshake or the payment of restitution or a symbolic act is the mark of finality and success.

Culture and Conflict

Human behavior is greatly influenced by underlying beliefs, values, and assumptions. These beliefs, values, and assumptions are, largely, a by-product of culture. Ting-Toomey and Chung (2005) define culture as a learned meaning system that consists of patterns of traditions, beliefs, values, norms, meanings, and symbols that are passed on from one generation to the next and are shared to varying degrees by interacting members of a community. Most of the time we are not conscious of how culture influences our values, beliefs, assumptions and our behaviors because culture is so all-encompassing.

Through empirical research, different cultures have been found to have different communication styles. Some studies about the efficacy and nature of conflict across cultures have been done, with early work by Gudykunst and Ting-Toomey (1988) and Augsburger (1989) indicating that some cultures are considered to be along a continuum from Low-context to High-context, depending on their focus of whether they see themselves as part of the group or independent from it.

High-context Cultures. Individuals from high-context cultures favor an indirect verbal style; prefer ambiguous, cautious, and non-confrontational ways of working through communication issues; they rely on nonverbal behaviors and subtleties, and are very listener-oriented. High context cultures tend to place a higher value on harmony, tactfulness, and saving face. Someone from a high-context culture will likely ease into a conversation, will wait to be invited to speak or request permission. Individuals will first connect on a relational level and only after that has occurred, introduce substantive issues.

Low-context cultures. Low-context cultures prefer communication that is direct and frank. An open confrontation of issues is ideal and a speaker-orientation is valued. Directness and self-assertion are preferred in low-context cultures so an individual will likely verbally assert him or herself into a conversation and will promptly acknowledge content issues. One communication style is not better or worse than another is but they are different. Parties in conflict, due to ethnocentrism, may judge the other party's style to be inferior and even offensive. In addition, parties with these different communication styles may have problems communicating with each other therefore making interventions such as mediation more challenging.

Further study and research needs to be conducted on the levels of conflict within and between cultures, including interpersonal, intergroup, and national and international disputes. Success may be measured incrementally through a lessening of conflict over time rather than a sweeping and sudden solution. This is not always an easy concept for Westerners who are used to a more expedient and rapid process of conflict resolution in our culture which is low-context and more self- than group-based within the mainstream, but due to changing trends in demographics may be more or less so depending upon the actual disputants.

The signing of the MOA is a goal in the *inAccord* model. This does not necessarily mean all of the issues have been settled, and often to get a final outcome document, underlying issues and value conflicts have just gone underground ready to spring back into action after the signing. Is this then a failure? We think not, although it could be a limitation of our model which will have to be changed to adapt for use in other cultures. As Kreisberg (1998) pointed out, success in conflict resolution often rests on two factors – equity and stability. If the agreements reached are both, whether the outcome document is signed or not, it might meet this definition of success.

Our contribution with the introduction of the *inAccord* model is to work with disputants to create a common understanding, a common language, with accepted research methods, data and statistical analysis. Our hope is that the MOA will build in language that encourages continued discussion and modification, be it weeks, months, decades or generations. When we review the failed mediations in the Palestinian and Israeli conflict, one can also highlight there has not been a formal war since the 1960's. Can we not consider this a success as the global community continues to work toward a "grand" solution? And, can we accept that the grand solution will not be sudden but incremental and timeless?

Self-Verification Theory

Although global conflicts sets many of these issues on a much grander scale, the field of psychology alerts us to other possible impediments to conflict resolution that occur at a more personal level that involve the protections of the individual "self". In a book entitled *Self Traps,* Swann, (1996), a social psychologist, challenged the commonly-held assumption that people are consumed by an overwhelming desire to enhance the self, by having people think highly of them, support them, and capitulate to their needs. However, Swann countered this often-held perception, arguing, persuasively, that far from a self-enhancement motive, people are more likely to seek self-verification. In this sense, they want others to confirm or validate their own core evaluations of themselves, including their negative self-judgments. Swan argues that they do not want feedback that will contradict their highly personal and entrenched self-identities.

Why such a stance, particularly if one views the self as imbued with negative characteristics? Because these self-identities provide a psychological blueprint for action, they are the very guideposts by which to navigate how one is to behave within one's family and personal relationships, in one's work environment, within one's primary community, and in one's nation. These guideposts set the stage for how a person's motivational energies are to be deployed, consistent with that person's core perceptions of who he or she is as a person. In more collectivistic nations or communities, one may not deviate from the shared perceptions of one's personhood. This author (Harter, 2012), frames a discussion of the self from a cross-cultural perspective. In the extreme, a person's personal sense of self is enmeshed within the larger community persona or identity, as identified by Augsburger (1989).

To extrapolate from Swann's (1996) self-verification theory, in the totem pole of life, certain individuals occupy a lower status, where they are not highly revered; however, they are respected for the role they play. They fulfill their mission within their community to which they are devoted. They have dutifully crafted and accepted a self, consistent with the role that their society has assigned them. Those who may occupy a lower status are threatened by anything or anyone who would deny their need for self-verification; they require feedback as to their less than favorable status, simply because it violates their entrenched view of who they are as a person. On a broader scale, such societal mechanisms insure that more collectivist societies function because everyone is cognizant of their role and plays it out, leading to harmony within. The boundaries within and across societies are clear, and they exquisitely define the individual self, with great clarity.

One can appreciate, in this brief excursion into self-verification theory, how the tenets may be relevant to attempts at mediation not only on the interpersonal and group levels, but also on the scale of national or international disputes. Suppose that the disputants are from different countries, or different tribes, or different ethnic groups with a country, as is common on the contemporary global landscape. If Rothman's (1997) theory of self-identity, coupled with Swann's (1996) concept of self-verification, has any validity, one can predict a challenge for the mediator. Here we may have two disputants or groups of disputant parties who have deeply entrenched perceptions of their core self, their identity, each resistant to change that would be far too threatening to alter. The edifice of the self would crumble and with it negotiating power. Thus, profound cultural forces, supported by socialization practices that lead to the construction of a self and an identity must be thoughtfully considered (see Harter, 2012, on the construction of the self).

Harter (2012 traces the developmental and sociocultural foundations of the self, including how cultures can shape an intractable self, resistant to change. Therefore, in national and international negotiations, the mediator needs to be sensitive to different cultural conceptions of self, and their implications for the initial frame and the potential for a reframe. It is particularly important that a mediator not assume that one disputant feels disempowered due their lower socioeconomic or political status nor that the disputant of higher status displays more empowering feelings. This makes the use of the *My Feelings Pre-Survey* prior to mediation not only imperative but potentially groundbreaking in terms of research results, especially if it reveals high levels of empowerment in lower- status populations and high levels of disempowerment in higher- status populations. In either case, this survey and others used in the *inAccord* model will help validate or challenge mediator assumptions about empowerment based on social status or participation or perception of belonging to a group. It may also help to support the theory of self-verification as it relates to identity-based conflict in global disputes.

The Implications of False- Self Behavior

Earlier in this book, we emphasized the important of authenticity, linking it to the concept of *transparency*, an important concept in the *inAccord* model. The disputant is encouraged to be honest and open, to attempt to identify characteristics of their typical styles for dealing with conflict, as well as the natural emotions they experience in dealing with conflict, particularly those that brought them to mediation. Our goal, in inviting disputants to explore their own styles and emotions, through responses to our surveys, was designed, in part, to bring greater transparency or authenticity to the mediation process. These would seem to be important lessons, identifying skills of self-awareness, which will bring greater clarity to the process for disputants and mediators, alike.

What impediments might there be that could stand in the way of such lofty and practical goals? Within the United States, a talented therapist and analyst of American culture, Lerner (1993) in her book entitled The *Dance of Deception* has put forth a provocative commentary on the depths of deception within our language. The premise of this book is that it delineates the needs of partners and people in conflict to *deceive* one another. As someone who pays great attention to the language of a given culture, she points to the inordinate number of words in our English language that communicate deception.

For example, verb forms make reference to fabricating, withholding, concealing, distorting, falsifying, pulling the wool over someone's eyes, posturing, charading, faking, and hiding behind a façade. Adjectives include evasive, elusive, wily, phony, fake, artificial, two-faced, hypocritical, manipulative, calculating, pretentious, crafty, conniving, duplicitous, deceitful, and dishonest. Noun forms include charlatan, chameleon, imposter, hypocrite, a fake, and a fraud.

So what might Lerner's fascinating linguistic foray tell us of these needs in terms of mediation? First, it sensitizes us to the fact that in our culture, people steeped in these negative frames may have difficulty switching to reframes, more constructively. Secondly, some of these more negative terms imply direct action against another, for example, being evasive, manipulative, conniving, or hypocritical in their dealings with the other party. These natural language tendencies in our language, sadly, can well undermine the mediator's goals of instilling more positive language and associated actions. Requiring that the disputants alter their vocabulary or abandon certain language and terminology can potentially send the conflict underground, leading to a less transparent process. However, from a global perspective, it is important to acknowledge the potential language barriers in different countries or cultures.

Our English language also does not naturally cooperate with the goals of mediation in that there are far more negative emotion terms than positive. The most common negative emotions terms include anger, frustration, regret, despair, hopelessness, resentment, anxiety, depression, and the list goes on. Positive emotions are fewer in number, an interesting observation, in and of itself. We have happiness, love, pride, gratefulness, hope, but the list is far shorter.

What are the implications for mediation to resolve disputes? One such approach would be to sensitize disputants and mediators that in our own culture, our very language stacks the deck against a more positive reframe. We naturally frame our conflicts and concerns within the native language given to us. Constrained to a language that emphasizes words of deceit, and a vocabulary of negative emotions, we are prone to couch our own concerns in that parlance. Thus, it is all the more important for mediators, and for our own surveys, to counter this negativity by highlighting positive alternatives that can lead to a more positive reframe.

For this reason, our approach to identifying the various emotions that may define disputant's initial reactions contain a list of not only the typical negative reactions that many mediators focus on, but a list of potential *positive* emotions that may be empowered in the course of the mediation process, for example, hope, optimism, gratitude, and serenity. Our own findings, presented earlier, indicate that these positive emotions do, in fact, increase as a function of the mediation experience, whereas the negative, disempowering emotions decrease in strength. These positive emotions need to be fostered as part of the mediation process, in addition to the decrease of the most destructive emotions.

Folk Theories About Whether People Can Change

Individual differences can also influence the effectiveness of the mediator's efforts to guide disputants toward the resolution of a conflict. Such differences are apparent when one asks people about their "folk theories" of human behavior, for example, their views of whether it is possible to *change* one's personality or cognitive-behavioral attributes. Dweck (1999) has proposed that people hold one of two theories about the malleability of the nature of human qualities. Those who hold what Dweck labels as an *entity theory* believe that qualities such as goodness or intelligence are *fixed*, that is, they are entities that people simply do or do not possess. These are considered to be immutable traits that cannot be altered.

In contrast, other people hold what Dweck calls an *incremental theory* of human qualities, that is, they believe that people's characteristics are malleable and can be altered or developed. This more dynamic view of human nature implies that through effort or education, anyone can change or improve upon attributes that they wish to nurture. Dweck and Ehrlinger (2006) apply this distinction to conflict resolution, illuminating how one's theory about the ability of people to change can impact the goals of mediation. Depending upon which type of theory one holds about the nature of human qualities, people's strategies of conflict resolution will differ.

Interestingly, when serious conflicts arise, for example, between a couple, those who hold an *incremental* view of their partner's qualities are more likely to express their frustrations, but they are also more willing to try to work through the differences toward a reasonable solution. That is, they see the potential for change, in their partner as well as in themselves. They display an openness toward alternative ways of thinking which is particularly conducive to promoting understanding between parties and is, therefore, useful in resolving conflicts. Those with an incremental view are open to mutual negotiation, to the possibility that both they and their partner can change, toward an acceptable solution.

In contrast, those who hold an *entity* perspective about the immutability of human characteristics are less likely to express their anger or to explore possible solutions. Given that they believe that their partner cannot change, they decide either to stoically live with his/her flaws or to leave the relationship. There is little room for negotiation or growth. Thus, the reluctance to revise one's impressions of others makes conflict resolution particularly difficult for entity theorists. The rigidity of their thinking can hinder reconciliation. Given this mind set in which they do not believe in the capacity of people to change, the only solution to the conflict is to marginalize, subjugate, or psychologically eliminate the other party. As an alternative, they may simply leave the relationship.

Given this distinction, it follows that those who hold the perspective that people's attributes are fixed or immutable entities will be more resistant to the skills that the *inAccord* mediation model hopes to instill, in the resolution of conflicts. Fortunately, and perhaps paradoxically, Dweck and Ehrlinger (2006) find that the implicit theory that human nature is predetermined or an immutable entity can be altered through intervention. When such a view is gently challenged by teaching such individuals a more incremental view of human nature, they may move toward a greater willingness to entertain the possibility of change in others, as well as in themselves. They manifest decreased defensiveness and greater openness to learning which fosters more effective negotiation and conflict resolution. Although those who hold an entity perspective represent a challenge to the mediator, it is possible that they will respond to the mediation intervention if the nature of their thinking is sensitively explored, in the spirit of change that will facilitate conflict resolution.

The Path Forward

The goal of Mediators Without Borders is not only to offer an educational solution and contribute to complimentary systems of justice, but also to find ways of delivering the *inAccord* model to a wider international audience who may be ready to start alternative dispute resolution processes. Our business model, which is still in its early stages of development, is based on the creation of a system of integrated virtual, as well as physical conflict resolution ADR Centers

206

which will train mediators who will then be able to deliver *inAccord* education and mediation services to couples, companies, and countries. The path forward for *inAccord* as a mediation practice and the setting up of the ADR Center initiative along with the establishment of the University of Professional Studies will surely experience unforeseen challenges and may not always follow a direct route. However, we believe the data collection from the research component built into the model will help us with continuous course corrections along the way.

The field of conflict management and resolution is both old and new, and although mediation has now over a half century of use in family courts across the U.S and is routinely used in business, workplace and environmental and social disputes, and has been institutionalized into the fabric of our justice system along with arbitration, its efficacy is still under scrutiny. Often this scrutiny focuses on that fact that there has been little systematic research. It may appear overly ambitious to some to embark on such a bold plan as ours, setting up ADR Centers in other nations and creating a University, yet we continue to follow the word of first Century Jewish scholar, Hillel who asked, "If not now, when?" (Marcus, 2002). We believe it is time for this field to be both brave and measurable of its strengths, while also addressing the impediments and the challenges of the process and the outcome.

We continue to build on the insightful concepts of such conflict resolution greats as Deutsch, Rothman, and others who have started a course which we should continue to pursue. Much of our *inAccord* mediation model is a reworking and adaptation of these great thinkers in our field, and we want to articulate the theoretical positions under our practice. We do not claim we have the definitive answer as to what mediation techniques are applicable to all situations. Rather, we want to look carefully and design our on-going research assembling what we think we do know along with questions regarding each phase, each stage, which we hope will provide a clearer understanding of the mediation process. This is a first step, and we have much work ahead. We are humbled to take our first steps and introduce the formulation of mediation called the *inAccord* model. The three phases of the *inAccord* model create a procedural framework we will work from unless or until the data shows us how to change the model to be more effective. The overview on Table 1 in Chapter Two outlines the specific research methods that are naturally embedded in the process, which measures issues of expectations, emotion, fairness, understanding, satisfaction and outcomes into the process.

A Case for Hope

This returns us to our opening question: *What then is Justice?* As we close this first edition of *In Justice, inAccord*, we remain both interested and optimistic about our ability as researchers to accurately pose the questions and try to find the answers. As humans in the profession of helping, we hope to successfully navigate the many conflicts that permeate couples, companies, and countries and provide a process we believe will help manage or resolve conflicts, to bring about more interpersonal justice to the disputants, and more harmony to the context in which the conflict resides.

This book is based on a deeply held common belief, that we have an obligation to live our lives in a way that respects not only the lives of others but the lives of those yet to come who will inherit the consequences of our decisions, good and bad. This is founded on values consistent among many of the indigenous peoples of the Americas, that are commonly referred to as the Seventh Generation Principle. It states that the manner in which we live our lives today is based on decisions that were made by the previous seven generations of our people. Furthermore, the decisions we make in our lives will have a similar effect on the seven generations that follow us. This is a guiding principle of Mediators Without Borders and the *inAccord* model.

All times are challenging, and the times we live in have unique and important issues for us on many levels. It is easy to fall into an apathy born not from lack of caring but from a paralysis to deal with problems that seem insurmountable. Climate change, diminishing resources, broken governments, poverty and death on epic scales can leave us breathless and broken. Yet, we must not give up hope and fall into the abyss of making excuses for why we should not actively address these issues.

We stand on the shoulders of many who came before to expand the field of conflict resolution and take special inspiration from the United Nations Universal Declaration of Human Rights which we include in the following section of our book. We have a deep hope and optimism that *inAccord* and Mediators Without Borders ADR Centers will take on a life of their own and add to the expanding dialogue of how to create and sustain a more peaceable world. This is our hope, our dream, and our vision for the future.

Universal Declaration of Human Rights

PREAMBLE

Whereas recognition of the inherent dignity and of the equal and inalienable rights of all members of the human family is the foundation of freedom, justice and peace in the world,

Whereas disregard and contempt for human rights have resulted in barbarous acts which have outraged the conscience of mankind, and the advent of a world in which human beings shall enjoy freedom of speech and belief and freedom from fear and want has been proclaimed as the highest aspiration of the common people,

Whereas it is essential, if man is not to be compelled to have recourse, as a last resort, to rebellion against tyranny and oppression, that human rights should be protected by the rule of law,

Whereas it is essential to promote the development of friendly relations between nations,

Whereas the peoples of the United Nations have in the Charter reaffirmed their faith in fundamental human rights, in the dignity and worth of the human person and in the equal rights of men and women and have determined to promote social progress and better standards of life in larger freedom,

Whereas Member States have pledged themselves to achieve, in cooperation with the United Nations, the promotion of universal respect for and observance of human rights and fundamental freedoms,

Whereas a common understanding of these rights and freedoms is of the greatest importance for the full realization of this pledge,

Now, therefore,

The General Assembly

proclaims

This Universal Declaration of Human Rights

as a common standard of achievement for all peoples and all nations, to the end that every individual and every organ of society, keeping this Declaration constantly in mind, shall strive by teaching and education to promote respect for these rights and freedoms and by progressive measures, national and international, to secure their universal and effective recognition and observance, both among the peoples of Member States themselves and among the peoples of territories under their jurisdiction.

Article I

All human beings are born free and equal in dignity and rights. They are endowed with reason and conscience and should act towards one another in a spirit of brotherhood.

Article 2

Everyone is entitled to all the rights and freedoms set forth in this Declaration, without distinction of any kind, such as race, color, sex, language, religion, political or other opinion, national or social origin, property, birth or other status.

Furthermore, no distinction shall be made on the basis of the political, jurisdictional or international status of the country or territory to which a person belongs, whether it be independent, trust, non-self-governing or under any other limitation of sovereignty.

Article 3

Everyone has the right to life, liberty and security of person.

Article 4

No one shall be held in slavery or servitude; slavery and the slave trade shall be prohibited in all their forms.

Article 5

No one shall be subjected to torture or to cruel, inhuman or degrading treatment or punishment.

Article 6

Everyone has the right to recognition everywhere as a person before the law.

Article 7

All are equal before the law and are entitled without any discrimination to equal protection of the law. All are entitled to equal protection against any discrimination in violation of this Declaration and against any incitement to such discrimination.

Article 8

Everyone has the right to an effective remedy by the competent national tribunals for acts violating the fundamental rights granted him by the constitution or by law.

Article 9
No one shall be subjected to arbitrary arrest, detention or exile.
Article 10
Everyone is entitled in full equality to a fair and public hearing by an independent and impartial tribunal, in the determination of his rights and obligations and of any criminal charge against him.
Article 11
(1) Everyone charged with a penal offence has the right to be presumed innocent until proved guilty according to law in a public trial at which he has had all the guarantees necessary for his defense.
(2) No one shall be held guilty of any penal offence on account of any act or omission which did not constitute a penal offence, under national or international law, at the time when it was committed. Nor shall a heavier penalty be imposed than the one that was applicable at the time the penal offence was committed.
Article 12
No one shall be subjected to arbitrary interference with his privacy, family, home or correspondence, nor to attacks upon his honor and reputation. Everyone has the right to the protection of the law against such interference or attacks.
Article 13
(1) Everyone has the right to freedom of movement and residence within the borders of each State.
(2) Everyone has the right to leave any country, including his own, and to return to his country.
Article 14
(1) Everyone has the right to seek and to enjoy in other countries asylum from persecution.
(2) This right may not be invoked in the case of prosecutions genuinely arising from non-political crimes or from acts contrary to the purposes and principles of the United Nations.
Article 15
(1) Everyone has the right to a nationality.
(2) No one shall be arbitrarily deprived of his nationality nor denied the right to change his nationality.

Article 16

(1) Men and women of full age, without any limitation due to race, nationality or religion, have the right to marry and to found a family. They are entitled to equal rights as to marriage, during marriage and at its dissolution.

(2) Marriage shall be entered into only with the free and full consent of the intending spouses.

(3) The family is the natural and fundamental group unit of society and is entitled to protection by society and the State.

Article 17

(1) Everyone has the right to own property alone as well as in association with others.

(2) No one shall be arbitrarily deprived of his property.

Article 18

Everyone has the right to freedom of thought, conscience and religion; this right includes freedom to change his religion or belief, and freedom, either alone or in community with others and in public or private, to manifest his religion or belief in teaching, practice, worship and observance.

Article 19

Everyone has the right to freedom of opinion and expression; this right includes freedom to hold opinions without interference and to seek, receive and impart information and ideas through any media and regardless of frontiers.

Article 20

(1) Everyone has the right to freedom of peaceful assembly and association.

(2) No one may be compelled to belong to an association.

Article 21

(1) Everyone has the right to take part in the government of his country, directly or through freely chosen representatives.

(2) Everyone has the right to equal access to public service in his country.

(3) The will of the people shall be the basis of the authority of government; this shall be expressed in periodic and genuine elections

which shall be by universal and equal suffrage and shall be held by secret vote or by equivalent free voting procedures.

Article 22
Everyone, as a member of society, has the right to social security and is entitled to realization, through national effort and international co-operation and in accordance with the organization and resources of each State, of the economic, social and cultural rights indispensable for his dignity and the free development of his personality.

Article 23
(1) Everyone has the right to work, to free choice of employment, to just and favorable conditions of work and to protection against unemployment.

(2) Everyone, without any discrimination, has the right to equal pay for equal work.

(3) Everyone who works has the right to just and favorable remuneration ensuring for himself and his family an existence worthy of human dignity, and supplemented, if necessary, by other means of social protection.

(4) Everyone has the right to form and to join trade unions for the protection of his interests.

Article 24
Everyone has the right to rest and leisure, including reasonable limitation of working hours and periodic holidays with pay.

Article 25
(1) Everyone has the right to a standard of living adequate for the health and well-being of himself and of his family, including food, clothing, housing and medical care and necessary social services, and the right to security in the event of unemployment, sickness, disability, widowhood, old age or other lack of livelihood in circumstances beyond his control.

(2) Motherhood and childhood are entitled to special care and assistance. All children, whether born in or out of wedlock, shall enjoy the same social protection.

Article 26
(1) Everyone has the right to education. Education shall be free, at least in the elementary and fundamental stages. Elementary education

shall be compulsory. Technical and professional education shall be made generally available and higher education shall be equally accessible to all on the basis of merit.

(2) Education shall be directed to the full development of the human personality and to the strengthening of respect for human rights and fundamental freedoms. It shall promote understanding, tolerance and friendship among all nations, racial or religious groups, and shall further the activities of the United Nations for the maintenance of peace.

(3) Parents have a prior right to choose the kind of education that shall be given to their children.

Article 27

(1) Everyone has the right freely to participate in the cultural life of the community, to enjoy the arts and to share in scientific advancement and its benefits.

(2) Everyone has the right to the protection of the moral and material interests resulting from any scientific, literary or artistic production of which he is the author.

Article 28

Everyone is entitled to a social and international order in which the rights and freedoms set forth in this Declaration can be fully realized.

Article 29

(1) Everyone has duties to the community in which alone the free and full development of his personality is possible.

(2) In the exercise of his rights and freedoms, everyone shall be subject only to such limitations as are determined by law solely for the purpose of securing due recognition and respect for the rights and freedoms of others and of meeting the just requirements of morality, public order and the general welfare in a democratic society.

(3) These rights and freedoms may in no case be exercised contrary to the purposes and principles of the United Nations.

Article 30

Nothing in this Declaration may be interpreted as implying for any State, group or person any right to engage in any activity or to perform any act aimed at the destruction of any of the rights and freedoms set forth herein.

G.A. res. 217A (III), U.N. Doc A/810 at 71 (1948)

Adopted on December 10, 1948
by the General Assembly of the United Nations (without dissent)

References

Augsburger, D. (1989). *Conflict mediation across cultures: Pathways and patterns.* Louisville, Kentucky: Westminster/John Knox Press.

Bandura, A. (1977). *Self-efficacy: The exercise of control.* New York: Freeman Press.

Bandura, A. (2006). Toward a psychology of human agency. *Perspectives on Psychological Science, 1,* 164-180.

Bandura, A., & Locke, E. A. (2003). Negative self-efficacy and goal effects revisited. *Journal of Applied Psychology, 88,* 87-99.

Bennett, M. & Hermann, M. (1996). *The art of mediation.* Notre Dame, IN: National Institute for Trial Advocacy .

Berreby, D. (2005) *Us and them: Understanding your tribal mind.* New York; Little, Brown & Company.

Blake, R. & Mouton, J. (1964). *The managerial grid: The key to leadership excellence.* Houston: Gulf Publishing Co.

Bolton R. (1979). *People Skills.* New York: Simon & Schuster, Inc.

Boyatzis, R., Goleman, D., & Rhee, K. (2000). Clustering competence in emotional intelligence: insights from the emotional competence inventory (ECI). In R. Bar-On & J.D.A. Parker (Eds.), *Handbook of emotional intelligence* (pp. 343-362). San Francisco, CA: Jossey-Bass.

Braithwaite, J., & Parker, C. (1999). Restorative justice is republic justice. In L. Walgrave & G. Gordon (Eds.), *Restoring Juvenile Justice: An Exploration of the Restorative Justice Paradigm for*

Reforming Juvenile Justice. Monsey, New York: Criminal Justice Press.

Bunker, B. & Rubin, J. (Eds.). (1995). *Conflict, cooperation, & justice*. San Francisco, CA: Jossey Bass.

Bush, R., & Folger, J. (1994). *The promise of mediation*. San Francisco, CA: Jossey-Bass.

Bush, R., & Folger, J. (2005). *The promise of mediation*. (2nd ed.). San Francisco, CA: Jossey-Bass.

Campos, J. J., Mumme, D., Kermoian, R., & Campos, R. G. (1994). A functionalist perspective on the nature of emotions. In N. Fox (Ed.), *The development of emotion regulation* (pp. 284-303). Chicago, IL: University of Chicago Press.

Carstarphen, N., Zelizer, C., Harris, R. & Smith, D. (2010). *Graduate education and professional practice in international peace and conflict (246)*. Washington, D.C.: United States Institute of Peace.

Cohn, M. A., & Fredrickson, B. L. (2009). Positive emotions. In S. J. Lopez & C. R. Snyder (Eds.), *Handbook of positive psychology* (pp. 13-24). Oxford, England: Oxford University Press.

Cornell Empowerment Group. (1989, October). Empowerment and family support. *Networking Bulletin*, 1(1)2.

Cowan, N. (2001). The magical number 4 in short-term memory: A reconsideration of mental storage capacity. *Behavioral and Brain Science, 24*, 87-114.

Darwin, C. (1965). *The expression of the emotions in man and animals*. Chicago, IL: University of Chicago Press. (Original work published in 1872.)

Davis, A. & Salem, R. (1984) Dealing with power imbalances in the mediation of interpersonal disputes. *Mediation Quarterly, 17,* 18-23.

Deutsch, L. (2012). *LA County Court Layoffs: Hundreds of Employees to Receive Pink Slips.* Retrieved at Huffington Post. http://www.huffingtonpost.com/2012/06/15/la-county-court-layoffs_n_1599865.html

Deutsch, M. (2006). Cooperation and competition. In M. Deutsch, P. T. Coleman, & E. C. Marcus (Eds.). *The handbook of conflict resolution: Theory and practice* (pp. 23-42). San Francisco, CA: Jossey-Bass.

Donovan, J. (Host). (2012, March 12). The challenges of aid workers in conflict zones. *Talk of the Nation.* Washington, DC: National Public Radio. Retrieved from http://www.npr.org/2012/03/12/148460539/the-challenges-of-aid-work-in-conflict-zones

Dweck, C. S. (1999). *Self-theories: Their role in motivation, personality, and development.* Philadelphia, PA: Psychology Press/Taylor and Francis.

Dweck, C. S. & Ehrlinger, J. (2006). Implicit theories and conflict resolution. In M. Deutsch, P. T., Coleman, & E. C. Marcus (Eds.). *The handbook of conflict resolution: Theory and Practice* (pp. 317-331). San Francisco, CA: Jossey-Bass.

Fischer, M., (2001). *Conflict transformation by training in nonviolent action. Activities of the Centre for Nonviolent Action (Sarajevo) in the Balkan Region.* Berghof Occasional Paper No. 18. Berlin: Berghof Research Center.

Fischer, R., & Ury, W. (1991). *Getting to yes: Negotiating agreement without giving in.* New York: Penguin Books.

Folberg, J., & Taylor, A. (1984). *Mediation: A comprehensive guide to resolving conflicts without litigation.* San Francisco, CA: Jossey-Bass.

Folger, J.P., Poole, M.S., & Stutman, R.K. (2005). *Working through conflict: strategies for relationships, groups, and organizations.* 5th ed. Boston: Pearson.

Fonagy, P., Target, M., Steele, M., & Gerber, A. (1995). Psychoanalytic perspectives ondevelopmental psychopathology. In D. Cicchetti & D. J.Cohen (eds.), *DevelopmentalPsychopathology* (Volume 1: Theory and methods, pp. 504-554). New York: Wiley &Sons.

Fredrickson, B. L. (1998). What good are position emotions? *Review of General Psychology, 2,* 300-319.

Freud, S. (1952). *A general introduction to psychoanalysis.* New York: Washington Square Press.

Friedman, E. H. (1990). *Friedman's fables.* New York: Guilford Press.

Furlong, G. (2005). *The Conflict Resolution Toolbox.* Ontario: John Wiley & Sons.

Goodman, A. H. (1994). *Basic skills for the new mediator.* Rockville, MD: SolomonPublications.

Gordon, T. (1970). *Parent effectiveness training: The "no-lose" program for raising responsible children.* New York: Peter H. Wyden.

Gottman, J., Ryff, C. D., Singer, B. (Eds), (2001). Meta-emotion, children's emotional intelligence, and buffering children from marital conflict. *Emotion, social relationships, and health. Series in affective science.,* (pp. 23-40). New York, NY, US: Oxford University Press.

Gray, B. (2004). Strong opposition: frame-based resistance to collaboration. *Journal of Community & Applied Social Psychology, Vol. 14:3,* pp. 166-176.

Greenberg, J. (1987). Reactions to procedural injustice in payment distributions: So the means justify the ends? *Journal of Applied Psychology, 75,* 55-61.

Gudykunst, W., Ting-Toomey, S., Sudweeks, S., & Stewart, L. (1995). *Building Bridges Interpersonal Skills for a Changing World.* Boston: Houghton Mifflin Company.

Gudykunst, W. & Ting-Toomey, S. (1988). *Culture and interpersonal communication.* Newbury Park, CA.: Sage Publications.

Harter, S. (1999). *The construction of the self: A developmental perspective (lst ed.).* New York: Guilford Press.

Harter, S. (2012). *The construction of the self: Developmental and sociocultural foundations* (2nd ed.). New York: Guilford Press.

Hawkins, D. R. (2002). *Power vs. force.* Carlsbad, CA: Hay House.

Hicks, Esther and Jerry (2004). *Ask and it is given.* Carlsbad, CA: Hay House.

Hoffman, L., Stewart, S., Warren, D., & Meek, L. (2009). Toward a sustainable myth of self: An Existential response to the postmodern crisis. *Journal of Humanistic Psychology, 49,* 135- 173.

Irving, I. M., Snyder, C. R., & Crowson, J. J. Jr. (1998). Hope and the negotiation of cancer facts by college women. *Journal of Personality, 66,* 195-214.

Isen, A. M. (2000). Positive affect and decision making. In M. Lewis & J. M. Haviland-Jones (Eds.), *Handbook of emotions* (2nd ed., pp. 417-435). New York: Guilford Press.

James, W. (1890). *Principles of Psychology.* Chicago, IL: Encyclopedia Brittanica.

Kals, E., & Jiranek, P. (2010). In E. Kals & J. Maes (eds.). *Justice and conflicts.* Berlin and Heidelberg: Springer-Verlag.

Klein, M. (1976). *Psychoanalytic theory: An exploration of essentials.* New York: International Universities Press.

Kovach, K. & Love, L. (1996). "Evaluative" mediation is an oxymoron. *Alternatives to High Cost Litigation*, 31, 31.

Kriesberg, L. (1998). *Constructive conflicts: from escalation to resolution.* Langham, MD: Rowman & Littlefield.

Kriesberg, L. (2007). *Constructive conflict: From escalation to resolution* (3rd ed.). Langham, MD: Rowman & Littlefield.

Kurtz, R. (1990). *Body-centered Psychotherapy: The Hakomi method.* LifeRhythm.

Lang, M., & Taylor, A. (2000). *The Making of a mediator: Developing artistry in practice.* San Francisco: Jossey-Bass.

Lazarus, R. S. (1982). Thoughts on the relations between emotions and cognition. *American Psychologist, 37,* 1019-1024.

Leary, M. (2004). *The curse of the self: Self-awareness, egotism, and the quality of human life.* Oxford, England: Oxford University Press.

Lewis, M. (2008). Self-conscious emotions: Embarrassment, pride, shame, and guilt. In M. Lewis, J. M. Haviland-Jones, & L. F. Barrett (Eds.), *Handbook of emotions* (3rd ed., pp. 742-756). New York: Guilford Press.

Lindner, E. G. (2006). Emotion and conflict: Why it is important to understand how emotions affect conflict and how conflict affects emotions. In M. Deutsch, P. T. Coleman, & E. C. Marcus (Eds.). *The handbook of conflict resolution: Theory and practice* (pp. 317-331). San Francisco, CA: Jossey-Bass.

MacFarlane, J. (2008). *The new lawyer: How settlement is transforming the practice of law.* Vancouver: UBC Press.

Maddux, J. E., & Gosselin, J. T. (2012). Self-efficacy. In M. R. Leary & J. P. Tangney (Eds.), *Handbook of self and identity (2nd ed.).* New York: Guilford Press.

Marcus (Eds.). *The handbook of conflict resolution* (2nd ed., pp. 268-293). San Francisco, CA:Jossey-Bass.

Marcus, Y. (Ed.) (2002). *Pirkei avot: Ethics of the fathers.* New York: Kehot Publishing Society.

Mayer, B. (2000). *The dynamics of conflict resolution.* San Francisco, CA: Jossey-Bass.

McKinney, B.C., Kimsey, W.D., & Fuller, R. (1995). *Mediator communication competencies: Interpersonal communication and alternative dispute resolution.* Edina, MN: Burgess.

Mindell, A. (1992). *Leader as martial artist: An introduction to deep democracy* (1st ed.). San Francisco: Harper.

Moffitt, M. (1998). Mediation transparency helps parties see where they are going. *Alternatives to the High Cost of Litigation*, Vol. 16, Issue 6, pp. 81-86.

Moore, C. (1985). *The mediation process: Practical strategies for resolving conflict.* New York: Jossey-Bass.

Moore, C. (2003). *The mediation process: practical strategies for resolving conflict.* San Francisco: Jossey-Bass.

Piaget, J. (1960). *The psychology of intelligence.* Patterson, NJ: Littlefield-Adams.

Pinker, D. (2011). *The better angels of our nature: Why violence has declined.* New York: Viking Penguin.

Rand, K. L., & Cheavens, J. S. (2009). Hope theory. In S. J. Lopez & C. R. Snyder (Eds.). *Oxford Handbook of Positive Psychology* (2nd ed.), (pp. 323-334)

Rappaport, J. (1987). Terms of empowerment/exemplars of prevention: Toward a theory for community psychology. *American Journal of Community Psychology,* 15, 121-148.

Rees, C. (2010). Mediation in business related human rights disputes: Objections, Opportunities, and Challenges. *Harvard Kennedy School*, Working Paper no.56.

Ries, S., & Murphy, G. (1999). *Quality of life: How to get it, how to keep it.* New York: William Morrow Publishers.

Riskin, L. (1996). Understanding mediators' orientations, strategies, and techniques: A grid for the perplexed. 1:7 *Harvard Negotiation Law Review* 7 at 13.

Rothman, J. (1997). *Resolving identity-based conflict in nations, organizations, and communities.* San Francisco, CA: Jossey-Bass.

Rudolph, (2012). *Pennsylvania Public Defenders Rebel Against Crushing Caseloads.* Retrieved from Huffington Post. http://www.huffingtonpost.com/2012/05/30/pennsylvania-public-defenders_n_1556192.html

Rummel, R.J. (1976). *Understanding Conflict and War, Volume 2: The Conflict Helix.* Beverly Hills, California: Sage Publications.

Saarni, C., Campos, J. J., Camras, L. A., & Witherington, D. (2006). In N. Eisenberg (Vol. ed.) and in W. Damon & R. M. Lerner (editors in chief), *Handbook of child psychology, Social, emotional, and personality development* (Vol.3, pp. 226-299). New York: Wiley.

Salovey, P., & Mayer, J. D. (1990). Emotional intelligence. *Imagination, Cognition, and Personality, 9,* 185-211.

Seaomone, E. (2000). *Bringing a smile to mediation's two faces: How aspiring mediators might jump-start careers immediately following law school.* III.B www.uiowa.edu/-cyberlaw/elp00Evan/mediation.

Shaver. P., Wu., S., & Schwartz, J. C. (1992). Cross-cultural similarities and differences in emotion and its representation. In M. Clark (Ed.), *Review of personality and social psychology* (Vol. 13, pp. 175-212). Newbury Park, CA: Sage.

Slaikeu, K. (1996) *When push comes to shove.* San Francisco. CA: Jossey-Bass.

Snyder, C. R. (1989). Reality negotiation: From excuses to hope and beyond. *Journal of ADR Central and Social Psychology, 8,* 130-157.

Snyder, C. R. (1994). *The psychology of hope: You can get there from here.* New York: Free Press.

Snyder, C. R., Rand, K. L., & Sigmon, D. R. (2002). Hope theory: A member of the positive emotion family. In C. R. Snyder & J. Lopez (Eds.), *Handbook of positive psychology (1st ed.),* (pp. 231-243). New York: Oxford University Press.

Spreitzer, G. M., & Doneson, D. (2005). Musings on the past and future of employee empowerment. In T. Cummings (Ed.), *Handbook of Organizational Development.* London: Sage Publishing.

Sturm, S., & Gadlin, H. (2007). Conflict resolution and systemic change. *Journal of Dispute Resolution,* Vol. 1, Issue 3.

Stuhlberg, J. (1997). Facilitative versus evaluative mediator orientations: Piercing the "grid" lock. *Florida State University Law Review, 985,* p. 1001.

Swann, W. B. (1996). *Self-traps.* New York: Freeman.

Taylor, A. (2002). *The handbook of family dispute resolution.* San Francisco: Jossey Bass.

Thomas, K., & Kilman, R. (1974). *Thomas-Kilman Conflict Mode Instrument.* New York: Xicom.

Ting-Toomey, & Chung, L. C. (2005). *Understanding intercultural communication.* Los Angeles, CA: Roxbury Publishing Company.

Tyler, T. (1989). The psychology of procedural justice: A test of the group-value model. *Journal of Personality and Social Psychology, Vol. 5,* pp. 830-838.

Tyler, T., & Belliveau, J. (1995). Tradeoffs in justice principles: Definitions of fairness. In B. Bunker & J. Rubin (Eds.), *Conflict, cooperation, & justice: Essays inspired by the work of Morton Deutsch* (pp. 291-314).

Tyler, T. R., & Lind, E. A. (1992). A relational of authority of groups. In M. Zanna (Ed.), *Advances in Experimental Social Psychology, Vol. 25,* pp. 115-191. New York: Academic Press.

Wall, P. (2009). *Law vs., Justice: Retrieved from* author's website http://www.peterwall.net/2009/05/02/law-vsjustice/.

Warren, P. (2001). *A systems approach to mediation.* Virginia: Commercial Mediation Association.

Weiner, B. (1985). An attributional theory of achievement motivation and emotion. *Psychological Review, 92,* 548-573.

Whitmore, E. (1988). Empowerment and the process of inquiry. A paper presented at the annual meeting of the Canadian Association of Schools of Social Work, Windsor, Ontario.

Wilmot, W. & Hocker, J.(1978). *Interpersonal conflict.* New York: McGraw Hill.

Winslade, J., & Monk, G. (2000). *Narrative mediation: A new approach to conflict resolution.* San Francisco: Jossey-Bass.

Zajonc, R. B. (1980). Feeling and thinking: Preferences need no inferences. *American Psychologist, 35,* 151-175.

Zinck, A. (2008). Self-referential emotions. *Consciousness and Cognition,* June:17, 496-505.

Coda: Conversations with the Authors

How it All Began

The authors' collaboration began at the Denver Botanical Gardens where first author Ries' began to share details of her *inAccord* model. As they mapped out the model and potential research study, they each noted how much their perceptions of justice and remedies to injustice were influenced by their educational and work backgrounds in psychology, sociology, and social work. These influences form much of the research behind this book and the measurement tools used in the *inAccord* model. The authors' commitment to work together on *In Justice, inAccord* deepened while attending the play, *Les Miserables,* in Denver, Colorado, which sparked long conversations about a shared passion for justice and scholarship. In subsequent meetings, they worked together to create a series of survey instruments that would measure a disputant's satisfaction with, and understanding of, the *inAccord* mediation process, each step of the way. This book is the first presentation of this model and the research and scholarship underlying its premises.

In Justice, inAccord has its roots deep within the business model that has become Mediators Without Borders®. The business grew out of first author Ries' commitment to provide students with a more comprehensive training in mediation and conflict resolution. One goal was to enhance professional excellence that would build on the foundational forty hour national standard training in the United States through creating a Graduate Certificate Program in Alternative Dispute Resolution. Mediators without Borders is currently listed in over 900 university catalogues and has a growing alumni of two thousand plus students. In Chapter Six, we will highlight our ADR Center initiative for international services and internships. The ultimate goal is to create a fully accredited Master and Doctoral Program under *Mediators without Borders International University of Professional Studies*. The Mediators Without Borders team's commitment to adding increasing value to alternative dispute resolution education and research also contributes to the field of Alternative Dispute Resolution (ADR) in a unique new model of facilitation, mediation and arbitration named *inAccord* which is disputant-focused, valuing transparency, empowerment, and underscoring the role of emotions.

A Conversation with Shauna Ries

The author and president of a company teaches peace talks, about why everyone needs conflict in their lives, the importance of going with your gut, and frogs.

Interviewer: You'd think that with nearly 750,000 lawyers in the country, we would have disputes pretty well covered. But Mediators Without Borders, the Boulder, Colorado-based company you co-founded as President, is more in-demand than ever. Why do you think people are looking beyond lawyers these days?

Ries: There are some disputes, ones in which there is no longer going to be a relationship in the future, that can go to court if need be, but if there is a *future* relationship – whether it is family, work, a friend – and you will be seeing the person you have the dispute with, I think there is a quality of life issue to settle the dispute with dignity and grace. Besides, mediation and other types of alternate dispute resolution save considerable money and time.

Interviewer: Wouldn't it just be easiest if we tried to *eliminate* conflict and the disputes that arise?

Ries: No. Conflict is *good*. So is anger. When my partner Genna [Murphy] and I were researching for our 1999 book entitled *Quality of Life* published by William Morrow & Company, we realized that anger and conflict were constructive. Those emotions help discern where you are versus where you want to be. Feelings of anger can inform you and serve to clarify and provide the energy you need to grow and change. It is when we're in conflict, whether with ourselves, our family or our boss that our anger can teach us about ourselves. Conflict and anger inform you your instincts are working and that you care enough to modify a situation. It's the people closest to us that we tend to have the most conflict with. This role of emotions in conflict is where the inAccord Conflict Analysis Model originated.

Interviewer: So conflict is good, but there are varying levels of conflict. What do you do to keep conflict constructive?

Ries: Communicate directly with the person you are in conflict and stay with the discussion until both sides have shared their *underlying* interests.

Interviewer: This is easier said than done.

Ries: Not really. inAccord teaches disputants three very important skills, we refer to as the Touchstone Skills: reflecting, reframing and questioning. We value the idea of transparency in the negotiation. By this, we make the covert, overt. Again, this is where exploring the role of emotions, in particular your disempowering emotions and try to articulate what those emotions require for a feeling of relief. People have problems trusting their own instincts. Most people feel angry yet need help to clarify their thinking behind what it is they're feeling. Trusting your instincts when faced with an injustice seems simple, but most of us have to learn how to put words around it.

Interviewer: So what's the Cliff Notes version of how to trust your instincts?

Ries: Look for the emotion of relief: explore what it is you require that would give you relief, at the beginning of the conflict. This is at the core of our Accord Conflict Analysis Model. Many are able to identify the conflict, yet are not clear what precisely they need for remedy.

Interviewer: You and Genna founded the precursor to Mediators Without Borders, Ries/Murphy Associates, in 1994 to provide conflict resolution and stress management services. What made you decide to branch into teaching others the inAccord Conflict Analysis model for mediators, arbitrators and alternative dispute resolution specialists?

Ries: With communication, negotiation, mediation, and arbitration skills comes great personal power. Successful mediators are able to resolve, what appear to be intractable situations. Our follow up research provides us with insight as to whether the inAccord is effective for disputants.

Interviewer: What kinds of people are enrolling in the Mediation and Arbitration Trainings?

Ries: Mediators Without Borders enrolls a diverse range of students. Some students are looking to make a career change into mediation while others want to advance within their profession, through a certificate in mediation or arbitration. Still others are taking courses to better their personal communication skills.

Interviewer: With 38 states currently requiring or recommending mediation to resolve civil and/or family disputes, the Administrative Dispute Resolution Act of 1996 mandating mediators receive training on a regular basis and over 1,500 law firms and 800 companies pledging to explore mediation before litigating there's no doubt mediators are in high demand. You could have gone gangbusters with Mediators Without Borders but instead you chose to grow the company slowly. Why?

I wanted a business my son and my grandchildren would be proud of. I wanted to build a principled company based on sound business practices. As corny as it sounds, I wanted to build a company with the intention of the world being a little bit better of a place because Mediators Without Borders exists. I, personally, wanted to live a life I could be proud of.

Interviewer: Making the world a better place – that's a pretty hefty goal for a company these days. What kinds of personal goals do you have?

Ries: Be transparent and congruent with others. Trust my instincts, while being pragmatic. Be in charge of my own destiny.

Interviewer: And what do all those things do for you?

Ries: They contribute to the high my quality of my life.

Interviewer: Quality of Life is the subject of the book you and Genna co-authored in 1999 and something in which you both counseled hundreds of clients in your mediation, arbitration and psychotherapy practice. How do you define it?

Ries: Quality of life is when you are integrated; when what you're thinking, saying, doing and feeling match.

Interviewer: What takes away from someone's quality of life?

Ries: Life is complicated and unpredictable. Usually it's not one thing, person or event that harms someone's quality of life. There is a story about frogs that kind of explains this idea. If dropped into scalding water, a frog will jump out immediately. But if you put a frog in a pot of water and slowly turn up the heat one degree at a time, it will stay. Eventually, it will die. The same thing happens to people. Conflicts and unhappiness come on and heat the water one degree at a time, building until one day they realize their water is scalding.

Interviewer: What is a first step for someone looking to reclaim their quality of life?

Ries: To understand the system of things. There is not one thing – a promotion, a new car, and a better job- that in and of itself is going to make everything all right. People often have this notion of a magic pill to fix problems. That's not reality however. It's not that concrete. Look, instead, at the different facets of your life and take those conflicts that you have control over and tackle those first. After you do that, you'll see the other pieces naturally start to change or become more manageable. This momentum will begin the reclamation process of your life.

Interviewer: It sounds like the struggle for quality of life is as self-revealing as conflict can be.

Ries: Conflict and quality of life go hand-in-hand. To have a high quality of life, you need to be able to move and navigate through conflict. Every time I've been through a difficult conflict in my life it has made me clearer, stronger and, eventually, happier. Now when I am faced with something that is difficult I know something clarifying will come, as a result. As Kahlil Gibran mentions, joy and pain are from the self- same well. The deeper your sorrow, the deeper your joy will be. Besides, I enjoy controlling my own destiny, even if it's not always easy.

A conversation between Shauna Ries and Susan Harter

Ries: I am delighted that you have joined our Mediators Without Borders team. We have always felt that the field of Psychology was central to mediation and your own expertise as a Professor of Psychology, including your extensive research experience has been a real plus. Tell me a little bit about your background.

Harter: I, too, am thrilled at the opportunity to work with you and your team on our research project designed to examine the effectiveness of the inAccord model. My background, I think, is well-suited for our project. After graduating from Oberlin College, I did my graduate work at Yale University where I obtained my Ph.D., trained in both in child-clinical and *developmental* psychology programs, each of which had a strong emphasis on research. I accepted an invitation to remain on the Yale faculty, as the first woman to do so. I left Yale after six years, accepting an offer to join the faculty at the University of Denver, where I crafted an exciting Developmental Program that trained both graduate students and post-doctoral trainees in research. I was honored to receive the highest academic award that the University of Denver bestows upon a faculty member, acknowledging one's international and national recognition for scholarly work and research. So I bring quite a bit of relevant experience to our project at Mediators Without Borders.

Ries: As someone with a career that has focused on both ADR Central and developmental psychology, what attracted you to the inAccord Model of *conflict* and its resolution?

Harter: My first answer would be that both our illustrious developmental and clinical theories, historically, were based on models of *conflict.*. Jean Piaget, the giant for many years in the field of cognitive- developmental psychology, saw conflict as essential. He used an interesting French word, *perturbation*, to refer to the fact that the infant's and child's worlds, their environments, are constantly posing challenges that "perturb" their existing repertoire of skills, by which he meant that they demand a stretch in the form of new learning.

So conflict really propelled development and learning, from his perspective. And of course from a psychoanalytic perspective, Sigmund Freud's well-known concepts of the *id, ego,* and *super-ego* defined the *intrapsychic conflict* that individuals experience. The *id* was the repository of instincts such as sex and aggression in "battle" or in conflict with the *superego,* one's *conscience* or moral values. The super ego's job goal was to tame unacceptable id impulses and behaviors. Then the *ego's* job definition was to literally be a mediator, attempting to resolve and balance the conflicts between the id and the superego, a harrowing task to be sure. Therefore, conflict for humans is *inevitable* from both developmental and clinical perspectives. And thus, my general interest in conflict. Of course, beginning in childhood and continuing into adolescence and adulthood, one observes a great deal of normative *interpersonal conflict.* In recent years, psychologists have developed intervention programs to help children and adolescents learn new social skills, allowing them resolve such disputes. For all of these reasons, I come by my interest in Mediators Without Borders very naturally.

Ries: In addition to your obvious interest in conflict, what other concepts from our inAccord model did you find interesting or compelling and why?

Harter: There were a number of concepts that I found intriguing and that stemmed from my own interests and research. One is the notion of *authenticity,* the capacity to be one's *true self,* acknowledging and expressing one's innermost thoughts, feelings, and opinions appropriately. By appropriate I mean in a way that others can actually listen to and hear, if they are expressed in a manner that is not interpersonally destructive. The inAccord concept of *transparency* is very analogous, promoting the goal that disputants as well as mediators access their authentic self as clearly as possible. To do so appropriately, one needs to learn specific skills, which are captured precisely by those emphasized in the model, reflecting, reframing, and questioning, the *Touchstone Skills.* However, in today's society, authenticity is in short supply, there are many challenges and impediments compromising our ability to access and display our true selves. We are bombarded with media messages and images that dictate how we should act, what we should look like, in order to meet the punishing standards of appearance for women and men in our culture. We are assaulted with dictates about what we should buy according to the latest trends, what we should think and say and what we should not say. In short, we are given a societal blueprint for who we should be as a person, as a self.

Ries: These are interesting cultural demands. But what are some of the more psychological impediments to being one's true self, as you see it?

Harter: I describe many of these barriers to authenticity in my recent 2012 book entitled *The development of the self: Developmental and sociocultural foundations* published by the Guilford Press. The contemporary self is cause for concern. Social psychologists studying adults have identified numerous self-enhancement strategies, self-serving biases, unrealistic or inaccurate self-perceptions, as well as narcissistic tendencies that compromise the authenticity of the self and, in the process, dilute the quality of one's interpersonal relationships. In my book, I trace the developmental origins of these pernicious paths to self-deception, many of which are actively supported by our socialization practices. For example, there has been a startling national initiative to raise the self-esteem of our nation's children and adolescents in recent years, with our schools at the hub of this movement, which began in California a number of years ago. Critics of this craze have argued that children's sense of self-esteem and competencies are being inflated unrealistically, rather than focusing on the acquisition of actual skills and abilities. Studies also reveal that narcissism is on the rise in our nation, beginning in adolescence. Too many of our youth are encouraged by their parents to feel entitled when they do not deserve this mantle.

Ries: How do you view these societal tendencies to encourage self-aggrandizement, in light of the principles espoused by the inAccord Model?

Harter: Quite simply, they are totally and directly *antithetical*. The inAccord model emphasizes *transparency*, akin to authenticity as I mentioned earlier. Toward this goal, the inAccord model identifies specific skills to encourage disputants to get in touch with their true feelings, and to do so with clarity. Inflated self-enhancement has no place in this model, given that it compromises those types of authentic interpersonal interactions necessary if disputants are to actively resolve the conflict. But before one can move to the acquisition of new skill sets, many of which are cognitively based, there is some groundwork that needs to be laid.

Ries: What kind of groundwork, what do you see as necessary before the skill training?

Harter: That is a critical question. The answer is at the heart of another theme that has dominated my own thinking and research. People must first learn to get in touch with their *emotions* that are powerful forces in their lives, some of which can be destructive, some of which can be constructive. Disputants must first be encouraged to acknowledge their own emotional states, as realistically as possible. Mediators must be trained to assist disputants in labeling and expressing their feelings rather than moving too quickly to cognitive skill development. Thus, the design and inclusion, in our collaborative research, of a self-report survey to enquire about disputants' perceptions of their own emotion is critical, as a first step. As you have described, often the initial emotions are intense and not always manageable. Moreover-, your own contribution of addressing two categories of emotions, those that are *empowering* as well as those that are *disempowering* is a major innovation in the field of mediation. A major contribution of your own thinking has been to illuminate the notion of a *match* or a *mismatch* between disputant emotions, where a match means that both disputants report the same type of emotions, that is, both indicate that they experience either empowering emotions or disempowering emotions. In contrast, a mismatch is observed when one party reports empowering emotions but the other party reports disempowering emotions. You have presented a very convincing case that the issue of a match versus a mismatch has profound implications for the intervention approach that a mediator selects. This focus on emotions represents a very creative contribution to the field of mediation.

Ries: Do you see our new focus on emotions or any other aspects of the inAccord model that interface with current trends in your own field of Psychology?

Harter: Most definitely! There is a clear convergence between the inAccord Model's new focus on identifying both positive *and* negative emotions and two present trends in the field of Psychology. The first is the acknowledgement that positive emotions play an important role in people's lives, that they have a *function*. For years, the field was dominated by an inordinate emphasis on *negative emotions*, for example, fear, anger, and depression. These affects were highlighted because they were assumed to be the major players on the stage of one's psychological life, they were touted as highly *functional*, from an evolutionary perspective (for example, the fight or flight reaction to fear, as emphasized by Charles Darwin and later by William James). Positive emotions were given short shrift, they were viewed as relatively non-functional and, as a result, were simply not studied. Recent work counters this belief and identifies several functions that are critical to the inAccord Model. For example, Frederickson's *broaden-and-build* theory of positive emotions makes the claim that positive affects serve to widen the array of thoughts and actions available to the individual, they produce more *flexible* tendencies and solutions to life's challenges. As a result of a broadened mind set, one has access to more personal coping resources and one is more receptive or open to new information that promotes creativity. These capacities, in turn, enhance the likelihood of decision-making success in the future. The second *building* function first requires broadening, toward the goal of providing a source of *agency* or self-determination, akin to the concept of empowerment in the *inAccord* model. It spurs one toward the creation of solutions. As a result, this new trend dovetails very nicely with the new focus on positive emotions in the *inAccord* Model, granting them legitimacy as powerful forces in resolving conflict. Each of these functions is front and center, in the *inAccord* Model.

The second recent trend has been the identification of a new subfield in psychology, labeled Positive Psychology. Martin Seligman spearheaded this movement, as its founder. Seligman and followers decried the over-emphasis on *negativity* within the field at large, urging psychologists to shift their focus to positive topics such as optimism, gratitude, serenity, hope, precisely those psychological commodities that have found their way into the *inAccord* model.

Beyond the traditional emphasis on negative emotions, the field has historically been consumed by negative diagnostic labels that are pejorative, that are demeaning and stigmatizing for individuals who come to therapy. The *inAccord* model as applied to mediation offers an alternative to the potentially negative effects of some therapies. Individuals are not viewed as helpless, pathological creatures with deep-seated problems that are resistant to change. Mediation offers an alternative that provides a hopeful path to conflict resolution, one that encourages self-determination, as individuals are empowered to take active role in solving one's own problems, and in so doing, are granted a sense of dignity. Empowerment has much in common with another relatively new concept in the field of psychology, the concept of *self-efficacy*, first introduced by Albert Bandura. Self-efficacy refers to the belief that the person has the power to personally make positive goals actually happen in his/her life. This is precisely what the inAccord Model fosters.

Ries: We have been talking about a number of issues that relate to the field of Psychology and to your own scholarly work and its application to the goals and principles underlying the inAccord model of conflict resolution and mediation. This has been extremely interesting. Have these goals and principles affected your *personal* life, as you navigate your way through your own life's challenges?

Harter: I'm glad you asked that question, because my involvement in our collaborative project has had a profound impact on me, personally. I see four such arenas. First, it has enhanced my own commitment to being an authentic self in my daily interactions with others. Second, and relatedly, it has sensitized me to the importance of acknowledging my emotions, first to myself, and then in my interpersonal relationships where emotions must be expressed in a constructive manner, in a way that strengthens the relationship rather than compromising it negatively. This, at times in my life, has been a challenge. Third, I have always been a proponent of self-determination and feel that my own life and career bear that out. The notion of empowerment in the *inAccord* model has, therefore, been particularly appealing. Seeing its power in the model, as it applied to mediation, has strengthened my resolve to appreciate the importance of empowerment in my own life. Furthermore, as a professor, it is a quality that I hope to encourage and nurture in my students. Fourth, my new knowledge about specific skills that can foster authenticity and can improve my own interpersonal negotiation abilities has been invaluable. I have become better at reflecting as well as reframing issues that may be problematic, and clearly notice the positive benefits of these skills in my own interpersonal interactions. Finally, enacting these various principles has definitely had a major impact on my own enhanced ability to live and love.

APPENDIX A: DISPUTANT SURVEY INSTRUMENTS

MEDIATORS WITHOUT BORDERS®

INACCORD CONFLICT ANALYSIS MODEL
Conflict Styles*

Name of   **Date:**
Party:

People sometimes handle conflict differently depending on the context (for example, if conflict arises in the home, we may handle it differently than we would handle conflict at work). For this survey, we would like you to reflect on how you typically handle conflict in each of five contexts: in your family of origin, at home, with friends, during play or recreation, and at work. All conflict styles have advantages and disadvantages, so it is important to note that **there is no right or wrong answer**.

•*Avoidance:* When I have a conflict, I tend to avoid it or refuse to engage in it.

•*Competition:* When I have a conflict, I tend to be competitive and feel that it is important to obtain my goals and/or ensure that the problem gets solved.

•*Compromise:* When I have a conflict, I prefer a "give and take" approach where we try to find middle ground between two differing positions, even if the outcome does not fully meet either party's goal.

•*Accommodation:* When I have a conflict, I tend to give in to another's wishes or sacrifice my own goals to minimize conflict.

•*Collaboration:* When I have a conflict, I prefer to work cooperatively with the other party until a mutually agreeable solution is found.

For each context listed below, please choose the conflict style that you use **most often**. If you feel that two responses might apply, please decide on which one **is TRUER for you**. Do not check more than one box.

1.Growing up in my **family of origin**, if conflict arose, the conflict style I used most often was:

☐ Avoidance   ☐ Competition   ☐ Compromise
          ☐ Accommodation   ☐ Collaboration

2.In my **home** life right now, when conflict arises, the conflict style I use most often is:

☐ Avoidance   ☐ Competition   ☐ Compromise
          ☐ Accommodation   ☐ Collaboration

3.If conflict arises when spending time with **friends**, the conflict style I use most often is:

☐ Avoidance   ☐ Competition   ☐ Compromise
          ☐ Accommodation   ☐ Collaboration

4.During **recreation or play**, if conflict arises, the conflict style I am most likely to use is:

☐ Avoidance   ☐ Competition   ☐ Compromise
          ☐ Accommodation   ☐ Collaboration

5.If conflict arises at **work**, the conflict style I am most likely to use is:

☐ Avoidance   ☐ Competition   ☐ Compromise
          ☐ Accommodation   ☐ Collaboration

*NOTE: We have adapted the framework of Wilmot and Hocker (1998) in the design of this survey instrument.

MEDIATORS WITHOUT BORDERS®

INACCORD CONFLICT ANALYSIS MODEL
My Feelings Scale: Pre Survey

Name of Party: **Date:**

You will fill out several surveys during the inAccord mediation process. These surveys are about personal opinions; therefore, there is no right or wrong answer. Please review each word or statement below and choose *ONLY ONE RESPONSE FROM THE FOUR*. If you feel that two responses might apply, please decide on which one *is TRUER for you*. Do not check in between the words or statements.

Please check the box next to the words that best describe how often you experience each of the feelings **with regard to this conflict**.

1)Serenity

☐ Most of the time ☐ Some of the time ☐ Not that often ☐ Hardly ever

2)Understanding

☐ Most of the time ☐ Some of the time ☐ Not that often ☐ Hardly ever

3)Forgiveness

☐ Most of the time ☐ Some of the time ☐ Not that often ☐ Hardly ever

4)Optimism

☐ Most of the time ☐ Some of the time ☐ Not that often ☐ Hardly ever

5)Hopefulness

☐ Most of the time ☐ Some of the time ☐ Not that often ☐ Hardly ever

6)Contentment

☐ Most of the time ☐ Some of the time ☐ Not that often ☐ Hardly ever

7)Trust

☐ Most of the time ☐ Some of the time ☐ Not that often ☐ Hardly ever

8)Happiness

☐ Most of the time ☐ Some of the time ☐ Not that often ☐ Hardly ever

9)Discouragement

☐ Most of the time ☐ Some of the time ☐ Not that often ☐ Hardly ever

10)Jealousy

☐ Most of the time ☐ Some of the time ☐ Not that often ☐ Hardly ever

11)Anger

☐ Most of the time ☐ Some of the time ☐ Not that often ☐ Hardly ever

12)Depression

☐ Most of the time ☐ Some of the time ☐ Not that often ☐ Hardly ever

13)Insecurity

☐ Most of the time ☐ Some of the time ☐ Not that often ☐ Hardly ever

14)Despair

☐ Most of the time ☐ Some of the time ☐ Not that often ☐ Hardly ever

15)Blame

☐ Most of the time ☐ Some of the time ☐ Not that often ☐ Hardly ever

16)Humiliation

☐ Most of the time ☐ Some of the time ☐ Not that often ☐ Hardly ever

My Expectations Scale

1.What is the level of your *Expectations* of **saving money** by choosing mediation as opposed to litigation?

☐ Very high expectations ☐ Pretty high ☐ Pretty low ☐ Very low

2.What is the level of your *Expectations* of **saving time** by choosing mediation as opposed to litigation?

☐ Very high expectations ☐ Pretty high ☐ Pretty low ☐ Very low

3.What is the level of your *Expectations* of **saving the relationship** with the other party or parties by choosing mediation as opposed to litigation?

☐ Very high expectations ☐ Pretty high ☐ Pretty low ☐ Very low

MEDIATORS WITHOUT BORDERS®

INACCORD CONFLICT ANALYSIS MODEL
STAGE 1
Understanding and Satisfaction Scale

Name of   **Date:**
Party:

This survey asks questions related to your experience of Stage 1 of the inAccord mediation model. This survey is about your personal opinions; therefore, there is no right or wrong answer. Please review each word or statement below and choose *ONLY ONE RESPONSE FROM THE FOUR*. If you feel that two responses might apply, please decide on which one *is TRUER for you*. Do not check in between the words or statements.

Stage 1: Sharing of Perspectives: Issues, Positions, and Interest Identification

1.How well did you understand the **issues** identified (the reasons you are seeking mediation)?
☐ Very well   ☐ Pretty well   ☐ Not very well   ☐ Not at ALL well

2.How well do you now understand *your own* **underlying interests or goals** (why you are taking the position you are taking)?
☐ Very well   ☐ Pretty well   ☐ Not very well   ☐ Not at ALL well

3.How well do you now understand the *other party's* **underlying interests or goals** (why the other party is taking the position that he/she is taking)?
☐ Very well   ☐ Pretty well   ☐ Not very well   ☐ Not at ALL well

4. How *Satisfied* were you with the *process* of sharing perspectives, including your own *issues, positions, and interests*?
☐ Very satisfied   ☐ Somewhat   ☐ Not very   ☐ Not at ALL

248

MEDIATORS WITHOUT BORDERS®

INACCORD CONFLICT ANALYSIS MODEL
STAGE 2
Understanding and Satisfaction Scale

Name of   **Date:**
Party:

This survey asks questions related to your experience of Stage 2 of the inAccord mediation model. This survey is about your personal opinions; therefore, there is no right or wrong answer. Please review each word or statement below and choose **ONLY ONE RESPONSE FROM THE FOUR.** If you feel that two responses might apply, please decide on which one *is **TRUER for you.*** Do not check in between the words or statements.

Stage 2: Option Generation and Developing the Agenda

1. How well do you understand the **questioning techniques** you received from the mediator for clarifying your issues?

☐ Very well   ☐ Pretty well   ☐ Not very well   ☐ Not at ALL well

2. How well can you now **reframe hurtful statements?**

☐ Very well   ☐ Pretty well   ☐ Not very well   ☐ Not at ALL well

3. How well can you now **brainstorm options?**

☐ Very well   ☐ Pretty well   ☐ Not very well   ☐ Not at ALL well

4. How *Satisfied* were you with the **list of issues** identified for the agenda?

☐ Very satisfied   ☐ Somewhat   ☐ Not very   ☐ Not at ALL

5. How *Satisfied* were you with the **order** in which the issues were addressed?

☐ Very satisfied   ☐ Somewhat   ☐ Not very   ☐ Not at ALL

MEDIATORS WITHOUT BORDERS®

INACCORD CONFLICT ANALYSIS MODEL
STAGE 3
Understanding and Satisfaction Scale

Name of Party: **Date:**

This survey asks questions related to your experience of Stage 3 of the inAccord mediation model. This survey is about your personal opinions; therefore, there is no right or wrong answer. Please review each word or statement below and choose **ONLY ONE RESPONSE FROM THE FOUR**. If you feel that two responses might apply, please decide on which one **is TRUER for you**. Do not check in between the words or statements.

Stage 3: Joint Solution Statements: Testing the Agreements in Principle

1. How well do you understand the following statement? *It is not important for the parties in a dispute to agree on the facts or recollections in order to create a joint solution.*

☐ Very well   ☐ Pretty well   ☐ Not very well   ☐ Not at ALL well

2. How well did the skills of reflective listening and reframing help you to **clarify the options** for resolving your dispute?

☐ Very well   ☐ Pretty well   ☐ Not very well   ☐ Not at ALL well

3. To what extent do you now feel able to create a Joint Solution Statement that will **represent your interests**?

☐ Very much so   ☐ Pretty much so   ☐ Not very much   ☐ Not at ALL

4. To what extent do you now feel able to create a Joint Solution Statement that will **represent the other party's interests**?

☐ Very much so   ☐ Pretty much so   ☐ Not very much   ☐ Not at ALL

5. Please rate your **overall satisfaction** with the Joint Solution Statement agreed upon.

☐ Very satisfied   ☐ Somewhat   ☐ Not very   ☐ Not at ALL

250

MEDIATORS WITHOUT BORDERS®

INACCORD CONFLICT ANALYSIS MODEL
STAGE 4
Understanding and Satisfaction Scale

Name of   **Date:**
Party:

This survey asks questions related to your experience of Stage 4 of the inAccord mediation model. This survey is about your personal opinions; therefore, there is no right or wrong answer. Please review each word or statement below and choose *ONLY ONE RESPONSE FROM THE FOUR*. If you feel that two responses might apply, please decide on which one *is TRUER for you*. Do not check in between the words or statements.

Stage 4: Crafting the Memorandum of Agreement

1.How well do you understand the **compromises** you made in order to arrive at an agreement?

☐ Very well ☐ Pretty well ☐ Not very well ☐ Not at ALL well

2.To what degree do you **understand the terms** of the final Memorandum of Agreement?

☐ Very much so ☐ Pretty much so ☐ Not very much ☐ Not at ALL

3.How well will you be able to **implement and comply with** the terms of the Memorandum of Agreement?

☐ Very well ☐ Pretty well ☐ Not very well ☐ Not at ALL well

4.To what degree are you *Satisfied* with the **skills you learned** in this process to help you resolve future conflicts?

☐ Very satisfied ☐ Somewhat ☐ Not very ☐ Not at ALL

MEDIATORS WITHOUT BORDERS®

INACCORD CONFLICT ANALYSIS MODEL
Exit Survey

Name of Party: **Date:**

This survey asks questions related to your overall impression of the inAccord mediation experience. This survey is about your personal opinions; therefore, there is no right or wrong answer. Please review each word or statement below and choose ***ONLY ONE RESPONSE FROM THE FOUR***. If you feel that two responses might apply, please decide on which one ***is TRUER for you***. Do not check in between the words or statements.

1. How well do you *understand* the inAccord Conflict Analysis model?

  ☐ Very well   ☐ Pretty well   ☐ Not very well   ☐ Not at ALL well

2. To what extent was the mediator *fair?*

  ☐ Very fair   ☐ Pretty fair   ☐ Not that fair   ☐ Not at ALL fair

3. The mediation process was made very *clear* to us.

  ☐ Very true   ☐ Pretty true   ☐ Not very true   ☐ Not at ALL true

4. How ***Successful*** was the inAccord Conflict Analysis model for you?

  ☐ Very successful ☐ Pretty successful ☐ Not that successful ☐ Not at ALL

5. I liked the fact that I personally had a lot of say in the negotiations.

  ☐ Very true   ☐ Pretty true   ☐ Not very true   ☐ Not at ALL true

6. How **Satisfied** were you with the inAccord *process*?

☐ Very satisfied ☐ Somewhat ☐ Not very ☐ Not at ALL

7. How **Satisfied** were you with the inAccord *outcome*?

☐ Very satisfied ☐ Somewhat ☐ Not very ☐ Not at ALL

8. To what extent was the mediator **Impartial?**

☐ Very impartial ☐ Pretty impartial ☐ Not that impartial ☐ Not at all

9. I had a good understanding of what was expected at each stage of the mediation.
☐ Very true ☐ Pretty true ☐ Not very true ☐ Not at ALL true

10. It was important to me to know that I had some control as we went through the mediation process.
☐ Very true ☐ Pretty true ☐ Not very true ☐ Not at ALL true

11. How much has your relationship with the other party or parties *improved* as a result of the inAccord Conflict Analysis model?

☐ Very much ☐ Pretty much ☐ Not very much ☐ Not at ALL

12. As a result of the inAccord Conflict Analysis model, how much more **Effective** do you feel you will be at handling future conflicts?

☐ Very effective ☐ Pretty effective ☐ Not very ☐ Not at ALL

13. How much more do you now understand the *other party's perspective* about this dispute?

☐ Very much so ☐ Pretty much so ☐ Not very much ☐ Not at ALL

14. To what extent was the mediator **Neutral?**

☐ Very neutral ☐ Pretty neutral ☐ Not that neutral ☐ Not at ALL

15. As a result of the *inAccord* Conflict Analysis model, how much are you better **Able** to prevent destructive and negative responses to conflict?

☐ Very much more able   ☐ Pretty much ☐ Not really ☐ Not at ALL

16. Although mediation is challenging, the *transparency* or clarity of the process was very helpful in guiding me to a decision.

☐ Very true   ☐ Pretty true   ☐ Not very true   ☐ Not at ALL true

17. I appreciated the fact that I was partly in charge of what was happening throughout the various stages.

☐ Very true   ☐ Pretty true   ☐ Not very true   ☐ Not at ALL true

MEDIATORS WITHOUT BORDERS®

INACCORD CONFLICT ANALYSIS MODEL
My Feelings Scale: Post Survey

Name of   Date:
Party:

This survey is about personal opinions; therefore, there is no right or wrong answer. Please review each word or statement below and choose *ONLY ONE RESPONSE FROM THE FOUR*. If you feel that two responses might apply, please decide on which one *is TRUER for you*. Do not check in between the words or statements.

Please check the box next to the words that best describe how you are feeling about this conflict **now that you have completed the mediation process**.

1)Serenity

☐ Most of the time ☐ Some of the time ☐ Not that often ☐ Hardly ever

2)Understanding

☐ Most of the time ☐ Some of the time ☐ Not that often ☐ Hardly ever

3)Forgiveness

☐ Most of the time ☐ Some of the time ☐ Not that often ☐ Hardly ever

4)Optimism

☐ Most of the time ☐ Some of the time ☐ Not that often ☐ Hardly ever

5)Hopefulness

☐ Most of the time ☐ Some of the time ☐ Not that often ☐ Hardly ever

6)Contentment

☐ Most of the time ☐ Some of the time ☐ Not that often ☐ Hardly ever

7)Trust

☐ Most of the time ☐ Some of the time ☐ Not that often ☐ Hardly ever

8)Happiness

☐ Most of the time ☐ Some of the time ☐ Not that often ☐ Hardly ever

9)Discouragement

☐ Most of the time ☐ Some of the time ☐ Not that often ☐ Hardly ever

10)Jealousy

☐ Most of the time ☐ Some of the time ☐ Not that often ☐ Hardly ever

11)Anger

☐ Most of the time ☐ Some of the time ☐ Not that often ☐ Hardly ever

12)Depression

☐ Most of the time ☐ Some of the time ☐ Not that often ☐ Hardly ever

13)Insecurity

☐ Most of the time ☐ Some of the time ☐ Not that often ☐ Hardly ever

14)Despair

☐ Most of the time ☐ Some of the time ☐ Not that often ☐ Hardly ever

15)Blame

☐ Most of the time ☐ Some of the time ☐ Not that often ☐ Hardly ever

16)Humiliation

☐ Most of the time ☐ Some of the time ☐ Not that often ☐ Hardly ever

My Expectations Scale

1.To what extent was your expectation of **saving money** through mediation *Realized*?

☐ Fully realized ☐ Partially ☐ Not really realized ☐ Not at ALL

2. To what extent was your expectation of **saving time** through mediation *Realized*?

☐ Fully realized ☐ Partially ☐ Not really realized ☐ Not at ALL

3. To what extent was your expectation of **saving the relationship** with the other party or parties *Realized*?

☐ Fully realized ☐ Partially ☐ Not really realized ☐ Not at ALL

APPENDIX B: MEDIATOR SURVEY INSTRUMENTS

MEDIATORS WITHOUT BORDERS®

INACCORD CONFLICT ANALYSIS MODEL
Mediator Analysis of Pre Survey Feelings Ratings

Name of   **Date:**
Mediator:

Name of Party   **Name of**
A: **Party B:**

My Feelings Pre Survey Four Blocks of Empowerment/Disempowerment

The following table represents four distinct blocks of responses to the *My Feelings* Pre Survey. The inAccord Model is a Facilitative Approach, guiding the Mediator through step-by-step facilitation and which approach to use, based on parties' empowering and disempowering emotions regarding the conflict. If disputants have similar emotions, meaning both parties are empowered or disempowered (a balance of power indicated by having both in the *same quadrant*), you will want to begin with an interest-based *relational approach* (where all parties stay at the table except to fill out the Stage 1 survey; Stages 2-4 surveys can be completed at the table together). If there is a mismatch, (parties fall in *different quadrants*), particularly if one party is in Quadrant A (high empowering/low disempowering) and the other party is in Quadrant D (low empowering/high disempowering), then you will want to begin with a more rights-based *directive approach* (BATNA; WATNA; MLATNA; use of shuttle negotiation).

According to their responses in the My Feelings Pre Survey, in which quadrant does each party fall?

Check only one quadrant for each party below:

A: High Empowering and Low Disempowering	B: High Empowering and High Disempowering
Mostly **high** responses to questions **1 – 8** (indicated by party choosing statements "Most of the time" or "Some of the time") combined with mostly **low** responses ("Not that often" or "Hardly ever") to questions **9 – 16**. ☐ Party A ☐ Party B	Mostly **high** responses to questions **1 – 16** ("Most of the time" or "Some of the time"). ☐ Party A ☐ Party B
C: Low Empowering and Low Disempowering	D: Low Empowering and High Disempowering
Mostly **low** responses to questions **1 – 16** ("Not that often" or "Hardly ever"). ☐ Party A ☐ Party B	Mostly **low** responses to questions **1 – 8** ("Not that often" or "Hardly ever") combined with mostly **high** responses to questions **9 – 16** ("Most of the time" or "Some of the time"). ☐ Party A ☐ Party B

Based upon the parties' *My Feelings* Pre Survey, which approach are you more likely to employ:

☐ *Directive Approach* ☐ *Relational Approach*

Did your parties display a:

☐ *Mismatch of Emotions* ☐ *Match of Emotions*

MEDIATORS WITHOUT BORDERS®

INACCORD CONFLICT ANALYSIS MODEL
STAGE 1
Understanding and Satisfaction Scale: Mediator Analysis of Stage 1 Responses

Name of Mediator: **Date:**

Name of Party A: **Name of Party B:**

Please review each word or statement below and choose **ONLY ONE RESPONSE FROM THE FOUR**. If you feel that two responses might apply, please decide on which one *is TRUER for that disputant*. Do not check in between the words or statements. *Be sure to answer each question for each party.*

Stage 1: Sharing of Perspectives: Issues, Positions, and Interest Identification

1. How well does the party understand the **issues** identified (the reasons they are seeking mediation)?

Party A:	☐ Very well	☐ Pretty well	☐ Not very well	☐ Not at ALL well
Party B:	☐ Very well	☐ Pretty well	☐ Not very well	☐ Not at ALL well

2. How well does the party now understand *their own* **underlying interests or goals** (why they are taking the position they are taking)?

Party A:	☐ Very well	☐ Pretty well	☐ Not very well	☐ Not at ALL well
Party B:	☐ Very well	☐ Pretty well	☐ Not very well	☐ Not at ALL well

3. How well does the party now understand the *other party's* **underlying interests or goals** (why the other party is taking the position that he/she is taking)?

Party A:	☐ Very well	☐ Pretty well	☐ Not very well	☐ Not at ALL well
Party B:	☐ Very well	☐ Pretty well	☐ Not very well	☐ Not at ALL well

4. How **Satisfied** were the parties with the *process* of sharing their own perspectives, including their own *issues, positions, and interests*?

Party A:	☐ Very satisfied	☐ Somewhat	☐ Not very	☐ Not at ALL
Party B:	☐ Very satisfied	☐ Somewhat	☐ Not very	☐ Not at ALL

INACCORD CONFLICT ANALYSIS MODEL
STAGE 2
Understanding and Satisfaction Scale: Mediator Analysis of Stage 2 Responses

Name of Mediator: **Date:**

Name of Party A: **Name of Party B:**

Please review each word or statement below and choose *ONLY ONE RESPONSE FROM THE FOUR.* If you feel that two responses might apply, please decide on which one *is TRUER for that disputant.* Do not check in between the words or statements. *Be sure to answer each question for each party.*

Stage 2: Option Generation and Agenda Setting

1.   How well does the party understand the **questioning techniques** they received from you for clarifying their own issues?

Party A: ☐ Very well   ☐ Pretty well   ☐ Not very well   ☐ Not at ALL well
Party B: ☐ Very well   ☐ Pretty well   ☐ Not very well   ☐ Not at ALL well

2.   How well can the party now **reframe hurtful statements**?

Party A: ☐ Very well   ☐ Pretty well   ☐ Not very well   ☐ Not at ALL well
Party B: ☐ Very well   ☐ Pretty well   ☐ Not very well   ☐ Not at ALL well

3.   How well can the party now **brainstorm options**?

Party A: ☐ Very well   ☐ Pretty well   ☐ Not very well   ☐ Not at ALL well
Party B: ☐ Very well   ☐ Pretty well   ☐ Not very well   ☐ Not at ALL well

4.   How *Satisfied* was the party with the **list of issues** identified for the agenda?

Party A: ☐ Very satisfied   ☐ Somewhat   ☐ Not very   ☐ Not at ALL
Party B: ☐ Very satisfied   ☐ Somewhat   ☐ Not very   ☐ Not at ALL

5.   How *Satisfied* was the party with the **order** in which the issues were addressed?

Party A: ☐ Very satisfied   ☐ Somewhat   ☐ Not very   ☐ Not at ALL
Party B: ☐ Very satisfied   ☐ Somewhat   ☐ Not very   ☐ Not at ALL

264

INACCORD CONFLICT ANALYSIS MODEL
STAGE 3
Understanding and Satisfaction Scale: Mediator Analysis of Stage 3 Responses

Name of Mediator: **Date:**

Name of Party A: **Name of Party B:**

Please review each word or statement below and choose *ONLY ONE RESPONSE FROM THE FOUR*. If you feel that two responses might apply, please decide on which one *is TRUER for that disputant*. Do not check in between the words or statements. *Be sure to answer each question for each party.*

Stage 3: Joint Solution Statements: Testing the Agreements in Principle

1.   How well does the party understand the following statement? *It is not important for the parties in a dispute to agree on the facts or recollections in order to create a joint solution.*

Party A: ☐ Very well   ☐ Pretty well   ☐ Not very well   ☐ Not at ALL well
Party B: ☐ Very well   ☐ Pretty well   ☐ Not very well   ☐ Not at ALL well

2.   How well did the skills of reflective listening and reframing help the party to **clarify the options** for resolving their dispute?

Party A: ☐ Very well   ☐ Pretty well   ☐ Not very well   ☐ Not at ALL well
Party B: ☐ Very well   ☐ Pretty well   ☐ Not very well   ☐ Not at ALL well

3.   To what extent does the party now feel able to create a Joint Solution Statement that will **represent their interests?**

Party A: ☐ Very much so   ☐ Pretty much so   ☐ Not very much   ☐ Not at ALL
Party B: ☐ Very much so   ☐ Pretty much so   ☐ Not very much   ☐ Not at ALL

4.   To what extent does the party now feel able to create a Joint Solution Statement that will **represent the other party's interests?**

Party A: ☐ Very much so   ☐ Pretty much so   ☐ Not very much   ☐ Not at ALL
Party B: ☐ Very much so   ☐ Pretty much so   ☐ Not very much   ☐ Not at ALL

5.   Please rate the party's **overall *Satisfaction*** with the Joint Solution Statement agreed upon.

Party A: ☐ Very satisfied   ☐ Somewhat   ☐ Not very   ☐ Not at ALL
Party B: ☐ Very satisfied   ☐ Somewhat   ☐ Not very   ☐ Not at ALL

265

INACCORD CONFLICT ANALYSIS MODEL

STAGE 4
Understanding and Satisfaction Scale: Mediator Analysis of Stage 4 Responses

Name of Mediator: **Date:**

Name of Party A: **Name of Party B:**

Please review each word or statement below and choose **ONLY ONE RESPONSE FROM THE FOUR**. If you feel that two responses might apply, please decide on which one *is TRUER for that disputant*. Do not check in between the words or statements. *Be sure to answer each question for each party.*

Stage 4: Crafting the Final Memorandum of Agreement

1.   How well does the party understand the **compromises** they made in order to arrive at an agreement?

Party A: ☐ Very well   ☐ Pretty well   ☐ Not very well   ☐ Not at ALL well
Party B: ☐ Very well   ☐ Pretty well   ☐ Not very well   ☐ Not at ALL well

2.   To what degree does the party **understand the terms** of the final Memorandum of Agreement?

Party A: ☐ Very much so   ☐ Pretty much so   ☐ Not very much   ☐ Not at ALL
Party B: ☐ Very much so   ☐ Pretty much so   ☐ Not very much   ☐ Not at ALL

3.   How well will the party be able to **implement and comply with** the terms of the Memorandum of Agreement?

Party A: ☐ Very well   ☐ Pretty well   ☐ Not very well   ☐ Not at ALL well
Party B: ☐ Very well   ☐ Pretty well   ☐ Not very well   ☐ Not at ALL well

4.   To what degree is the party *Satisfied* with the **skills they learned** in this process to help them resolve future conflicts?

Party A: ☐ Very satisfied   ☐ Somewhat   ☐ Not very   ☐ Not at ALL
Party B: ☐ Very satisfied   ☐ Somewhat   ☐ Not very   ☐ Not at ALL

266

MEDIATORS WITHOUT BORDERS®

INACCORD CONFLICT ANALYSIS MODEL
Mediator Exit Survey

Name of Mediator: **Date:**

Name of Party A: **Name of Party B:**

Please review each word or statement below and choose **ONLY ONE RESPONSE FROM THE FOUR**. If you feel that two responses might apply, please decide on which one *is TRUER for that disputant*. Do not check in between the words or statements. *Be sure to answer each question for each party.*

1. How well does the party *understand* the inAccord Conflict Analysis model?

Party A: ☐ Very well   ☐ Pretty well   ☐ Not very well   ☐ Not at ALL well
Party B: ☐ Very well   ☐ Pretty well   ☐ Not very well   ☐ Not at ALL well

2. To what extent were you perceived as *fair* to this party?

Party A: ☐ Very fair   ☐ Pretty fair   ☐ Not that fair   ☐ Not at ALL fair
Party B: ☐ Very fair   ☐ Pretty fair   ☐ Not that fair   ☐ Not at ALL fair

3. The mediation process was made very *clear* to this party.

Party A: ☐ Very true   ☐ Pretty true   ☐ Not very true   ☐ Not at ALL true
Party B: ☐ Very true   ☐ Pretty true   ☐ Not very true   ☐ Not at ALL true

4. How ***Successful*** was the *inAccord* Conflict Analysis model for the party?

Party A: ☐ Very successful ☐ Pretty ☐ Not that successful ☐ Not at ALL
Party B: ☐ Very successful ☐ Pretty ☐ Not that successful ☐ Not at ALL

5. The party liked the fact that he/she personally had a lot of say in the negotiations.

Party A: ☐ Very true ☐ Pretty true ☐ Not very true ☐ Not at ALL true
Party B: ☐ Very true ☐ Pretty true ☐ Not very true ☐ Not at ALL true

6. How ***Satisfied*** was the party with the inAccord *process*?

Party A: ☐ Very satisfied ☐ Somewhat ☐ Not very ☐ Not at ALL
Party B: ☐ Very satisfied ☐ Somewhat ☐ Not very ☐ Not at ALL

7. How ***Satisfied*** was the party with the inAccord *outcome*?

Party A: ☐ Very satisfied ☐ Somewhat ☐ Not very ☐ Not at ALL
Party B: ☐ Very satisfied ☐ Somewhat ☐ Not very ☐ Not at ALL

8. To what extent were you perceived as ***Impartial*** by this party?

Party A: ☐ Very impartial ☐ Pretty impartial ☐ Not that impartial ☐ Not at ALL
Party A: ☐ Very impartial ☐ Pretty impartial ☐ Not that impartial ☐ Not at ALL

9. The party had a good understanding of what was expected at each stage of the mediation.

Party A: ☐ Very true ☐ Pretty true ☐ Not very true ☐ Not at ALL true
Party B: ☐ Very true ☐ Pretty true ☐ Not very true ☐ Not at ALL true

10. It was important to this party to know that he/she had some control as they went through the mediation process.

Party A: ☐ Very true ☐ Pretty true ☐ Not very true ☐ Not at ALL true
Party B: ☐ Very true ☐ Pretty true ☐ Not very true ☐ Not at ALL true

11. How much did the party's relationship with the other party or parties *improve* as a result of the inAccord Conflict Analysis model?

Party A: ☐ Very much ☐ Pretty much ☐ Not very much ☐ Not at ALL
Party B: ☐ Very much ☐ Pretty much ☐ Not very much ☐ Not at ALL

12. As a result of the inAccord Conflict Analysis model, how much more *Effective* do you feel the party will be at handling future conflicts?

Party A: ☐ Very effective ☐ Pretty effective ☐ Not very ☐ Not at ALL
Party B: ☐ Very effective ☐ Pretty effective ☐ Not very ☐ Not at ALL

13. How much more does the party now understand the *other party's perspective* about this dispute?

Party A: ☐ Very much so ☐ Pretty much so ☐ Not very much ☐ Not at ALL
Party B: ☐ Very much so ☐ Pretty much so ☐ Not very much ☐ Not at ALL

14. To what extent were you perceived as *neutral* by this party?

Party A: ☐ Very neutral ☐ Pretty neutral ☐ Not that neutral ☐ Not at ALL
Party B: ☐ Very neutral ☐ Pretty neutral ☐ Not that neutral ☐ Not at ALL

15. As a result of the inAccord Conflict Analysis model, how much better *Able* do you believe the party is to prevent destructive and negative responses to conflict?

Party A: ☐ Very much more able ☐ Pretty much ☐ Not really more ☐ Not at ALL
Party B: ☐ Very much more able ☐ Pretty much ☐ Not really more ☐ Not at ALL

16. Although mediation is challenging, the *transparency* or clarity of the process was very helpful in guiding this party to a decision.

Party A: ☐ Very true ☐ Pretty true ☐ Not very true ☐ Not at ALL true
Party B: ☐ Very true ☐ Pretty true ☐ Not very true ☐ Not at ALL true

17. This party appreciated the fact that he/she was partly in charge of what was happening throughout the various stages.

Party A: ☐ Very true ☐ Pretty true ☐ Not very true ☐ Not at ALL true
Party B: ☐ Very true ☐ Pretty true ☐ Not very true ☐ Not at ALL true

MEDIATORS WITHOUT BORDERS®

INACCORD CONFLICT ANALYSIS MODEL
Mediator Analysis of Post Survey Feelings Ratings

Name of   **Date:**
Mediator:

Name of Party   **Name of**
A: **Party B:**

My Feelings Post Survey Four Blocks of
Empowerment/Disempowerment

The table on the next page represents four distinct blocks of responses to the *My Feelings* Post Survey.

According to their responses in the My Feelings Post Survey, in which quadrant does each party fall?

Check only one quadrant for each party below:

A: High Empowering and Low Disempowering Mostly **high** responses to questions **1 – 8** (indicated by party choosing statements "Most of the time" or "Some of the time") combined with mostly **low** responses ("Not that often" or "Hardly ever") to questions **9 – 16**. ☐ Party A ☐ Party B	B: High Empowering and High Disempowering Mostly **high** responses to questions **1 – 16** ("Most of the time" or "Some of the time"). ☐ Party A ☐ Party B
C: Low Empowering and Low Disempowering Mostly **low** responses to questions **1 – 16** ("Not that often" or "Hardly ever"). ☐ Party A ☐ Party B	D: Low Empowering and High Disempowering Mostly **low** responses to questions **1 – 8** ("Not that often" or "Hardly ever") combined with mostly **high** responses to questions **9 – 16** ("Most of the time" or "Some of the time"). ☐ Party A ☐ Party B

Which approach was most appropriate for this case?

☐ Directive Approach   ☐ Relational Approach

Did the parties at the end of the case show a:

☐ Mismatch of Emotions   ☐ Match of Emotions

Appendix B

Sample Mediator's Opening Statement

Welcome. My name is _____ and I have been selected by you to serve as mediator. First, how would you prefer that I address each of you during our time together? You may address me as _____.

A bit about my background.... [Describe background and experience]

I want to commend you on your willingness to give the mediation process a chance. You are here voluntarily, and you will voluntarily decide whether to come to an agreement in this matter. If you come to an agreement, you will jointly decide what that agreement looks like.

Unlike going to court and having a case decided by a judge or having the matter arbitrated before a third party who decides the outcome, mediation presents the unique opportunity for the parties to a dispute to determine how the matter gets resolved. In mediation, the parties also control the process, and are able to address issues and explore options for resolution that might not be allowed in a more formal, legal setting.

It is important that all parties necessary to come to a resolution of this matter are here either in person or by authorized representative. If we do, then we can begin.

I have provided each of you with an Agreement to Mediate, which I will ask you to sign after reading. Among other things, it provides that you agree to enter into the mediation session in good faith, and to commit to attempt to resolve the issues before you, including considering reasonable solutions that are presented.

I will also have you each sign the Fee Agreement, which contains the parties' prior agreement regarding sharing the cost of this mediation.

You need to know that, with limited exception, any discussions that take place during this mediation are confidential and cannot be used by any of us or any third party in a court of law or in any other proceeding outside of this room. As a condition of participating in this mediation, you agree not to subpoena me, my company, or any documents used in this mediation into any court of law. Also, I will destroy any notes I may take at the conclusion of this mediation.

The sole exception is that if I learn of the abuse of another that occurred in the past, or if I am made aware of a threat of violence or harm against another person or their property, I am authorized to disclose otherwise confidential information to appropriate authorities.

My role today is basically that of an impartial set of ears and eyes. This is *your* mediation, and my purpose for being here with you is to watch and listen and to help guide the process with a minimum of interference. I want to be clear that I am not here today as a judge or decision maker; nor am I acting as an attorney or financial advisor for any party. If you should feel at any point that you need to seek professional advice in order to come to a decision, I encourage you to ask to take a break in order to allow that to happen.

That being said, would you each permit me to interrupt your discussions only in order to help focus and guide the communication process? Thank you.

In order to keep the focus of this mediation firmly on you, the disputants, I would ask that you agree to the following ground rules:
First, to listen to one another respectfully, without interruption, and to avoid any inflammatory language
Second, to share relevant information openly with the other
Finally, to be open to the possibility of moving off a fixed position you might have, even one that you believe to be completely valid

I can guarantee you that someone else sees their position to be completely valid as well. The existence of diversity of points of view is something we acknowledge from the outset.

For my part, I promise to help keep the focus of your mediation squarely on YOU.

Okay, let's talk about the procedure for today's mediation.

Be assured that you will each have your opportunity to be heard. First, each of you will give your statement of your interpretation of the dispute. Once each of you has had an opportunity to give your statement, there will be an opportunity for each of you to respond to the other's statement, and to ask any questions of the other for purposes of clarification. It is just as important for purposes of your mediation to *understand the other* as it is to *be understood* by the other. I have given each of you a yellow pad and a pen if you'd like to take notes as the other speaks, or for you to jot down any thoughts of your own.

After it is agreed that each person has had ample time to be heard and has been understood by the other, you will then jointly develop a list of issues for discussion, including items that might go into a written agreement. With your agenda in hand, you can then go about generating options for resolution.

Now, if in the course of discussions, anyone feels they would like to speak to me out of the presence of the other, just let me know, and I will have a private conversation called a caucus with each of you in turn. Just as the contents of our joint discussions are confidential to the rest of the world, I will not disclose the contents of any private conversations I have with you to anyone else, UNLESS you give me permission to do so. I will always ask you at the conclusion of any private caucus whether I am permitted to disclose any part of what you told me in joint session.

Finally, the ultimate goal of your mediation is to jointly craft a written document called a Memorandum of Agreement or MOA that commemorates the points of agreement you have mutually and voluntarily come to regarding resolution of this matter. Once the MOA contains all the points that you each feel need to be included, you will each sign the agreement and agree to be bound by its terms.

Let me tell you a little about the *inAccord* Conflict Analysis Model that I will be using throughout this process. People come to mediation with varying levels of understanding of the goals and the process. Typically, the average person comes to mediation with little experience; that is, they have had little reason to develop such skills until now, because there was no clear dispute. So we do not expect--at least at the outset of this process--that people will have an understanding of the STAGES AND STYLES we will be sharing with you.

So I am going to ask you some questions to determine what needs more clarification before we proceed. During and at the end of the *inAccord* process, we will be asking you, individually in a private meeting called a caucus, if your understanding of the principles has changed in either direction. This will help us to evaluate whether we have presented the material effectively. Further, your insights will assist our research, which will assist others in similar situations, in determining the approaches and stages that were helpful for their particular conflict.

Are there any questions about today's mediation or any other concerns about the process as I have laid it out?

Now, if everyone could make sure their cell phones are on silent, we can begin your mediation session.

MEDIATORS WITHOUT BORDERS®

Agreement to Mediate

This agreement is between _____ and
_____,
hereinafter referred to as the party or parties, and
_____ and _____, of
Mediators without Borders (MwB), hereinafter referred to as mediator, to
work towards a settlement of a dispute between the parties. This agreement
shall act as a binding contract between the parties.

1. **Good Faith**: In consideration of receiving services from MwB, the
parties agree to enter into this mediation in good faith. Each party agrees to
undertake to attempt to resolve the issues relevant to this dispute and will
consider reasonable solutions presented to them towards this goal.

2. **Mediator Role**: The role of the mediator is to assist the parties to reach
a mutually acceptable resolution of this dispute. The parties understand that
the mediator is not acting as an attorney or psychotherapist in this process and
will not offer legal or developmental advice to the parties.

3. **Legal Advice**: Each party is advised to retain counsel to determine any
rights and responsibilities of the party and any legal consequences resulting
from any agreement made pursuant to this mediation before, during and after
the mediation. In the event that the mediator drafts a Memorandum of
Agreement documenting the agreements made in mediation, this document is
not for the purpose of giving legal advice. Also, a party may wish to have any
agreement between the parties reviewed by counsel prior to execution. This is
a personal decision of each party based upon the party's own judgment.

4. **Financial Advice**: Each party is advised to obtain independent financial advice to determine any rights or responsibilities of the party and any financial consequences resulting from any agreement made pursuant to this mediation before, during and after the mediation. In the event that the mediator drafts a Memorandum of Agreement documenting the agreements made in mediation, this document is not for the purpose of giving financial advice. Also, a party may wish to have any agreement between the parties reviewed by a financial advisor prior to execution. This is a personal decision of each party based upon the party's own judgment.

5. **Legal Rights**: The parties understand that the mediator is not obliged to identify or resolve legal issues, whether or not raised by either or both parties in the course of the mediation. Each party understands that he or she may be waiving or compromising legal rights by settlement of the dispute and the parties' claims.

6. **Disclosure of Information**: The parties understand that for mediation to be successful, full disclosure of all relevant information, written and oral, is essential. Therefore, each party agrees to be open and honest as to all such relevant information. This includes providing each other and the mediator with all information and documentation that would be available through the discovery process in a litigation proceeding. Should either party fail to disclose any such information, the parties agree to hold the mediator harmless for any agreements made pursuant to this mediation.

7. **Confidentiality**:
A. The parties agree that they will not at any point during the mediation process or thereafter call the mediator, including anyone affiliated with Mediators without Borders, as a witness in any legal or administrative proceeding relative to this dispute. The parties further agree that they will not subpoena or otherwise call for the production of any records, notes or work product relevant to this dispute in the possession of the mediator or Mediators without Borders in any such legal or administrative proceeding. To the extent that the parties may have such rights, those rights are hereby waived by each party. If an attempt to subpoena the mediator or Mediators without Borders is made in violation of this agreement, the violating party agrees to reimburse Mediators without Borders for any and all expenses incurred pursuant to such violation, including, but not limited to expenses incurred to quash such subpoena. Expenses will include actual expenses plus an hourly rate of $____.

B. The parties understand that the mediator will keep all information revealed pursuant to the mediation confidential as to any and all third parties, unless permission to reveal is given by both parties. The parties understand that disclosure of otherwise confidential information can be made by the mediator to the proper authorities if there are concerns of the likelihood of past, present, or future physical harm to an individual or his or her children, or the past, present, or future commission of a felony. *The parties understand that MwB staff, faculty, and/or students may observe this mediation for educational purposes, and that all relevant information regarding names and the nature of the dispute will be kept confidential by such observers.*

8. **Restraining Orders**: The parties will disclose to the mediator at the outset of the mediation any past or present restraining orders against either party. The parties will obtain an exception to any current restraining orders so that they can meet together in mediation. If such an exception cannot be obtained, the parties will make other arrangements with the mediator in advance of the mediation.

9. **Termination of Mediation**: The parties understand that either or both may withdraw from mediation at any time. If in the opinion of the mediator it is determined that it is not possible to resolve the dispute through mediation, after full discussion of the reasons for this conclusion has taken place and been confirmed in writing, the mediation may be terminated.

10. **Release of Liability**: The parties enter into this Agreement with the full understanding that they agree to hold MwB and the mediator harmless for the outcome of the mediation, including, but not limited to legal or financial consequences, irrespective of whether or not the mediation process is successful or whether or not an agreement is reached between the parties.

By signing below, I agree that I have read, understand, and agree to each of the provisions of this Agreement:

_____   _____

Signature of Party   Date   Signature of Party   Date

MEDIATORS WITHOUT BORDERS®

Fee Agreement For Mediation

This is an agreement between _____ and
_____ (hereinafter referred to as the parties) and
Jane Doe, L.C.S.W (hereinafter referred to as the mediator.) The parties have
entered into mediation with Jane Doe, L.C.S.W. with the intention of reaching
a consensual settlement of their dispute regarding

_____.

The fee provisions of this agreement are as follows:

1. The parties agree to share the cost of mediation, which is documented as
follows:

    a. Face-to-Face mediation is charged at $___ per hour.

    b. Phone mediation is charged at $____ per hour and can be prorated at
$__ per 15-minute increments. This includes any and all phone calls from
the parties to the mediator except in the instance of scheduling
appointments.

    c. Preparation of paperwork is charged at a fee of $__ per hour.

2. The parties agree to pay a retainer of $____ prior to beginning mediation.

3. If mediation costs exceed the retainer, parties agree to pay the hourly fee
prior to the service being rendered.

I have read, understand and agree to each of the provisions of this agreement.

_____   _____
Signature of Party   Date   Signature of Party   Date

MEDIATORS WITHOUT BORDERS®

Authorization to Release of Information

By signing below, I give my permission for mediator, Tom Jones, to contact the following agencies, caseworkers, therapists, or attorneys in order to gain information that may be helpful in designing an appropriate mediation intervention in order to promote a non-adversarial resolution of my dispute.

_____

_____

_____

_____

_____

_____

SignatureDate

_____

Print Name

_____

Address CityState Zip

_____

Mediator's NameDate

_____

Contact Number

MEDIATORS WITHOUT BORDERS®

Court Ordered Mediation Follow Up

DATE:
TO THE HONORABLE JUDGE:
COURT:
CASE NUMBER:

Thank you for referring this case to mediation. In consideration of your interest and in the spirit of cooperation, we would like to provide you with the following information:

Date of Referral to Mediation:

Outcome:

_____Parties engaged in mediation and successfully negotiated agreements. All parties participating in mediation have a copy of this signed agreement in their possession.
_____Parties engaged in mediation but did not negotiate agreements.
_____Parties did not show up for the mediation session.
_____MwB staff screened out the case as not appropriate for mediation at this time.

We appreciate your support of this valuable program!

Sincerely,

John Doe, Mediators without Borders

CPSIA information can be obtained
at www.ICGtesting.com
Printed in the USA
FSOW02n2307210116
15848FS